HIGH/SCOPE
EDUCATIONAL RESEARCH FOUNDATION
Ypsilanti, Michigan

Monographs of the
High/Scope Educational Research Foundation
Number Eight

CHANGED LIVES
The Effects of the Perry Preschool Program on Youths Through Age 19

John R. Berrueta-Clement
Lawrence J. Schweinhart
W. Steven Barnett
Ann S. Epstein
David P. Weikart

with a preface by
David P. Weikart

and commentaries by
Marie Skodak Crissey

Edward Gramlich
University of Michigan

Julius Richmond and Milton Kotelchuck
Harvard University

THE
HIGH/SCOPE
PRESS

Library of Congress Cataloging in Publication Data

Main entry under title:

Changed lives.

   (Monographs of the High/Scope Educational Research Foundation; no. 8)
   Bibliography: p.
   1. Perry Preschool Project—History. 2. Socially handicapped children—Education—Michigan—Ypsilanti. 3. Socially handicapped children—Michigan—Ypsilanti—Psychology. 4. Students—Michigan—Ypsilanti—Socio-economic status. 5. Youth—Michigan—Ypsilanti—Psychology. I. B.-Clement, John R.B.- (John R. Berrueta-), 1943-   . II. Series.
LC4092.M42C46   1984   371.96'7   84-12945

ISBN 0-931114-28-4

Printed in the United States of America

Contents

Tables and Figures

Tables

Figures

Acknowledgments

Members of the High/Scope staff collaborated to write this monograph. In Chapter 1, Lawrence Schweinhart wrote about the background of the study and Ann Epstein wrote the history of Ypsilanti. John Berrueta-Clement and Steven Barnett wrote Chapters 2 through 5, reporting the analysis of data. John Clement conducted the general data analysis, and Steven Barnett conducted the economic analysis. Lawrence Schweinhart wrote the review of research in Chapter 6 and joined with David Weikart in writing Chapter 7 on the lessons of early childhood research. Ann Epstein wrote the case studies and conclusions in Chapter 8. Lynn Spencer and Marge Senninger provided valuable editorial assistance. Shirley Barnes, Barbara Bruemmer, Sandy Grenier, and Pamela Woodruff assisted with word processing.

We owe special gratitude to the two interviewers, Van Loggins and Elinor Jackson, who collected interviews from an unprecedented 98 percent of the members of the sample.

Margaret Farnworth helped us develop our thinking and strategies for analyzing crime and delinquency. Hakim Rashid formulated and conducted several of the case study interviews. Lawrence Lopes interviewed several community members to compile information concerning the history of Ypsilanti. Melissa Hopp assisted in collecting economic data. Barbara Bruemmer collected some data and coded all of the data. The economic analysis reported here was facilitated by Carol Weber's gathering of the relevant data through 1973, for our earlier cost-benefit analysis (Weber, Foster, & Weikart, 1978).

We thank the consultants and others who gave us advice as the research progressed. Economists included Edward Gramlich, Norton Grubb, Gerald Musgrave, and Mary Rowe. Delinquency researchers included Delbert Elliott, Darnell Hawkins, and Rosemary Sarri. Other educators and researchers included Walter Allen, Norman Freeberg, Alice Hayden, Asa Hilliard, and Herbert Weisberg. We would also like to express gratitude to project officers and other representatives of funding agencies who provided us with useful advice, among them Barbara Finberg of Carnegie Corporation of New York, James Hamilton of the U. S. Office of Special Education and Rehabilitative Services, James Breiling of the National Institute of Mental Health, Kirke Wilson of the Rosenberg Foundation, and Thomas Harris of the Levi-Strauss Foundation.

Financial support for the work reported herein was provided from 1980 to 1984 through the Field Initiated Program of the Office for Special Education and Rehabilitative Services in the U.S. Department of Education. A grant to examine data pertaining to delinquency was provided from 1980 to 1982 by the Center for Studies in Crime and Delinquency of the National Institute of Mental Health. A grant to conduct an economic analysis of the Perry Preschool program and disseminate findings of the study was co-funded from 1980 to 1982 by the Rosenberg Foundation and the Levi-Strauss Foundation of San Francisco. The study and other such research have been widely disseminated by High/Scope's Voices for Children Project, an effort to inform citizens about the documented benefits of high quality early childhood education. Core funding for this project has come from Carnegie Corporation of New York from 1979 to 1984. The opinions expressed in this monograph are those of the authors and do not necessarily represent the opinions or policies of the funding organizations.

The study has enjoyed excellent cooperation from schools, employers, the police and courts, and the Michigan Department of Social Services Staff of the Ypsilanti, Willow Run, Van Buren, and Ann Arbor Public Schools—along with the Washtenaw Intermediate School District—were most helpful in providing data from school records and data on school costs. Special thanks go to Iona Shea and Thomas Korn of the Ypsilanti schools and Beautohn Wilson of the Willow Run schools.

Assistance with crime data was provided by police officers of the Ann Arbor, Belleville, Inkster, Jackson, Lansing, Livonia, Ypsilanti, and Michigan State Police Departments; by officers of the Washtenaw and Wayne County Sheriffs' Departments; and by personnel of the Washtenaw County Juvenile Court. Deputy Chief Dan Heliker of the Ypsilanti Police Department provided information about police procedure.

Assistance in obtaining data on welfare was provided by the Planning and Evaluation Division of the Michigan Department of Social Services.

Most basically, we acknowledge and express tremendous gratitude to the 123 participants in the study itself. They cooperated with our unusual requests and helped us make, through the Perry Preschool study, a unique contribution to knowledge about the long-term effects of early childhood education.

Preface

Historically, education has been a means by which individuals improved their prospects for a more productive and personally satisfying life. Our society, investing in education, has reaped the benefits of meaningful progress in all aspects of our nation's development. Led by the report of the National Commission on Excellence in Education, public debate about education took on a new urgency in 1983. Today, people are seeking new ways to improve the quality of education and thereby improve the quality of life.

In this light, there is growing public recognition that early childhood education programs can help students to be more successful throughout their school careers than would be possible without early education. The evidence generated by longitudinal research on the effectiveness of early childhood education programs of high quality strongly supports decisions by policymakers to use public funds to expand such programs.

In particular, research concerning the key importance of early childhood education to learning and success in life for low-income children began a few years before the advent of the national Head Start program, in a series of specially designed and controlled research projects. Later, evaluation studies were funded to study the impact of the national Head Start program. These two streams of work came to fruition recently with remarkable evidence of long-term effectiveness (Lazar, Darlington, Murray, Royce, & Snipper, 1982; Hubbell, 1983). The basic finding is that early childhood education of high quality can improve the lives of low-income children and their families; most important from the public viewpoint, it has payoffs for society as well in that it can enhance the quality of life for the community as a whole.

The High/Scope Perry Preschool Project, the subject of this monograph, is from that group of studies begun early in the 1960s. It is one of the principal studies supporting the value of early education.

The Perry Preschool Study

The High/Scope Foundation's Perry Preschool study is a longitudinal study designed to answer the question, Can high quality early childhood education help to improve the lives of low-income children and their families and the quality of life of the community as a whole? The project has progressed through four of five phases. Each phase has examined issues that reflect the growth of the children as they move from family to school to the wider world of adulthood. As new phases begin, new variables gain central importance.

Phase One focused primarily on the operation of a high quality program of early childhood education, with extensive curriculum development and annual replication of program components. Importance was placed on the documentation of the curriculum and the home visits. The principal measurement concern was the early childhood development of intellectual ability. This phase coincided with the operation of the program from 1962 to 1967 (Weikart, Deloria, Lawser, & Wiegerink, 1970; Weikart, Rogers, Adcock, & McClelland, 1971).

Phase Two began the longitudinal follow-up of the project as the children and parents were tracked into elementary school through third grade or age 8. The principal measurement concerns of this phase were intellectual development, school achievement patterns, and social maturity. This phase also included an examination of parental attitudes and demographic information. The project's first "real-world" measures were introduced: scholastic placement and the first cost-benefit analysis (Weikart, Bond, & McNeil, 1978; Weber, Foster, & Weikart, 1978).

Phase Three extended the longitudinal study of children and families from age 8 to age 15. The emphasis continued to be on intellectual development, school achievement patterns, and family attitudes. The real-world measures grew in importance and included examinations of scholastic placement, delinquent behavior, after-school employment, and cost-benefit analysis (Schweinhart & Weikart, 1980).

Phase Four is reported in this volume. It continues the focus on the longitudinal development of the study participants, now young adults, through school departure and subsequent experience at age 19. The shift from psychological to real-world variables is all but complete by age 19. Instead of an intelligence or traditional achievement test, study participants took a test of functional competence that focused on information and skills used in the real world. Other measures focused on social behavior in the community at large, job training, college attendance, pregnancy rates, and patterns of crime. For the first time, the cost-benefit analysis is based on actual data from complete school records, police reports, and state records of welfare payments. Employment histories and birth records have been verified. While projections of lifetime earnings are still necessary, the basic patterns of the subjects' adult lives are beginning to unfold.

Phase Five, the next piece of work, will follow subjects into adulthood—through age 26. Their life patterns will have stabilized; they will have formed clear patterns of family functioning, employment, use of welfare assistance, crime, and social behavior. A cost-benefit analysis at that time will provide a final reckoning of the economic value of the preschool program, with a strong base in actual data for projections into the future.

Strengths of the Perry Preschool Study

The Perry Preschool study has become the cornerstone of a body of longitudinal research that permits definitive statements about the value of early childhood education for children from low-income families. This body of research is having major impact on federal policies as expressed, during the Reagan Administration, in steadily increasing funding for the national Head Start program. There are certain facts about the Perry Preschool study that support its strong position in this group of studies in influencing policy development.

First, the study was designed as a true experiment with random assignment of subjects to experimental or control groups. Rarely are social experiments established in such a fashion outside artificial laboratory settings. This experimental design was created during a simpler time: We had not yet learned how difficult experimental designs are in field research. Also, President Johnson's War on Poverty had yet to be conceived, and the old authoritarian institutional structures were still in place, allowing an experimental approach to service to be accepted by participants. Thus, the community accepted the project for what it was—a study of low-income children growing up and a school district trying to find ways to help them.

Second, the study repeated the experimental/control group design annually for five successive waves of children. This design pattern was natural to a special services division of a school system, to which each year brought a new group of students and renewed funding from state resources.

Third, while the study sample (123 subjects) is small compared to cross-sectional surveys, nearly all of the sample subjects are still available to the project. Such availability eliminates the problem of attrition that plagues so many longitudinal studies, even those that last only a few years.

Fourth, during follow-up, although both control-group and experimental-group children were sometimes recognized by teachers as participants in a child development study, there was no reason for teachers to attach importance to the fact that some children had attended a preschool program and some had not. At the time, early education was a rare occurrence for any child. Teacher bias toward one group or the other was essentially nonexistent. Further, beyond the reach of any potential bias are the important data on employment, pregnancy, welfare, crime, and postsecondary education.

Fifth, data from the study have been internally consistent over the years, no matter how or by whom the data were collected. There are no indications that the control group did better than the experimental group under any circumstances. Also important is the fact that the data collected from subjects' self-reports have been corroborated by data collected by outside agencies. Arrest records, documented on police blotters, corroborate self-reports of arrest. Official school records confirm the findings of testing and interviews of subjects by project staff. Computer files of the Department of Social Services agree with self-reported welfare findings.

Sixth, the study includes the most complete cost-benefit analysis of early childhood education yet undertaken. A first, rudimentary effort was undertaken in 1971, by looking at scholastic placement from a cost-savings orientation. A second, major effort was carried out under the direction of an economist, with data collected from the schools through 1973 (Weber et al., 1978). This monograph presents a new economic analysis based on data collected through 1982 from schools, police and courts, and social services.

Seventh, the study has focused on collecting variables meaningful to society rather than variables meaningful only to psychologists. The effort has focused on real success in school as well as on test scores. Thus, we have used special education placement, school attendance, retention in grade, remedial education placement, and school completion as guides to outcomes. Outside of school we have focused on labor force participation, crime and delinquency, and arrest rates.

Hence, the Perry Preschool study has a number of features that make it worthy of special attention—experimental design repeated over five years, lack of attrition, consistency of findings regardless of source of data, cost-benefit analysis, and variables meaningful to society.

How the Study Was Accomplished

An interesting component of effective longitudinal work in a social science field is its ability to survive the changing times. The Perry Preschool study is a good example. When the study began, it operated outside the bounds of general social popularity. The project began in the early 1960s as a local attempt to solve a local problem of school failure and delinquency on the part of the disadvantaged segment of the school population. At that time, the advice of several outside consultants was not to initiate the project, because it might be harmful to the children and their families. Of course, with the great social movement of the late 1960s coming to fruition in the War-on-Poverty legislation passed by Congress in 1965, preschool education suddenly became a national effort (through Head Start), and the public's attitude shifted dramatically to favor such programs. During the 1970s things gradually tightened up both economically and philosophically, early childhood education for low-income children became less popular, and it barely survived the early cuts in social programs introduced by the Reagan Administration. Nevertheless, evidence of the cost-effectiveness of such high quality preschool programs has enabled them to become part of the social "safety net." So, the Perry Preschool Project began as a "suspect" innovation, then became one of a multitude in a surge of public support for such efforts, and has played a major role in legitimating preschool education through the research evidence of its cost-effective nature as a social investment.

Impossible to plan for in advance, an accident of history finds that a small midwestern project, carefully designed and executed, has the right data at the right time 20 years after its inception to join with similar carefully designed studies and actually affect social policy at a national (and increasingly international) level.

It is worth mentioning a particular difficulty involved in carrying out longitudinal research. Such research receives praise more often than it receives funding. Both government agencies and private foundations admire such efforts, but are wary of making the long-term funding commitments that such studies require. Thus, the researcher must constantly seek funds from all possible resources. In the Perry Preschool Project we have found a wide range of funding sources for our work; fundraising is a recurring process that begins again and again when we hear, "Our agency policy has changed" or "We've done our share, now find others to help."

More than three years of the study were totally unfunded. So how did the data collection continue? Some data collection was delayed. Staff were asked to increase their workloads. Reports were delayed until new funding sources were found. Although the recurring funding difficulties sometimes impede our progress, the work continues.

The Perry Preschool Project data demonstrate that preschool education of high quality can alter the lives of children living in poverty. I believe that high quality early childhood education programs can contribute to solving the major social problems of our times; the data support this belief. Preschool programs are well worth the investment required even in times of limited resources, because they have long-term, positive outcomes that make them cost-effective. The challenge we face now is to develop systems of early education provision that are consistently of the highest quality so they can be widely disseminated and can guarantee delivery on their promise.

David P. Weikart
Principal Investigator
1984

I Background and Context of the Perry Preschool Study

Summary of the Study

The Perry Preschool Project is a study of 123 black youths, from families of low socioeconomic status, who were at risk of failing in school. The purpose of the study is to explore the long-term effects on these young people of participation versus nonparticipation in a program of high quality early childhood education. Drawn from a single school attendance area, at ages 3 and 4 these youngsters were randomly divided into an experimental group that received a high quality preschool program and a control group that received no preschool program. Information about these youngsters on hundreds of variables has been collected and examined annually from ages 3 to 11, and again at ages 14, 15, and 19—assessing family demographics; child abilities, attitudes, and scholastic accomplishments; and involvement in deliquent and criminal behavior, use of welfare assistance, and employment. Earlier monographs on this study have reported findings through the end of preschool (Weikart et al., 1970), through fourth grade (Weikart et al., 1978), and through age 15 (Schweinhart & Weikart, 1980); an economic analysis was also reported (Weber et al., 1978).

Results to age 19 indicate lasting beneficial effects of preschool education in improving cognitive performance during early childhood; in improving scholastic placement and achievement during the school years; in decreasing delinquency and crime, the use of welfare assistance, and the incidence of teenage pregnancy; and in increasing high school graduation rates and the frequency of enrollment in postsecondary programs and employment. The age 19 findings are summarized in Table 1.

Preschool attendance altered performance by nearly a factor of two on four major variables at age 19. The rates of employment and participation in college or vocational training were nearly double for those with preschool as compared with those without preschool. For those who attended preschool, the rate of teenage pregnancy (including live births) and the percent of years spent in special education classes were slightly over half of what they were for those who did not attend preschool. Preschool attendance led to a reduction of 20 percentage points in the detention and arrest rate and nearly that much in the high school dropout rate. Those who attended preschool also did better on a test of functional competence.

These benefits considered in terms of their economic value make the preschool program a worthwhile investment for society. Over the lifetimes of the participants, preschool is estimated to yield economic benefits with an estimated present value that is over seven times the cost of one year of the program. The positive implications of these findings for improved quality of life for participating individuals, their families, and the community at large are of enormous importance.

In this chapter we introduce the Perry Preschool Project, its evaluation, and the community in which the research takes place. We begin by reviewing the conceptual framework of the study and presenting details of design and method for the present report. To provide the context in which the lives of study participants have unfolded, the chapter concludes with a brief history of Ypsilanti's black community.

Table 1

MAJOR FINDINGS AT AGE 19
IN THE PERRY PRESCHOOL STUDY

Category	Number[a] Responding	Preschool Group	No-Preschool Group	p[b]
Employed	121	59%	32%	.032
High school graduation (or its equivalent)	121	67%	49%	.034
College or vocational training	121	38%	21%	.029
Ever detained or arrested	121	31%	51%	.022
Females only: teen pregnancies, per 100	49	64	117	.084
Functional competence (APL Survey: possible score 40)	109	24.6	21.8	.025
% of years in special education	112	16%	28%	.039

[a]Total $n = 123$

[b]Two-tailed p-values are presented if less than .100.

Conceptual Framework

When the present study and other preschool research projects were undertaken in the 1960s, they were based on the hypothesis that human intelligence and the ability to do well in school could be improved during the early years. This hypothesis was derived from studies with animals (Scott, 1962; Krech, Rosenzweig, & Bennet, 1960), from Bloom's observation that "50 percent of [variance in intellectual] development takes place between conception and age 4" (1964, p. 88), and from the emerging work of Piaget on the development of the thinking process in young children (Hunt, 1961; Piaget & Inhelder, 1969). The hypothesis was also favored by the social context of the late 1950s and early 1960s, the drive for reform in institutional systems and procedures that seemed to hold back segments of our population from successful participation in the economic life of our country.

As the present study has continued, researchers have had to extend the study's conceptual framework, with two purposes in mind. The first has been to adapt the study's structure to late childhood, then to adolescence, and finally to adulthood, as continued positive findings have supported the extension of measurement and group comparisons. The second has been to adapt the study's scientific foundations to new ways of thinking about the determinants of growth and development in childhood.

The Transactional Approach

In the years since 1962, theorizing on the development of the thinking process has proceeded on many fronts. Most important has been the development of theory on the temporal unfolding of the relationship between a person's heredity and environment. No longer is the question simply whether a personal trait such as intelligence is inherited or the product of experience. Rather, a trait is best viewed as a dynamic relationship between genetic material and environmental opportunities (e.g., Sameroff & Chandler, 1975). Effects of genetic inheritance and effects of experience are inseparably intermixed and indistinguishable; all that can be observed and measured is an individual's performance in a setting. Human development may be modeled as a series of interactions or transactions between performance and setting.

This formulation can be enriched by very general concepts originally developed by Elliott and his associates to explain the causes of delinquency (Elliott, Ageton, & Canter, 1979). They speak of internal and external factors in the development of behavior. Internal factors (for example, commitment to schooling) come from within a person. External factors (for example, the opinions of peers) affect a person from outside. On the basis of these internal and external factors, social bonds develop between persons and settings in the course of human development. Strong social bonds to conventional settings, such as school, are seen as making delinquency less likely, whereas weak social bonds make delinquency more likely. In the previous monograph on the Perry Preschool study (Schweinhart & Weikart, 1980), we proposed a transactional framework with three factors: the internal factors of scholastic achievement and commitment to schooling and the external factor of student role reinforcement, especially as expressed in special education placement. In this monograph, we extend this thinking to the domains of employment and crime and delinquency.

Each domain of life may be viewed as a series of interactions between performance and setting. A *setting* is one of the several environments, physical and social, in which a person lives. Settings for children are usually determined for them by others. Parents decide when and where children live and receive child care and schooling; educators decide when and if children should go on to the next grade, when and if they need special or remedial classes. For the competent adult, placement in a setting is usually the result of a mutual choice by the individual and someone else, for example, the choice to take a job, to continue schooling, to buy a house, or to get married. *Performance* is behavior within a setting. The setting defines the appropriateness or inappropriateness of the behavior. For example, the school defines the appropriateness of behavior by evaluating performance according to its own criteria.

The Causal Model

A proposed causal model for the Perry Preschool study is presented in Figure 1, arranged according to settings and performances at various times

4

of life (see also Schweinhart & Weikart, 1980, pp. 5-15). The early child-hood setting for the children in this study is family poverty, defined as a relative lack of resources and measured in our study in terms of unfavora-ble levels of parental education, occupation, and housing.

Figure 1

TRANSACTIONAL MODEL OF PRESCHOOL'S EFFECTS

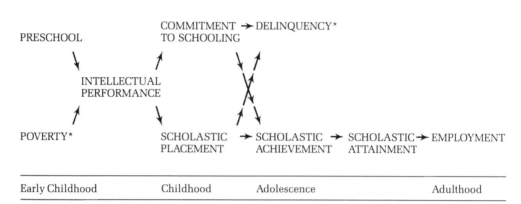

*These variables are negatively related to the other variables in the model. Thus, poverty depresses intellectual performance; strong commitment to schooling and favorable scholastic placement make delinquency less likely.

Preschool then comes as an intervention to prevent the deleterious effects of family poverty on school performance. For us "preschool" means any of a variety of programs that serve young children and their parents. The function they have in common is to better prepare the child for suc-cessful school performance and thereby create a foundation for life success.

For preschool to affect the child later on, it must have some immediate effect on the child and/or on the enduring family environment of the child. The best-documented immediate effect of preschool is an improve-ment in the child's intellectual performance, an effect that usually lasts no more than a few years. Yet these years include the crucial beginning of school, and children who have attended preschool exhibit better intellec-tual performance as they adapt to the highly demanding school setting. Hence we see the child's intellectual performance as the connecting link between preschool and later effects. (There is also appeal to the hypothesis that parents provide a connecting link by gaining improved parenting skills that support the child during schooling; however, there is insuffi-cient evidence in the present study to support this hypothesis.)

Preschool, then, enables children to better carry out their first scho-lastic tasks. This better performance is visible to everyone involved—the child, the teacher, the parents, and other children. Children realize they have this capacity for better scholastic performance and believe and act accordingly, developing a stronger commitment to schooling. Teachers recognize better scholastic performance and react to it with higher expectations and eventually with scholastic placements that reflect these higher expectations. If the child cannot carry out scholastic tasks, the teacher develops lower expectations for future performance. Sometimes placements are made within the classroom by seating or grouping children according to ability, or even by grade retention. Other placements involve assignment outside the classroom—to special education programs or to remedial education programs. In our model, ability as represented by intellectual performance evokes in the child the response of commitment to schooling and in teachers the response of rewarding performance and commitment with improved scholastic placement.

Commitment to schooling and scholastic placement then work together to influence scholastic achievement. Scholastic placement, by determining the setting, regulates exposure to content. The child's commitment determines how well the content is absorbed. Achievement then reflects performance in the setting and resultant mastery of content.

In our model, reduced delinquency is another effect of commitment to schooling and scholastic placement. To use Elliott's term, both commitment and placement represent bonds between the student and the school. The strength of these bonds keeps young people linked into the schooling process and away from delinquency. Delinquency is a kind of negative performance in the community setting.

Scholastic achievement is seen as leading to scholastic attainment, which is measured in our research by high school graduation. Scholastic attainment is based on a series of mutual choices by the student and educators. At least through high school graduation, these decisions grow out of consideration of the student's scholastic potential and achievement and consideration of the underlying commitment that permits potential to be realized. Of course, in decisions about postsecondary schooling involving private investment, the additional factor of financial resources comes strongly into play as well.

The final step in our model is from scholastic attainment to employment, indicating success in the community. One of the major purposes of education is to prepare young people for the world of work. Productive employment of one sort or another is one of the principal features of adult competence. Education does by and large prepare people for work and resultant earnings: U.S. population statistics for 1981 continue to show that the median income rises as scholastic attainment increases—with high school graduates, for example, earning $19,748 for the year and those not completing high school earning $13,155 (U.S. Bureau of the Census, 1982a).

Experimental Design

The Perry Preschool study has focused on the lives of 123 youths in five waves born each year from 1958 to 1962, as shown in Table 2. The study began in 1962 with the selection of a group of 4-year-olds designated Wave Zero and a group of 3-year-olds designated Wave One. The longitudinal sample was completed over the next three years by the annual selection of additional groups of 3-year-olds designated Waves Two, Three, and Four. Each wave was divided into an experimental (preschool) group and a control (no-preschool) group. The Wave Zero experimental group attended preschool for one school year; experimental groups of the remaining four waves each attended preschool for two school years. In the analysis reported here, the experimental groups of the five waves are combined (as are the control groups of the five waves) to enable us to base findings on a larger sample size. Most of the reported findings apply to each wave as well. This report emphasizes findings at age 19, an age reached by Wave Zero in 1977 and by Wave Four in 1981.

Table 2

CALENDAR YEAR STATUS OF WAVES

Wave	Number in Sample	Number in Preschool Group	Number in No-Preschool Group	Birth Year	Preschool Years	Age-19 Year
Zero	28	13	15	1958	1962-1963	1977
One	17	8	9	1959	1962-1964	1978
Two	26	12	14	1960	1963-1965	1979
Three	27	13	14	1961	1964-1966	1980
Four	25	12	13	1962	1965-1967	1981

Selecting Children for the Study

The children in the study lived in a neighborhood on the south side of Ypsilanti, Michigan, that was the attendance area of the Perry Elementary School. This area was (and is) an enclave of low-income black families. Children of preschool age were located for the study by identifying them on a Perry Elementary School census of families with youngsters attending the school, by referrals from neighborhood groups, and by door-to-door canvassing. Once children were identified as possibilities, their families were screened for socioeconomic level, which was computed on the basis of parents' scholastic attainment, the father's or single parent's level of employment, and the ratio of rooms to persons in the household. Children from families below a certain socioeconomic level were given the Stanford-Binet Intelligence Test. Children with IQ's between 60 and 90, with no evidence of organic handicap, were selected for the study.

Families whose children participated in the study were considerably less well-off than most people in the country, as reflected by comparisons with the U.S. Census. The parents had a median 9.4 years of schooling as the study began, only .4 years less than the national average for blacks in 1970, but 2.6 years less than the national average for all races. Fewer than 1 in 5 of the parents had completed high school, compared with national rates of 1 in 3 for blacks and 1 in 2 for all races. Forty-seven percent of the children in the study lived in single-parent families, compared with 14 percent for all races nationally. Residences were typical of local urban areas in size (median of 4.8 rooms), but were crowded, with more than twice the number of people in the typical household in the 1970 Census (6.7 vs. 2.7). For further details, see Schweinhart and Weikart (1980, pp. 17-19).

The available evidence indicates that these early conditions were persistent and that they were predictive of scholastic failure and other problems. In a parent survey 11 years after project entry (1973-1977), it was again found that in 2 out of 5 families, no parent was employed. Scholastic achievement scores at age 14 for those who had not attended preschool averaged at the third percentile on national norms; and the high school dropout rate for this group was 42 percent, as compared with national rates for 18- to 24-year-olds of 30 percent for blacks and nearly 18 percent for whites (National Center for Educational Statistics, 1982).

Assignment to Groups

The scientific strength of this study, its ability to determine preschool effects 20 years afterwards, is due primarily to an experimental design in which study subjects were randomly assigned to a group that went to preschool or to a group that did not go to preschool. Each year, children in the wave for that year were assigned to either one of two groups by forming pairs of children with similar pretest IQ's and assigning, at random, each pair member to one of the two groups. Then, pairs of similarly ranked children were exchanged between groups to equate within-group ratios of boys to girls and the average socioeconomic levels of the two groups. By flipping a coin, one group was assigned to the preschool condition and the other to the no-preschool condition. In Waves Two, Three, and Four, any siblings were assigned to the same group as their older siblings, to maintain the independence of the groups. Five children with single parents employed outside the home had to be transferred from the preschool group to the no-preschool group because of their inability to participate in the classroom and/or home-visit components of the preschool program. Once children were assigned to the groups, none of the families withdrew from the program. Clearly, neither teachers nor parents had influence in deciding who participated in the preschool program and who did not.

By these procedures, 58 children were assigned to the preschool group, also called the experimental group; and 65 children were assigned to the no-preschool group, also called the control group.

While the assignment procedures are a sufficient guarantee that group comparisons reflect the effects of the preschool program, group comparisons on background characteristics provide added assurance. At project entry, the two groups had no statistically significant (for statistical significance, $p < .100$) differences on the following background characteristics: ratio of boys to girls, child's age and IQ at project entry, family socioeconomic level, father's presence or absence, father's or mother's scholastic attainment, family welfare status, father's level of employment, household density, family size, and birth order (see also Schweinhart & Weikart, 1980, pp. 21-24). Because several children whose single parents were employed outside the home were reassigned from the preschool group to the no-preschool group, there was a statistically significant difference between groups on maternal employment, 9 percent in the preschool group versus 31 percent in the no-preschool group ($p = .002$).

Eleven years later, there were no differences between groups on demographic measures, such as father's presence or absence, father's employment, household density, neighborhood ratings by parents, and number of family moves since the child started school. Also, there was no difference between groups in maternal employment, with 27 percent employed in the preschool group versus 26 percent in the no-preschool group. In short, the difference between groups at entry was limited to maternal employment rates, and this difference was not permanent. The possibility still exists that the transitory difference in maternal employment rates might have had an impact on group differences in study outcomes. However, statistical analyses summarized in the Appendix on page 181 show this not to be the case.

The Preschool Program

The preschool program to which the 58 children in the preschool group were assigned was an organized educational program directed at the intellectual and social development of young children. Each year it was staffed by teaching teams of 4 teachers who received extensive managerial supervision and inservice training. Children participated in the program for two school years at ages 3 and 4, except in the case of the Wave Zero preschool group that received the program for one school year at age 4. The school year began in October and ended in May, a relatively short 7½ month period. Classes were conducted for 2½ hours each morning Monday through Friday; the staff-child ratio was 1 adult for every 5 or 6 children enrolled. Teachers made a home visit to each mother and child for 1½ hours weekly. The curriculum employed is described in the book *The Cognitively Oriented Curriculum* (Weikart et al., 1971). (The curriculum has continued to evolve since then; its current status is described in the book *Young Children in Action*, by Hohmann, Banet, & Weikart, 1979.)

Participation or nonparticipation in the preschool education program was the extent of differential treatment of members of the sample by the investigators. All participants in the study received the schedule of tests and interviews regardless of which group they were in. Testers, interviewers, and subsequent teachers were not informed by the investigators concerning the group membership of study participants. Any knowledge they did acquire about preschool attendance may be construed as a natural extension of the experimental treatment.

Data Collection, Analysis, and Presentation

Four major sources of information form the principal focus of the present report: a youth interview at age 19, primary and secondary school records, police and court records, and records of social service use. In addition, case interviews were administered to eight study subjects and to members of their families (see Case Study Data Collection and Analysis, page 11). The outcome variables of this study may be divided into three domains of measurement: scholastic success, socioeconomic success, and social responsibility. The instruments and principal variables used in the study through age 19 are delineated for scholastic success in Table 3 and for socioeconomic success and social responsibility in Table 4.

Attrition in the study sample has been a minimal factor in the study. The median rate of missing data across all measures has been only 5 percent. For example, the age-19 Young Adult Interview was administered to all but 2 study participants (both in the control group), and school records were found for all but 11 (4 in the preschool group, 7 in the no-preschool group). The low rates of missing data generally mean that attrition does not affect either sample representativeness or group comparisons. Analyses of differential attrition are mentioned briefly as

Table 3

OUTCOME VARIABLES:
SCHOLASTIC SUCCESS

Measure	Age[a] of Subject	Principal Variables
Stanford-Binet Intelligence Scale	3-9	intellectual performance
Wechsler Intelligence Scale for Children	14	intellectual performance
Leiter International Performance Scale	3-9	nonverbal intellectual performance
Illinois Test of Psycholinguistic Abilities	3, 5-9	psycholinguistic abilities
Peabody Picture Vocabulary Test	3-9	vocabulary
California Achievement Test	7-11, 14	scholastic achievement
Adult APL Survey	19	scholastic abilities in everyday life
School Records	5-19	scholastic attainment, scholastic placement, grades, absences, disciplinary incidents
Pupil Behavior Inventory	6-9	classroom conduct scholastic motivation
Ypsilanti Rating Scale	6-9	scholastic potential, social maturity
Youth Interview	15	commitment to schooling, homework, school conduct
Young Adult Interview	19	high school satisfaction
Case Study Interview	19 to 22	parental roles in discipline and education, role models

Note. Copies of the Pupil Behavior Inventory, Ypsilanti Rating Scale, Youth Interview, and Young Adult Interview are available through the High/Scope Press, at cost. Sources and references for the earlier measurement instruments can be found in Schweinhart and Weikart (1980, p. 25).

[a]A dash indicates annual assessments between the indicated ages.

Table 4

OUTCOME VARIABLES:
SOCIOECONOMIC SUCCESS AND SOCIAL RESPONSIBILITY

Measure	Age of Subject	Principal Variables
Socioeconomic success		
Youth Interview	15	current and past jobs
Young Adult Interview	19	current and past jobs, unemployment, income sources, savings, debt, ownership, job satisfaction, plans
Case Study Interview	19 to 22	attitudes toward money, goal orientation
Social responsibility		
Youth Interview	15	delinquent behavior, memberships, peer relations, activities, health, attitudes, life objectives
Young Adult Interview	19	crime and delinquency, arrests, memberships, help seeking, people problems, pregnancies, family relations, activities, health, general attitudes
Police and court records	19	juvenile detentions, petitions, dispositions; adult arrests, prosecution, sentences
State social services records	19	welfare assistance, use of social services
Interviewer questionnaire	19	behavior during interview
Case Study Interview	19 to 22	church and religion, sense of responsibility

appropriate in the text and discussed in further detail in the Appendix.

Our success in maintaining effective links with study subjects is due to a number of reasons that reflect characteristics of the study population as well as special features of the study itself. Since their migration into the area during World War II, Ypsilanti residents, and especially working-class blacks, have shown a strong tendency to remain in the local area. This trend may have changed recently, since our sample reached adulthood just as an automobile industry recession brought a massive series of layoffs in local factories. Even when study participants have moved, however, they have retained ties of family and friendship that have permitted our interviewers to retain contact. The interviewers involved in our study are themselves a principal reason for low attrition rates: They have been willing to immerse themselves in the life of the community and to go to extraordinary lengths to locate sample members. The wave design means that data collection occurs for a relatively small number of persons each year, permitting careful attention to individuals. Ultimately, of course, the continued collaboration and good will of schools, of courts and police, of social services providers, and of the study participants themselves are key elements of successful data collection.

Methods of Analysis

The principal analytic methods used in this report involve the straightforward comparison of differences between groups, without statistical adjustment. The study's experimental design and initial group comparability allow us to assume with confidence that on the average the behavior of control group members reflects patterns that would have characterized experimental group members in the absence of treatment. This assumption is supported by the consistent picture provided by analyses of group differences in previous reports; further corroboration is provided by analyses using various statistical techniques to control for initial differences between individuals within groups. These analyses are reported in the Appendix, which also includes a description of the statistical approaches used in all analyses. Throughout the report, statements that groups differ on a given variable are made only when the likelihood that such a difference would occur by chance is less than 1 in 10.

Case Study Data Collection and Analysis

A major component of the present report's data base is case study information. The case study task involved interviewing study subjects, family members, and friends, as well as analyzing the longitudinal information on participants that was available in our files. Eight persons were selected for inclusion in this report; their profiles appear as case studies in Chapter 8, with a number of vignettes used as illustrations elsewhere. It should be understood that these cases were not selected at random. The eight persons (whose names have been changed in this report) were chosen to portray the variety of lifestyles and situations in our study population: half are male, half are female; half attended preschool, half did not; half have been relatively successful in their lives to date, half have been relatively unsuccessful.

The purpose of the case studies is to supplement the insights provided by the analysis of group data with a more intensive look at how the lives of individual study participants have unfolded over time and at how these participants see themselves. Examination of the major features of the eight case studies has also served to generate hypotheses about common trends—hypotheses that may be tested with group data. Conclusions from case study analyses, however, should be treated with caution, both because of the intentional way in which cases were selected and because case materials inform by example or by contrast between individual cases, rather than by aggregation and statistical test.

The methods of case selection and data collection for the case studies were as follows. The most recent set of outcome data was examined for all study subjects to select from each of four groups one individual who had been relatively successful and one who had not. The four groups were: preschool males, no-preschool males, preschool females, no-preschool females. The final selection of cases to study involved judgments of the balance and variety between all the persons represented. A set of interview topics was prepared; interviewers were urged, however, to use these topics as a framework and to pursue topics further as it appeared worthwhile to do so during the interview.

Case analysis and report preparation were carried out by a researcher with considerable experience in case and clinical methods who happened not to have been involved in the interviews. The prepared case studies were then reviewed by the interviewer most familiar with the families, who read for accuracy and for appropriateness of the organizing themes in each case. Preliminary examination of interview and file data led the case analyst to set forth six areas, which have been used to organize and integrate the cases in Chapter 8; these areas are parental roles, attitudes toward money, role models, church and religion, sense of responsibility, and goal orientation. The case studies let these young adults and their families speak for themselves whenever possible and avoid conjecture about motivation in favor of descriptions of actual behavior.

Ypsilanti's Black Community

This historical summary focuses especially on the years in which our study participants were growing up and provides the setting for both case studies and aggregate analyses. Three types of sources were consulted in compiling this brief history. Population statistics were obtained from the U.S. Bureau of the Census for the decades from 1920 to 1980. Two written documents traced the history of the Ypsilanti area as a whole and that of the black community, respectively—*The History of Ypsilanti: 150 Years* (Tobias, Baker, & Fairfield, 1973); and *The Negro in Ypsilanti* (Howe, 1953). Finally, personal interviews were conducted with two prominent members of Ypsilanti's black community: A. P. Marshall, a noted black historian; and Eugene Beatty, an educator and principal of Perry School at the time of the Perry Preschool Project. We consider four major areas that affect the quality of life of a community's residents: employment and business, housing, politics, and education. Developments in each area are traced chronologically, setting the stage prior to 1960 (that is, up until the time the sample members were born) and then proceeding through the 1960s and 1970s into the present early 1980s. Where appropriate, events in one area are related to concurrent developments in other areas. Moreover, the history of Ypsilanti's black community is examined from the perspective of changes going on in the city, state, and nation as a whole during these years.

Ypsilanti: An Overview

The municipality of Ypsilanti was founded in 1823 as a trading post community called Woodruff's Grove. Commemorating its 150th year, the

Supervisor of Ypsilanti Township wrote, "In the past century and a half, Ypsilanti has grown from a backwoods outpost on the midwestern frontier to a thriving center where education, commerce, and industry work hand in hand in the best interest of the community" (Tobias et al., 1973). The dual importance of the auto industry and educational institutions is reflected in Ypsilanti's motto: "Where commerce and education meet."

As a neighbor of Detroit, Ypsilanti understandably has a pattern of development that has been affected by the automotive and related industries ever since the first Ford plant was opened at the beginning of the century. In the two decades of the Perry Preschool study, growth in Ypsilanti (city and township) has been steady. The population has gone from 46,907 to 78,546—an increase of 67 percent. Until recently, local employment rates have also been steady; however, the early 1980s have been characterized by massive layoffs in the auto industry, leading to increases in unemployment rates. Other local industries not associated with automotive manufacturing include paper products and stove production. Altogether, as of 1980, Ypsilanti had 75 industries employing over 24,000 workers.

Educationally, Ypsilanti has an active public school system as well as three institutions of higher learning. Approximately 7,400 pupils attend its nine elementary schools, two middle schools, and one high school. In light of the current publicity about the decline of our nation's schools, it is noteworthy that President Reagan in 1983 praised the Ypsilanti community for tightening its high school graduation requirements. Eastern Michigan University, founded in 1849 as Michigan State Normal School, serves approximately 19,000 students, 85% of them from southeast Michigan. In addition, 7,500 area students attend Washtenaw Community College, which was established in 1965. Cleary Business College has 600 students enrolled in secretarial, managerial, and accounting programs.

A black community first began forming in Ypsilanti in the early 1850s, when the city was a stop on the underground railroad for escaped slaves traveling north as far as Canada. There were two stations in Ypsilanti, including one at the home of George McCoy, a black man who fled from slavery in Kentucky and settled in the city. McCoy made cigars and transported them in a wagon with a false bottom, which he used to hide fugitive slaves. With limited employment opportunities, the black community in Ypsilanti remained small until the arrival of the automobile industry some 50 years later. Today, blacks make up 20 percent of Ypsilanti's population.

Employment and Business

There have been two major influxes of blacks to Ypsilanti, both due to employment opportunities. In the decade from 1920 to 1930, the number of blacks doubled from 627 to 1,294. It was during this time that Henry Ford became famous for his "$5 a day pay" on the assembly line. From 1940 to 1950, the black population again doubled—from 1,682 to 3,405—when blacks came north to work in the bomber plant at Willow Run (in Ypsilanti Township) during the war.

After the war, the automotive industry continued to provide steady employment. Ford plants were operative. Kaiser-Frazer Corporation

bought the bomber plant in 1946 and converted it to automobile manufac-
ture. General Motors took over the Kaiser-Frazer Plant in 1953, adding its
Chevrolet and Fisher Body divisions in 1959. This complex of automobile
and related manufacturing has been the primary employer of blacks in the
Ypsilanti community.

In the 1950s, a small black middle class began to grow, made up
primarily of long-time factory workers rather than retail businessmen or
educated professionals. Blacks who accumulated money did so through
land and property speculation—buying, renovating, and renting rooming
houses and apartments in their own community. As the 1960s and 1970s
were a time of general prosperity, so too did Ypsilanti's black community
find employment and prosper. The economic setbacks in the automobile
industry in the 1980s have hit the black population hard.

As late as the 1950s, in some areas of employment, blacks were
openly discriminated against in local hiring. For example, at that time the
local paper company and stove manufacturer did not hire blacks. No
blacks were employed by any of the utility companies or the bus line.
Clerical positions were closed off to blacks, and banks and chain stores
employed them only as maintenance workers. On a police force of 30
officers, there was 1 black policeman. It was not until the Civil Rights Act
of 1965 that open discrimination in hiring stopped; today blacks are employed at all levels of local business and industry.

Housing

At least through the 1960s, black housing was concentrated on the city's
south side (where Perry School is located) and in the Willow Run area of
Ypsilanti Township, near the major automotive plants. Substandard housing abounded; in 1947 more rigid enforcement of building codes was
instituted to stop this trend. Even so, in 1952, the Ypsilanti Housing
Commission called the south side "one of the worst congested slum dwell-
ing areas in the State of Michigan."

During the 1940s and 1950s, blacks who had enjoyed steady incomes
from working in the bomber plant and had stayed on in the automobile
factories wanted to build homes. However, no money was available to
them. Blacks could not get FHA or bank loans, even if they were professionals. Their only recourse was to pool their resources and build homes
over a long period of time. In the late 1950s and early 1960s, blacks were
able to borrow some money to complete these homes. But it really was not
until the Fair Housing Act of 1968 that federal loans became available to
black home-buyers.

It was also during this time that city-owned public housing was first
built in Ypsilanti. John H. Burton was elected Ypsilanti's first black mayor
in 1967 and spurred the development of more public housing. Construction of the projects began in 1967-68. At the same time, other low-income
housing was developed collaboratively by the churches and the Ypsilanti
Negro Business and Professional League.

Beginning in the 1970s, racially based housing patterns in Ypsilanti
started to break down. While the south side had always had white residents, it was in the early 1970s that the public housing projects them-

selves became more noticeably integrated. In a corresponding fashion, single family homes were opened up to blacks in other areas of the city. Recalls Ypsilanti historian A. P. Marshall, "In 1969 we found difficulty in finding a realtor who would show us a house. But by 1971 or 1972 realtors were showing us houses all over town. And as a result, blacks started moving all over town." Ironically, in the late 1970s and early 1980s, there has been an influx of whites buying homes and moving into Ypsilanti's south side.

Politics

Business and politics have a long history of being linked in Ypsilanti's black community. Most noticeable in this history is the role of the auto-motive industry and the unions. Says A. P. Marshall, "The opening of the automobile plants did not just create employment for the black commu-nity; it also may have been a catalyst for blacks politically in the area." The Congress of Industrial Organizations (CIO) opened up the labor unions to blacks on an equal basis; they were the first union to organize across racial lines. Locally, the CIO was involved in all industries, although it was almost exclusively the auto industry that employed blacks. In 1940, the first black was elected to the Ypsilanti City Council, and in 1952, two blacks served on the Council; both were elected with strong backing from the union.

Another vital political force was the Ypsilanti Negro Business and Professional League, created in 1952. This group was composed of profes-sional, semiprofessional, and skilled blacks who organized themselves politically. Their first success was to get the streets paved on the south side. In addition, they joined forces with the revitalized NAACP and the Commission on Human Relations in the 1950s to encourage local busi-nesses to make blacks more represented in the economic life of the com-munity. The League, later renamed the Ypsilanti-Ann Arbor Business and Professional League, has continued its political activities into the present. In the 1970s, pushing for affirmative action, they put pressure on the city manager and had a black man appointed as the Ypsilanti Chief of Police. They were also successful in getting a black man as the Housing Inspector. Today, their endorsement of local political candidates is a key factor in the black community's voting behavior.

The 1960s were active years for the civil rights movement in this country. From 1960 to 1970, when Martin Luther King dominated the movement and churches and students were in the civil rights vanguard, Ypsilanti's churchgoers and high school students reflected national trends. Significantly, John H. Burton, Ypsilanti's first black mayor, was also the first black mayor in Michigan and one of only a handful in the country at that time; his election was noteworthy enough to be reported in *Life* magazine.

Burton served one term, from 1967 to 1968. As described earlier, he was mostly noted for advancing public housing in Ypsilanti. But A. P. Marshall recalls that "Burton also gave the blacks a new sense of identity, a new sense of power, not to mention pride and all of that. I think he made them realize what kind of power they had."

Four years later, in 1972, a second black mayor was elected in Ypsilanti. George Goodman served as mayor until 1982, the longest term of anyone elected to this position. Historian Marshall believes Goodman was responsible for solidification of the gains made after the Civil Rights Act of 1965 and the increases in federal monies made available to blacks. "Goodman brought us dignity, from my point of view. He could run the business of the city, he could handle people; this is why he stayed in there so long." Mayor Goodman got blacks active and visible in city politics by getting them to volunteer for various citizens' groups and commissions. Under Goodman, blacks joined senior citizens' groups, firemen's examination boards, the historical society, the library commission, building code and sanitation commissions, and recreational study groups. As a result, at least at the professional level, Ypsilanti "began to see blacks socializing more with whites." And while social patterns at lower socioeconomic levels were not changed, black involvement in the city's political network did make a difference in the daily living conditions of the black community as a whole.

Education

Ypsilanti schools have never been deliberately segregated, but because of housing patterns before 1960, the schools on the south side (Harriet School, later Perry) had few white children. The few blacks living in other parts of the city attended neighborhood schools along with their white peers. The major effect of the 1954 U.S. Supreme Court decision (Brown vs. the Board of Education) was on black teachers in Ypsilanti rather than directly on the pupils. Up until that time, all the black teachers had been at Perry School or in Special Education Services. After the Supreme Court's decision, however, black teachers were hired at other elementary schools as well as at the high school. Eastern Michigan University also began hiring black professors in the late 1950s, although it wasn't until 1965, when Harold Sponberg became President, that large numbers of black teachers and administrators were hired and began to attract black students.

The 1950s were also a time when blacks first became active on the local school board. In 1953, Dr. Perry (a black dentist and the namesake of Perry School) was elected to the Board of Education; he served two terms until his death in 1956. Another black and former city councilman, Amos Washington, was appointed to finish Dr. Perry's term; he was subsequently elected to the Board of Education on his own. Thus, in Ypsilanti as in the rest of the nation, the effects of the civil rights movement in the 1950s were being felt. Blacks not only elected two members to the City Council, but were also beginning to enter the political world of the educational community.

Blacks active on the educational scene were concerned about reducing the large numbers of high school dropouts. Marshall recalls the tremendous dropout rate in the 1940s and the early 1950s. Part of the reason was that there was employment available in the plants but "also part of the reason had to be lack of emphasis or guidance on the part of parents." In the 1950s, while there was still high employment, "people began to look beyond what they were doing, beyond the bomber plant or the automobile factory, and to look at their opportunities." Marshall believes that this change in attitude prompted many black parents to encourage their youngsters to stay in school and the percentage of those graduating began to increase.

Eugene Beatty, himself an educator, has a complementary and very personal perspective on the problem of black youngsters dropping out of high school. Beatty became the first black principal of Perry School in 1940. He recalls that at that time, no more than two black students graduated from Ypsilanti High School each year. Beatty attributes this to a lack of incentive to graduate—there were no black teachers in the high school to motivate and encourage black pupils. So, working at the elementary level, Beatty began promoting the value of education with his students and their parents. In 1947, he staged the first "elementary school graduation ceremony" for his 48 sixth graders; by the mid-1950s, 45 of the 48 students in that graduation class had completed high school in Ypsilanti, Willow Run, or other places to which they had moved. Beatty instituted other changes during his tenure as principal at Perry School. He made the school operate more like a community center, enabling the people to use the building for a variety of recreational and organizational functions. Thus, Beatty sent out a message that the school, like the church, could serve as a focal point for the black community.

Myrne Howe, a white teacher, taught black students at one of Ypsilanti's junior high schools in the 1950s. Her perspective on education is interesting in that it agrees with both Marshall's observations on the importance of parents and Beatty's emphasis on supportive role models in the schools. Howe (1953) states, "When parent-teacher conferences were first initiated, there was poor attendance due to unfamiliarity with the plan. However, now 85 percent or more of the parents attend." At the same time, notes Howe, there was little black involvement in the Parent-Teacher Association. Howe goes on to say that "counseling is badly needed for the high school group. It might then be possible to keep more in high school for longer periods of time." She observes that informal counseling is given to black youths by interested community leaders, such as teachers and the director of the Parkridge Community Center on the south side. Howe also notes that the newly established Negro Business and Professional League was even then awarding three medals each year to black high school graduates with outstanding scholarship, leadership, and church participation records. Yet Howe laments that only about half of the blacks entering high school will graduate, that only half of the graduates will go on to college, and that of those entering college perhaps only 20 percent will complete their studies.

While the situation has improved in the 20 years since Howe's observations, Ypsilanti still has a high dropout rate when compared with the rest of Washtenaw County and the State of Michigan (data obtained from "Dropout rates," July 18, 1983). Statewide, school dropout rates are falling; from 1979-80 to 1980-81 the rate decreased from 6.5 percent to 5.6 percent. The present county rate of 4.5 percent is even lower than the state average. Ypsilanti, however, while following the downward trend, still shows a dropout rate of 13.1 percent (down from 15.7 percent in 1979-80). And though city statistics are not broken down by race, state figures show that dropout rates are much higher among blacks and Hispanics.

Summary

In sum, the 20 years during which the Perry sample was growing up were ones of significant change for Ypsilanti's black community, as they were for the rest of the nation. It was a time of expanding options in the areas of business, living conditions, political involvement, and educational advancement. Yet, as the most recent economic crisis in the nation has emphasized, opportunities for the poor black community have always lagged far behind the rest of America. Statistics on unemployment and school dropout rates show the continued vulnerability of black youth in today's society. The lives of eight of the study's black youngsters, as detailed in the case studies in Chapter 8 of this monograph, as well as the vignettes found in the other chapters, illustrate the striking differences in the ways the youngsters responded to their circumstances and used the opportunities available to them.

II Preschool's Effects on School Success

The conceptual framework of the study outlined in Chapter 1 postulated that preschool education leads to greater school success and, through school success, to greater socioeconomic success and increased social responsibility. This chapter deals with the first step in that linked sequence of events: the relation between early education and success in the school years.

Preschool led to greater school success for study subjects. The finding of school success through late adolescence is consistent with results reported for earlier ages, extending further in time and to broader domains. Improvement in the school performance of children who attended preschool is indicated by higher achievement test scores, by higher grade-point averages, and by lower numbers of failing marks. Greater parental satisfaction with how children have done in school is also viewed as indicative of greater school success. Greater commitment to schooling is reflected in more favorable attitudes toward high school, as well as in early evidence of reduced absences and of improvement in attitudes and behavior. Improved school placement is shown by a decrease in the proportion of time that individuals spent receiving special education services, and a decline in the number of persons classified by the school as mentally retarded. Higher educational attainment is indicated by more persons graduating from high school and by more persons pursuing college or vocational training after high school graduation. Finally, substantial reductions in per-pupil costs of elementary and secondary education are obtained, primarily as a result of the reduced need for special education.

Success in school, as a concept, includes improved academic achievement, changes in student attitudes and behaviors, and changes in attitudes

School Success from an Early Start

Bonita has a bachelor's degree in special education; she plans to obtain her master's degree and then teach. By her own account, school has always been an avenue of success for her. Bonita's father attributes at least some of his daughter's initial academic success to the early start she got through her preschool involvement: "I think it was the right help because she learned how to do a lot of the things when she got into kindergarten; see, they gave her a jump." When she, herself, becomes a teacher, Bonita believes it will be her job to challenge the intellectual capacity of each of her young pupils; she does not believe that the easy way out results in any lasting academic gains: "I know it's a lot of work and it's much harder, but I think maybe they would get more out of their education."

—from *Bonita Emerson: A Case Study*

and behaviors of teachers. Together, these lead to changes in student placements. Success at this age also includes special achievements in other life areas distinct from school: in sports, community life, family and social relations, employment and income. These areas are discussed in Chapters 3 and 4.

Processes Underlying School Success

School success is both a process and an outcome. The school process is embodied in the conception of a *school success flow*, consisting of a series of transactions between the student and the school setting. As depicted in Figure 2, the school success flow has four elements: intellectual performance, commitment to schooling, scholastic placement, and scholastic achievement. This process results in the outcome of scholastic attainment.

Intellectual performance is demonstrated when one carries out the first scholastic tasks presented by teachers in kindergarten and first grade.

School: Passing Through and Hanging Out

Although Yvonne has graduated from high school, her records are dotted with academic problems and disciplinary incidents from the time she entered kindergarten. She summarizes her school experiences as follows: "When I was coming up in school I should have knew what I wanted to do because now I kind of regret being bad in school and hanging out...." A series of offenses—smoking in the bathroom, fighting with peers, arguing with teachers—resulted in a total of three suspensions and two expulsions. Academically, Yvonnne coasted through school, just getting by: "I passed through, but I also did a lot of hanging out. I was skipping all the time, I'd do my work, I passed... You know, I do my work and then after I got the grade for that one semester, or that week, then I knew it would be time to hang out." She showed interest in sports and music in school, but never made these interests lead to anything; even today she expresses regret at the missed opportunities: "Well, I messed up in high school when I had a chance to be on the basketball team and try to do something for myself or make it to somebody's college or whatever. I was hanging out a lot, you know, just messing around, and I didn't accomplish what I wanted to, see, and I'm still mad at myself about that."

—from *Yvonne Barnes: A Case Study*

Figure 2
SCHOOL SUCCESS IN THE STUDY'S CONCEPTUAL FRAMEWORK

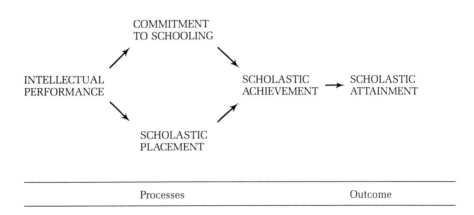

The student receives feedback almost immediately on whether this performance was successful or not, so that judgments of success and failure are intimately bound up with intellectual performance. Commitment to schooling represents those personal motives that define each student's relation to school and includes aspirations, ambition, and attitude towards school. Scholastic placement refers to the continuing actions of teachers and other school officials in reaction to the student's performance; these can be measured in terms of the provision of special education services. Scholastic achievement reflects the extent to which students meet the commonly accepted goals of school, as evidenced in standardized achievement test scores and school grades.

The outcome of school success is scholastic attainment. Attainment is measured by years of education successfully completed, high school graduation, and postsecondary education or vocational training.

Earlier Effects of Preschool on School Performance and Attitudes

Evidence that children attending preschool had a more positive school success flow is available from the earliest years of formal schooling (Schweinhart & Weikart, 1980, Chapter 3). These early findings are summarized here.

Preschool education improved children's intellectual performance during the period from preschool through first grade. Intellectual performance was assessed by IQ tests. Contrary to initial expectations based on early IQ changes, IQ's of the experimental and control group children were equivalent by second grade and remained so thereafter.

24

Study participants who attended preschool showed increased commitment to schooling through 15 years of age. During elementary school, their teachers rated them higher than their no-preschool counterparts in academic motivation; when they were interviewed at age 15, they placed a higher value on schooling, had higher aspirations for college, showed greater willingness to talk to their parents about school, spent more time on their homework, and rated themselves more highly on school ability.

Preschool education led to improved scholastic placement, as shown by a decreased rate of placement in special education classes. This finding is re-confirmed in this chapter. Preschool education contributed to increased scholastic achievement during the years of elementary and middle school, as measured by standardized achievement tests. At age 14, the average achievement test score of those youths who had attended preschool was 1.2 grade-equivalent units higher than the average score of those who had not attended preschool; significant differences between groups occurred not only for overall achievement but also for reading, language, and arithmetic subtests.

The improved school success of children who attended preschool was also evident to their parents, who reported greater satisfaction with the school performance of their children. In parent interviews, 51 percent of parents of 15-year-olds who had attended preschool said their children had done as well in school as they would have liked, while only 28 percent of parents of those who had not attended preschool said this.

Effects on School Performance

Preschool education contributed to improvements in academic performance in elementary, middle, and secondary school. Table 5 shows results obtained from the examination of school records not available in earlier reports.

Youths who had attended preschool had better marks through secondary school. School records were sufficiently complete to yield high school

Table 5

SCHOOL PERFORMANCE

Variable	Preschool	No-Preschool	p[a]
Mean high school grade-point[b] average	2.08 (n = 38)	1.71 (n = 39)	.018
Mean number of failing grades obtained per year (all school years)	.67 (n = 54)	1.01 (n = 58)	.073

[a]Tests in this table are Student's t tests; two-tailed p-values are presented if lower than .100.
[b]A = 4, B = 3, C = 2, D = 1, F = 0.

grade-point averages for 64 percent of the study sample;[1] the control group had a C- average, while the group attending preschool had slightly better than a C average. Similarly, individuals who attended preschool had fewer failing grades, on the average, in both elementary and secondary school.

Effects on School Placement and Experiences

Preschool education led study participants to have different school experiences. It led the preschool group to fewer absences, and more significantly, it reduced the incidence, time spent in, and level of special education services. The results of group comparisons are contained in Table 6 and in Figure 3.

During elementary school, individuals who had attended preschool had, on the average, fewer absences per year than those who had not attended preschool—12 days versus 16 days per year.

There was no difference between groups in the extent to which individuals in the study were retained in grade. The lack of findings of group difference in grade retention may reflect local school district policies discouraging retention. In fact, levels of retention are somewhat lower for the Perry Preschool study sample than for some other samples with populations at risk studied longitudinally through high school age (see Lazar et al., 1982).

Those persons who had attended preschool spent fewer of their school years in special education—that is, in integrated (mainstreamed) or self-contained classrooms after being classified as handicapped. Even among individuals receiving special education services, the mean number of years spent in special education was significantly lower: As Table 6 shows, for those who had gone to preschool and were later classified as handicapped, the average time spent in special education was about 5½ years, whereas for those who had not gone to preschool the average time spent was almost 7¼ years. The proportion of persons ever classified as mentally retarded was much lower for those who had attended preschool: 15 percent, compared with 35 percent for those who had not been to preschool. This reduction takes on special meaning if one bears in mind that participants were initially selected for the study on the basis of low IQ (among other factors), which is usually an indication of high vulnerability to placement in special education.

When other special services are considered in addition to special education—compensatory and remedial education, as well as early speech and language support—a somewhat different picture emerges. It is of special interest that children who went to preschool spent more time receiving remedial education. The contrast is suggestive: Children who

---

[1]Grade-point averages were obtained for 38 experimental and 39 control individuals. They were not available for individuals who had dropped out of school in the ninth or tenth grade or who had changed schools during high school. Values recorded were transformed as necessary to a common scale in which F = 0, D = 1, C = 2, B = 3, and A = 4.

Table 6

SCHOOL PLACEMENT AND EXPERIENCE[a]

Variable	Preschool (n = 54)	No-Preschool (n = 58)	p[b]
Mean number of days absent per year, in grades K-6	11.90	16.30	.088
Mean number of grades repeated	.52	.69	—
Percent of children ever classified as handicapped[c]	37%	50%	—
Percent of all years of education in which group members were in special education	16%	28%	.039
Mean number of years in special education programs, for persons ever classified as handicapped (n = 49)	5.45 (n = 20)	7.24 (n = 29)	.097
Percent of children ever classified as mentally retarded	15%	35%	.014
Percent of children ever receiving special services of all kinds[d]	65%	60%	—
Percent of all years of education in which group members received special services of all kinds	25%	32%	—
Percent of all years of education in which group members received remedial education services	8%	3%	.026

[a]Sample size for this table is n = 112, corresponding to the number of school records that could be located for the study sample.

[b]Tests in this table are Fisher's exact test for the comparison of group category proportions, and Student's t test for the comparison of group means. Two-tailed p values are presented if lower than .100.

[c]Placement in integrated (mainstreamed) special education or self-contained special education classrooms and/or direct evidence of classification were used to determine handicapped classification. Speech/language services or remedial/compensatory educational services are not included as special education.

[d]Special services include special education placements as defined in footnote c above, as well as remedial education, compensatory education, and speech/language support.

attended preschool were more often classified as in need of remedial support, whereas those who did not were more frequently classified as mentally retarded. A possible explanation is that children who have gone to preschool appear to their teachers in the early elementary grades to have more academic promise, more potential, than do those who have not attended preschool; with a little help, the former could perform well in school, while the latter require more extreme measures. In fact, teacher ratings of the two groups of children in early elementary school (Schweinhart & Weikart, 1980, p. 35) show just that: Teachers rated children who had been to preschool, on the average, as showing more academic potential and motivation than children who had not gone to preschool.

COMPARISON OF SCHOOL EXPERIENCES

Average School Years Spent	Persons who attended preschool (67% graduation rate)	Persons who did not attend preschool (49% graduation rate)

Effects on Commitment to Schooling

Earlier we reviewed evidence from prior reports of this study showing that preschool led to higher expressed commitment to schooling through age 15. Evidence from interview data at age 19 continues to show higher commitment to schooling on the part of individuals who attended preschool.

Preschool attendance led to a more favorable attitude toward high school at age 19. Sixteen items in the Youth Interview probed participants' feelings toward high school, and perceptions of its importance; the items were developed by High/Scope Foundation staff following work by Freeberg (1974) on job satisfaction. The items, and study subjects' responses, are presented in Table 7. Youths who had attended preschool gave a positive response more frequently for 14 of the 16 items, a result not likely to occur by chance. (Using a binomial distribution, the probability of 14 or more successes in 16 trials is .002.) A scale formed from these items showed reasonable internal consistency, even though the items appear to tap a variety of areas (α = .799). (The alpha coefficient is an index of internal consistency. See Cronbach, Gleser, Nanda, & Rajaratnam, 1972.) As Table 7 shows, scale totals show a mean of 21.3 for persons who attended preschool and 20.2 for persons who did not (with higher values indicating a more positive attitude). Three items showed statistically significant differences between groups, all favoring the preschool group.

28

Table 7

ATTITUDE TOWARD HIGH SCHOOL

Item	Preschool (n = 58)	No-Preschool (n = 63)	p[a]
What are your feelings about the high school you went to?			
It was great; liked it a lot.	33%	25%	—
It was okay/Didn't like it at all.	67%	75%	
If you could have, how much would you have changed your school?			
Hardly at all; it was really good.	28%	19%	—
A lot/Somewhat—good and bad things.	72%	81%	
How much studying did you do?			
More than enough to just pass.	22%	19%	—
Enough to get by/Less than needed to pass.	78%	81%	
How were your grades for the amount of studying you did?			
Good grades for the amount studied.	36%	25%	—
About what should/Less than deserved.	64%	75%	
Did you feel that you were part of the school, that you really belonged?			
Yes, that's just the way I felt.	46%	35%	—
Maybe sometimes/No; school just another place.	54%	65%	
How important was high school to you as a place to learn?			
Very important.	52%	43%	—
Somewhat important/Not at all important.	48%	57%	
How important was high school to you as a place to be with your friends?			
Very important.	29%	27%	—
Somewhat important/Not at all important.	71%	73%	
How important was high school to you as a place to get to know teachers and staff?			
Very important.	24%	29%	—
Somewhat important/Not at all important.	76%	71%	
How important was high school to you as a place for sports and athletics?			
Very important.	43%	25%	.031
Somewhat important/Not at all important.	57%	75%	
How important was high school to you as a place to join various clubs and organizations?			
Very important.	17%	21%	—
Somewhat important/Not at all important.	83%	79%	
How often did you try to change something that you didn't like about your school?			
Fairly often.	7%	5%	—
Sometimes/Almost never.	93%	95%	

Table 7 cont.

ATTITUDE TOWARD HIGH SCHOOL

Item	Preschool (n = 58)	No-Preschool (n = 63)	p[a]
How good was your education compared to what you feel you could have gotten at another high school?			
Better than most high schools.	22%	19%	—
About the same/Worse than most others.	78%	81%	
When you took a program of classes, like college prep or vocational, did you feel it was right for you?			
Yes, I'm glad I took the program.	54%	48%	—
Not sure/No.	46%	52%	
About how many of your high school teachers seemed to really care about students?			
Most of them.	36%	30%	—
Some of them/Very few of them.	64%	70%	
About how many of the counselors at your high school seemed to really care about students?			
Most of them.	48%	29%	.021
Some of them/Very few of them.	52%	71%	
When you finished a day at school, did you feel that you learned something worthwhile?			
Almost always felt that way.	36%	22%	.068
Sometimes/Amost never felt that way.	64%	78%	
Mean scale score:			
16 items, scored 16-32; α = .799[b]	21.3	20.2	.083

Note. Table entries for items are the percent of sample responding in a given category or category combination.

[a]Two-tailed p-values are presented if less than .100. Statistical tests in this table are Fisher's exact test for the comparison of category frequencies and Student's *t* test for the comparison of group means.

[b]α is an index of internal consistency for the scale.

The interviewer also asked study participants about their work and education plans over the next 6 months; 44 percent of the respondents stated that they planned to enroll (or to continue) in some training or education program. There were no differences between groups on responses to this question. Finally, area-specific self-esteem questions asked respondents to pick an area in which they wanted "to do well and get along with people"; for respondents who picked school as that area (45 percent of the total), neither ratings of how well they were doing nor ratings of how well others thought they were doing showed differences by group.

School as a Place for Success

Outside of his family, Jerry sees three major influences that have played a role in setting his goals: friends, teachers, and his high school guidance counselor. Jerry's friendships seem to have been based on shared academic interests, with the students reinforcing in one another the importance of learning and accomplishing something. His mother recalls that Jerry primarily chose his friends from school and had a racially mixed peer group. Jerry also claims that his teachers always rewarded and encouraged his academic accomplishments, especially in his elementary school years. He says of them as a group: "I guess the teachers helped a lot. Back then, I'd put them first." And in high school, it was his senior counselor who became aware of Jerry's mathematical ability and encouraged him to go into engineering and drafting when he entered college. Without the influence of this counselor, says Jerry, "I would have ended up going to school, but not knowing what I was going for. I would just have been taking classes."

—from *Jerry Andrews: A Case Study*

Effects on Educational Attainment

Two out of 3 individuals who attended preschool graduated from high school;[2] the comparable rate for persons in our sample who had not attended preschool was 1 out of 2. Educational attainment is summarized in Table 8; Figure 4 displays the distribution of attained educational levels for the study sample. High school graduation is very much the "bottom line" of school success at this age, and it is a necessary step for continuing education. Although age 19 is too early to confidently estimate the ultimate educational attainment of study subjects, failing to graduate from high school presents a significant obstacle to future educational progress. Graduation is also an important consideration, if not an absolute prerequisite, for many jobs or opportunities for vocational training.[3]

Preschool helped study participants overcome some of the disadvantages of coming from lower-income families and of being more educationally vulnerable than the national black population. The percent of high school graduates in the study sample can be compared to national

---

[2]Graduation here includes earning a graduate equivalency diploma (G.E.D.), which occurred in eight cases in our sample.

[3]A check of local employers and apprenticeship schools revealed that graduation is not viewed as a prerequisite to employment in local factories, although it may be important in securing later promotions. High school graduation is certainly required for apprenticeship into skilled job categories or for entry into the majority of local vocational programs.

Table 8

EDUCATIONAL ATTAINMENT

Category	National Data	Preschool $(n=58)$	No-Preschool $(n=63)$	p^a
Graduating from high school	66%	67%	49%	.034
Receiving postsecondary academic training	25%	19%	13%	—
Receiving postsecondary vocational training	13%	19%	10%	—
Receiving either academic or vocational training	n/a^b	38%	21%^{c}	.029

^{a}Test in this table is Fisher's exact test; two-tailed p-values are presented if lower than .100.

^{b}n/a means not applicable.

^{c}Figures for "Receiving either academic or vocational training" may be less than the sum of academic and vocational categories, since a person might receive both kinds of training. See text for definition of categories.

figures. In 1980 in the United States, 66 percent of all blacks aged 19 and 20 graduated from high school or received a graduate equivalency diploma,[4] while for the study's control group, the rate was 49 percent and for the experimental group, 67 percent. Preschool thus raised the rate of graduation to the national level for blacks.

Persons who attended preschool were more likely to have enrolled in some form of further education or vocational training after graduating from high school. If we consider either academic or vocational[5] training, Table 8 shows that the group who had been to preschool had a nonsignificantly higher percent of persons in each of these categories. However, the difference between groups reached statistical significance when both categories were considered together: 38 percent of those who had attended preschool undertook further education or training, as compared with 21 percent of those who had not attended preschool. Precisely comparable national figures on postsecondary education or training rates are not available; however, in 1980 the proportion of blacks aged 19 and 20 in college was 25 percent, versus 13 percent for our study's control group; and the proportion of blacks aged 18 to 24 in postsecondary vocational programs was 13 percent, as compared with 10 percent for our control group.[6] To the extent that these two national figures from different sources can be compared, it can be seen that preschool raised the rates of postsecondary

[4]Source: U.S. Bureau of the Census, "Current Population Surveys," unpublished data for 1980.

[5]Classification was based on content analyses of self-reported program descriptions. Academic programs involved subjects usually considered part of the college curriculum (e.g., engineering or teaching); vocational programs involved subjects usually viewed as specifically preparatory for an occupation for which a college degree is not required (e.g., secretary or medical assistant).

[6]Source of data on blacks aged 19 and 20: U.S. Bureau of the Census, "Current Population Surveys," unpublished data for 1980. Source of data on blacks aged 18 to 24: National Center for Education Statistics, 1982, p. 146, Table 4.11.

Figure 4

EDUCATIONAL ATTAINMENT THROUGH AGE 19[a]

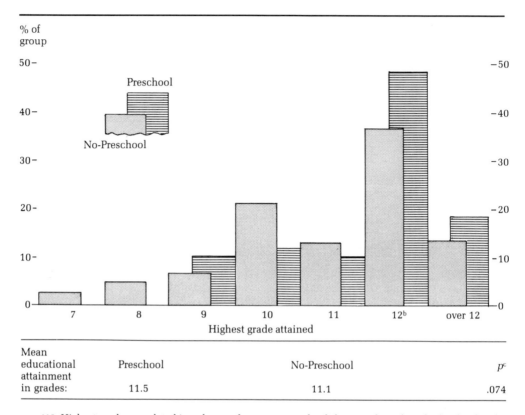

Highest grade attained

Mean educational attainment in grades:	Preschool	No-Preschool	p[c]
	11.5	11.1	.074

[a]n = 118. Highest grade completed is unknown for 3 persons who did not graduate from high school and 2 who were not interviewed.

[b]Attainment of grade 12 means high school graduation or G.E.D.

[c]The statistical test used was Student's *t* test.

education and training of the preschool group to approximately the national levels for blacks.

Effects on Competence in Skills of Everyday Life

The Adult Performance Level Survey (APL) is a multiple-choice test that was developed for students in adult education programs. It was designed to assess skills needed for educational and economic success in modern society (American College Testing Program, 1976). The functional competencies measured by the APL involve the application of five specific skills to five knowledge areas. A content-by-skills matrix showing examples of specific APL tasks is presented in Table 9. The domains of abilities and information sampled in the APL test are considerably narrower than those

Table 9

APL SURVEY: TASK EXAMPLES
ORGANIZED BY CONTENT AND SKILLS

| | Content Areas | | | | |
Skills	Community Resources	Occupational Knowledge	Consumer Economics	Health	Government and Law
Identification of facts and terms	Knowing what a time zone is	Knowing what skills are needed for clerical jobs	Knowing what "bait and switch" is	Knowing what the normal human temperature is	Knowing what the Bill of Rights says
Reading	Reading a bus schedule	Reading a want ad	Reading a contract	Reading a prescription label	Reading a ballot
Writing	Writing a letter to make hotel reservations	Filling out a W-4 Form	Filing a consumer complaint	Answering a medical questionnaire	Writing a letter to a legislator
Computation	Computing a plane fare	Computing overtime earnings	Finding the best buy	Computing a daily dosage	Computing a statute of limitations
Problem solving	Determining where to go for help with a problem	Deciding what to say to a bothersome co-worker	Deciding which of two decisions is better in economic terms	Deciding which meal is best, given a set of preconditions	Determining whether a given situation or action is legal

Note. This table is reproduced from the *User's Guide: Adult APL Survey* (American College Testing Program, 1976).

included in measures of general ability. In this respect, it is more akin to tests of scholastic achievement than to tests of intelligence. Because of our interest in understanding how academic achievement of study subjects is related to competence in life skills, we administered the APL at the end of the age-19 Young Adult Interview. The following is a typical APL item:

Q. What does it mean when people have the *right of way* in traffic?

a. They must stay in the right lane.
b. They must turn right at the next corner.
c. They have the right to turn in any direction they choose.
d. They do not have to yield to cross traffic.

Taken together, the 40 items of the APL appear to be reasonable pencil-and-paper simulations of important real-life terms and situations. One potential problem in interpreting test results is that items outside the reading skills category also require the test-taker to read words or numbers; thus persons with weak reading skills might do poorly on the test even though they had the functional competencies being tested. In the administration of the age-19 Young Adult Interview, the interviewer read each of the items to the respondent and could repeat them upon request. Reading skills were still required, however, to decode and interpret the supplementary information needed for some of the items. Eight individuals in our study sample stated they could not complete the test because they could not read. An additional four persons refused to take the test for a variety of reasons;[7] a contributing factor, certainly, was the fact that the test was administered at the end of an interview that itself took between 60 and 90 minutes.

A summary of between-group comparisons for the APL total score and subscale scores is presented in Figure 5. Preschool led, on the average, to an increase in the total number of items with correct responses, amounting to nearly ½ standard deviation. Persons who had attended preschool answered about 25 items correctly, whereas those who had not attended preschool answered about 22 items correctly. The difference between group score distributions can be compared by reference to the distribution obtained for the original APL norming sample.[8] Test developers divided total scores for the norming group (which consisted of a national sample of participants in adult education courses) into three categories: below average, average, and above average. As can be seen from Table 10, there were higher proportions of individuals in the two higher categories among those who had attended preschool than among those who had not, although the proportions in the norming sample in the two higher categories were even greater than the proportions of preschool attendees.

---

[7]The 12 persons who did not take the APL did not differ from the 109 who did on entry-level or outcome characteristics. Of the 12 persons who refused to take the test, 6 are from the preschool group. Of the 8 persons who stated they would not take the test because they could not read, 5 are from the preschool group. Of the 4 who gave other reasons, 1 is from the preschool group.

[8]Since testing conditions for the study sample differed from those used with the national norming group, the norm group scores provide only a set of reference points for interpreting the meaning of group differences within the study sample.

Persons who attended preschool also scored higher on APL subscales. Significant differences favoring preschool attendees appeared for three skill subscales: Identification of Facts and Terms, Reading, and Writing. They also appeared for two content subscales: Occupational Knowledge and Health Information.

Figure 5

APL SURVEY RESULTS

A. Total Score Comparisons

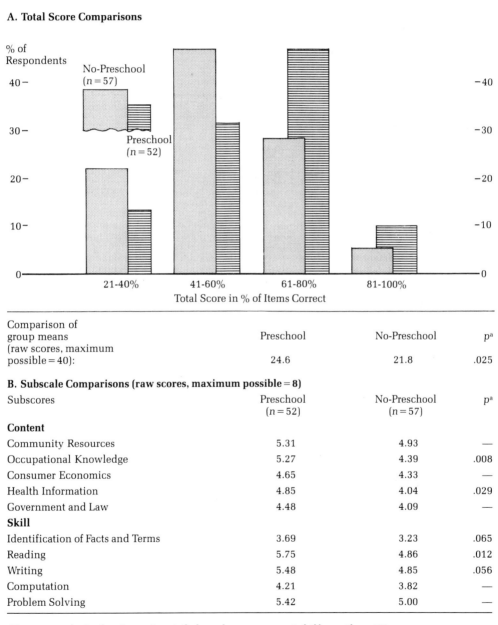

Comparison of group means (raw scores, maximum possible = 40):	Preschool	No-Preschool	p[a]
	24.6	21.8	.025

B. Subscale Comparisons (raw scores, maximum possible = 8)

Subscores	Preschool (n = 52)	No-Preschool (n = 57)	p[a]
Content			
Community Resources	5.31	4.93	—
Occupational Knowledge	5.27	4.39	.008
Consumer Economics	4.65	4.33	—
Health Information	4.85	4.04	.029
Government and Law	4.48	4.09	—
Skill			
Identification of Facts and Terms	3.69	3.23	.065
Reading	5.75	4.86	.012
Writing	5.48	4.85	.056
Computation	4.21	3.82	—
Problem Solving	5.42	5.00	—

[a]Tests are analysis of variance; two-tailed p-values are presented if lower than .100.

36

Table 10

COMPARISON OF APL SURVEY TOTAL SCORE DISTRIBUTIONS

APL Scores	Study Sample[a]		National Norm (n = 2,853)
	Preschool (n = 52)	No-Preschool (n = 57)	
Above-average	6%	5%	25%
Average	55%	33%	60%
Below-average	39%	62%	15%

Note. Response category groupings were formed by test developers on the basis of norming group scores (American College Testing Program, 1976).

[a]Comparison of the preschool group and no-preschool group indicated a statistically significant difference, $p = .051$ (x^2 statistic).

An Economic Analysis of Preschool's Effects on School Success

We consider in this section the effects of preschool on educational costs; specifically, we will examine the reductions in costs to the elementary and secondary education system related to preschool attendance. This is only a part of the economic analysis, since there are other effects of preschool to be considered—reductions in cost to the justice system, taken up in Chapter 4, and the complete analysis, reported in Chapter 5. Our analysis is also limited because study participants have not necessarily completed their education by age 19. Thus, we examine in this section the reductions in cost associated with differences in educational attainment only through the end of high school.

From an economic viewpoint, the primary effect of preschool is to increase the efficiency of the educational process. This increase in efficiency may be represented either as an increase in educational output for a given cost, or as a decrease in cost for a given educational output. In the Perry Preschool study the increase in educational efficiency is manifested in both cost decreases and output increases; we have used a framework derived from economic theory to link costs and outcomes together. Before presenting in detail our analyses and their results, we describe briefly both the theory and variables used for the economic analyses.

Our economic analysis of school success brought together two distinct types of information: data on individual educational outcomes and data on school costs. Information about the schooling experiences of study participants comes from school records.[9] These school histories specify

---

[9]Data on the remaining nine persons were collected from our other sources, and are used wherever possible in our analyses; without the school records, however, we lack the detail necessary to link outcomes to cost data.

educational status in a multifaceted way, including information about the schools attended, attainment, education program characteristics, special services, and disciplinary incidents. Cost computation procedures were dictated by the limitations of the available cost data.

School cost data were collected from the district (Ypsilanti) that accounted for 80 percent of the years of schooling of study subjects and also from three surrounding school districts (Ann Arbor, Willow Run, Van Buren) that accounted for all but 5 percent of the remaining schooling years. Data from surrounding school districts provide some indication of costs relative to those for the Ypsilanti schools but are not complete enough to use directly in our economic analysis. Thus only the Ypsilanti school district's cost data are used to estimate schooling costs. Information from district budgets, enrollment summaries, and personnel lists was combined to produce estimates of annual per-child costs for each educational program service-type, for each educational program delivery-type, and for psychological evaluations.[10]

The theoretical framework for the economic analyses views the educational process as a production process in which there are inputs and outputs. Inputs to this process are child, family, and community characteristics, along with the resources provided by the school system.[11] We have chosen to define **educational attainment** as the output, an output recognized in several production-process models currently in use. In this section we consider only the process of production of education through elementary and secondary school.

The effects of preschool on the efficiency of the educational production process can be seen in the difference between the cost of education for the preschool and no-preschool groups, shown in Table 11. Putting a child who went to preschool through elementary and secondary school cost the school system, on the average, $34,813 (in constant 1981 dollars); putting one who did not attend preschool through elementary and secondary school cost, on the average, $41,895. The difference is $7,082 per child; that is, preschool reduced the cost of elementary and secondary education by $7,082 per child. Since preschool also increased the average educational attainment, this cost difference understates the total increase in educational efficiency.

---

[10]The availability of cost data at the level of detail required for this analysis for Ypsilanti schools is due to the collection of such information in 1974 by Carol U. Weber under High/Scope auspices for an earlier economic analysis (reported in Weber et al., 1978). Such data were no longer available from official sources by 1980. Cost data for specific years were obtained from special residential schools in situations in which costs were known to be much greater than annual average figures for general education. Individual components of educational status used to estimate costs are educational program service-type (general education, correctional/disciplinary education, educable mentally impaired education); educational program delivery-type (full-time residential school, full-time special class, part-time teacher-consultant, full-time regular classroom); and psychological evaluation. The last is the only additional service of significant cost that can be reliably identified from school records and for which a cost can be calculated. Additionally, psychological evaluations are important because they generally indicate that the child has been referred for some problem. In later years, psychological evaluations are a part of formal special education evaluation procedures whose costs are underestimated by the cost of the psychological evaluations alone.

[11]As we specified the overall theoretical model, any effects of preschool must occur by way of these inputs (see Chapter 1). What inputs are affected and how such effects come about is discussed in Chapter 5, as we consider a causal model of these processes.

Table 11

AVERAGE COSTS PER CHILD (IN 1981 DOLLARS)
OF ELEMENTARY AND SECONDARY EDUCATION,
AND COSTS PER YEAR OF EDUCATION ATTAINED[a]

Cost	Preschool (n = 54)	No-Preschool (n = 58)	Difference	p[b]
Total Education Cost				
Undiscounted	$34,813	$41,895	$7,082 (17%)	—
Present value, discounted at 3%[c]	27,117	32,230	5,113 (16%)	—
Cost Per Year Attained				
Undiscounted	3,130	3,930	800 (20%)	.075
Present value discounted at 3%	2,439	3,026	588 (19%)	.070

[a]n = 112.

[b]Test of significance is Student's t test for comparison of group means; two-tailed p-values are presented if lower than .100.

[c]See footnote 13 for an explanation of discounted present value.

The effect of preschool on the efficiency of the school production process can be estimated more precisely by calculating the average *cost per year of school attainment* in both groups. The decrease in cost per year attained that is attributable to preschool is $800. In other words, preschool reduced the cost per student of successfully completing each additional year of school from $3,930 to $3,130; this difference corresponds to a little over 20 percent of the annual cost of elementary and secondary education without preschool. Thus we can say that preschool increased the efficiency of the educational process by about 20 percent.[12]

The reason for this reduction in costs can be found in Table 6, page 26: Notable reductions in the proportion of total years of education in which children were in more expensive, special education programs. These reductions come about in two ways: Proportionately fewer children who attended preschool were in special education, and those who were in special education received fewer years of service. This is particularly true for children classified by the school system as educable mentally retarded. Furthermore, reductions in per-child costs between the two groups occurred in spite of the fact that persons who attended preschool have gone to school longer—a situation that tends to raise the costs of education for the study's experimental participants.

These findings are highly encouraging. However, they require some further elaboration. In economic analyses, the timing of costs and of cost reductions must be taken into account as well as their magnitude. A dollar today or in the near future is worth more than a dollar many years from

[12]The figures in Table 11 cannot be used in a straightforward way to get an estimate of the relative total costs for the preschool and no-preschool groups reaching equal levels of educational attainment. The reason is that both the cost per year attained and the number of years attained differed for the two groups.

now. To take into account the timing of costs and benefits, we convert all dollar figures to their *discounted present value*.[13] The discounted present value of the $7,082 difference in total educational costs is $5,113 per child, using a discount rate of 3 percent. As we shall see in Chapter 5, $5,113 is greater than the present value of the cost of one year of preschool.

From the Case Studies: Insights on School Success

Two factors in the lives of youth—parent attitudes and role models—may play an important part in school success. Parents' attitudes about education surface during the early elementary years, as soon as youngsters begin school. In the families of successful children, school is seen as a place to "learn"; in the families of the less successful, opinions about school stop with the expectation that children "behave well." Parents of preschool and nonpreschool children might equally espouse the view that school is important. Parents of preschoolers, additionally, are quickly exposed to the phenomenon that learning in an academic sense begins at a very young age and continues, along with good behavior, to be a critical dimension of school performance.

Role models assume increasing importance for youths during high school years. Those role models that support education become part of the students' school success flow. The influence of educational role models may be both a cause and an effect of school experiences. Early role models, particularly those within the family, act as a source of encouragement and inspiration for youngsters to succeed in school. But as the students reach the upper grades, it is those who are already successful who have the greatest opportunity to interact with role models within the school system. Those who are not successful have literally or psychologically dropped out of school by this time. It is the academically successful youth whose grades are good enough to allow them to participate in sports and come under the guidance of an athletic coach, who join various clubs and take part in extracurricular activities, who become exposed to the special tutelage of teachers and counselors who will take individual interest in them. These educational role models from outside the family appear to be important influences at a time when youths are making decisions about their future after high school.

---

[13]Discounted present value or *present value* (as usually abbreviated) is a criterion for judging the worth of an investment at the time the money is invested, rather than at the time the returns are collected. Dollar values for returns are adjusted for inflation (put into constant-

Cost reductions reflect only part of preschool's effect on education; preschool also increased educational attainment. If this is taken into account, as Table 11 shows, the effect of preschool on costs per year attained is greater than the effect of preschool on total educational costs (19 percent instead of 15 percent). Thus preschool is an even better investment in terms of educational returns than the difference in total costs indicates. In later chapters the benefits of increased educational effectiveness are explicitly taken into account.

Summary

Early education can lead to increased school success. In the Perry Preschool study, persons who had attended preschool had better grades, fewer failing marks, and fewer absences in elementary school; they required fewer special education services, were more likely to graduate from high school, and were more likely to continue their education or get vocational training after school than their no-preschool counterparts. The picture of detailed and consistent improvement in school performance and placement is also reflected in increased commitment: Those youths who attended preschool had a more favorable attitude toward high school. The economic analysis of these findings indicates that early education can substantially increase the efficiency of later schooling and that the effect of preschool education on school system costs alone is sufficient to cover the costs of early education.

Thus, preschool programs can substantially increase the efficiency of elementary and secondary education, not only by reducing costs but also by increasing effectiveness. In addition to reducing costs, preschool will boost the school performance of children who have a relatively poor prognosis for school success. These children put more into education (school commitment) and they get more out (school achievement, educational attainment). On a large scale, improving the educational process for disadvantaged children seems likely to benefit all students by raising the average level of commitment and achievement in the environment in which education takes place.

---

dollar terms) and then discounted to adjust for the expected rate of return that would have been obtained had some other mode of investment been chosen. After these adjustments, costs and returns can be compared on an equal same-day basis. The selection of a discount rate is a matter of considerable debate; we have chosen to use a discount rate of 3 percent, representing a middle estimate among economists of a reasonable rate of return on investment over and above inflation. It is important to realize that present value is a considerably more stringent criterion than just the comparison of costs and benefits; to see the difference, the following example should be considered. If you buy a savings bond for $500 and cash it in for $1,000 ten years later, the return is 200 percent—but after ten years. To see if this is a good investment, we compute its present value. Assuming inflation of 5 percent per year and a discount rate of 3 percent per year, the present value of the bond is $463, which is less than its cost. Thus, if we anticipate 5 percent annual inflation and we think a reasonable rate of return on our investment is 3 percent, the bond is not a good investment.

Preschool offers the educational system and the society that funds it a way to allocate educational funds that is economically efficient as well as equitable. Even without counting the inherent benefits to the children and their families from increased school success, we may judge preschool to be a sound social policy investment on the basis of its effects on educational costs alone.

III Preschool's Effects on Early Socioeconomic Success

This chapter is the second of three dealing with the effects of the Perry Preschool Project as observed at the end of the study subjects' adolescent years. The conceptual framework for the study, described in Chapter 1, stated that preschool education led to greater socioeconomic success through success in school. In Chapter 2 we presented the evidence the study has amassed to show that preschool led to greater school success; in this chapter we describe evidence of preschool's effects on socioeconomic success through age 19. As in the other chapters of this book dealing with the effects of early intervention, we base our assertions on the examination of differences between two groups, initially the same on the average, one of which attended preschool while the other did not. In Chapter 5, where we bring together the project's measured inputs, processes, and outcomes into a comprehensive perspective, we examine the relation between school success and early socioeconomic success in our study sample.

Preschool led to greater socioeconomic success for study participants. An increase in levels of employment of persons who attended preschool is indicated by higher proportions of persons working at the time they were interviewed, by more months of employment at ages 18 and 19, and by fewer months of unemployment since leaving high school. One finding that resulted from the age-15 Youth Interview foreshadowed the results in this chapter. At that time, 29 percent of youths who had attended preschool reported current or recent employment, compared with 16 percent of those who had not attended preschool (Schweinhart & Weikart, 1980, p. 56, Table 12). As a result of differences in levels of employment, higher earnings are reported at age 19 by the preschool group. Finally, a greater degree of economic independence is indicated by a higher proportion of persons in the preschool group supporting themselves on their own (or their spouses') earnings, and by a lower incidence of use of certain kinds of social services. These findings are extrapolated into future years to project accumulating benefits from increased lifetime earnings and from reductions in welfare costs.

The Concept and Measurement of Early Socioeconomic Success

Regarding economic and social position, the major difference between late adolescence and early adulthood is a move toward independence, or at least a shift in dependence. Ties with the family of origin are loosened, and new bonds are formed. Members of our society pass from the stage in life in which they primarily attend school to the stage in life in which they work and/or raise a family. This is a time of transition; changes in personal situations can be quite abrupt, and examination of a group of subjects at any point in such a period will show that some have changed (for instance, have married) while others have not yet done so.

In the longitudinal examination of the lives of Perry Preschool study participants, we chose as our primary focus for this report the period during which they were 19 years old. This may be too early in the transition period to predict socioeconomic success with long-term accuracy, since adult roles are not completely assumed. As we shall see in the next chapter, the majority of study subjects were still living at home at this age, one third had children, and few were married. Many of the sample members also appear to have reached a hiatus in their educational progress; as we saw in the last chapter, no more than 1 out of 6 in the study sample have gone to college after graduation from high school. The non-college majority, therefore, have had some time in which to take or seek a job at this point. As survey studies have shown, there is a strong relation between first and later occupations (e.g., Blau & Duncan, 1967); we can believe on these grounds, then, that findings on early socioeconomic success at this age may have longer-term predictive value for this group.

Socioeconomic position has three interlinked components: employment, income, and occupational status.[14] In this population, employment is crucial, particularly continuity of employment. Due in part to the Midwest's economic shifts in the late 1970s, unemployment among black youth has been both serious and chronic. Income is closely related to employment, since earnings from employment are for most persons the principal source of income. There are, however, several possible income sources other than earnings—among them the family and the welfare system. Occupational status represents vocational choices that persons make, as well as those to which they aspire in the future.

Early Success: Working and Studying

Jerry is currently enrolled in a pre-engineering program at a community college; he plans to eventually enter the University of Michigan to obtain an engineering degree with a specialty in drafting. Jerry has always had jobs—beginning with neighborhood chores at age 10—but there is no feeling that money per se has taken on extraordinary importance for him. Instead he has saved most of what he has earned, and has limited purchases with his own money to small items. These days, Jerry works 20 hours a week as a packer at a large thrift store. His earnings have gone to buy a used car and, above all, to finance his college education. If the lure of working full-time occasionally tempts Jerry, his mother reasserts the essential values that strengthen this family: "I mean it's easy for him to say, 'Momma, I gotta work, I gotta get me a job, I'd rather get a job than go to school.' And I say, 'Jerry, just keep on going,' you know. 'Go to school.' Because I don't want him to quit school. I want him to keep on going."

—from *Jerry Andrews: A Case Study*

---

[14]A fourth component, education, has been discussed extensively in Chapter 2.

Early Failure: Obstacles and Rescue

Marlene is being divorced after three years of marriage. She has two children, aged 1 and 2, and is receiving Aid to Families with Dependent Children (AFDC) and food stamps. Marlene has never held a job. Before her marriage, she was enrolled in a secretarial program but dropped out after one year. Her future plans are vague and filled with excuses about the obstacles preventing her from achieving economic independence. Marlene talks about looking for a job—in the next breath saying why she cannot, or has not, done so: "I am going to try and find me a job; then I have to try and find me a babysitter. If I could get a job—but I haven't really had no transportation to go out there and look because our cars broke down on us—but as soon as I can get that opportunity to go look for a job, I am, because I need to get away from home to get my mind off things that are at home." The theme of escape from her troubles, even more than financial need, seems to be Marlene's primary motivation for wanting a job. Similarly, she sees finding a new mate as her means of rescue from her current situation. Marlene says she plans to find someone who will be better to her than her first husband and provide her with more money than she receives on public assistance.

—from *Marlene Franklin: A Case Study*

The study provides information on other concepts related to these three components—economic independence, consumer and other economic activities, and attitudes toward work and pay. Data on employment, economic activities, self-sufficiency, and attitudes were collected through the age-19 Young Adult Interview. Details were also obtained concerning a person's current or most recent job and three previous jobs. These work histories provide data on dates of employment, hours, wages, and occupational categories—all of which give a picture of the labor market experience of study participants through age 19.

The earliest reported employment is at age 12; however, few participants reported employment prior to age 16. This may be due, at least in part, to the structure of our age-19 Young Adult Interview question on this topic: Spaces were provided for the description of no more than four jobs. If a participant had a different job each year from age 16 to 19 (or had more than one job per year), there was no place to report earlier jobs. As a result, work in years prior to age 15 may be underrepresented in the age-19 interview. In any case, there were few jobs reported before age 16, and all jobs before age 16 are excluded from analysis.[15] The number of study subjects reporting some employment at each age is as follows:

[15]In a few cases, there is also available self-report information on employment from the age-15 Youth Interview; since the amount of information is relatively small, it is not included here.

	Age							
	12	13	14	15	16	17	18	19
Number (n = 121)	1	1	1	3	10	27	56	85
Percent	1%	1%	1%	2%	8%	22%	46%	70%

Some underreporting in these figures is to be expected; it should decrease with increasing age. A partial check of local CETA (Comprehensive Employment and Training Act) records revealed substantial underreporting, with 3 of 16 jobs reported. We did not have access to all local CETA records; CETA jobs not reported by study participants were not added to job histories. CETA employment underreporting may be atypical, however, because of the relatively brief duration of CETA jobs. There is no reason to expect substantial differences between the two treatment groups in job underreporting.

Effects of Preschool on Employment and Earnings

Preschool led to higher levels of employment, less unemployment, and higher earnings by age 19 for study subjects. As Table 12 shows, 50 percent of those who had attended preschool were working at the time of the age-19 Young Adult Interview, as compared to 32 percent of those who had not gone to preschool. Study participants who had been to preschool had spent fewer months without work since leaving high school: 4.9 months, compared with 10.3 months for those who had not attended preschool. In the calendar year in which they were 19, preschool attendees had been employed longer (6 months vs. 4 months) and had higher median annual incomes ($2,800 vs. $1,100). Similar trends occur for employment and earnings in earlier years.

Effects of Preschool on Occupational Aspirations

Occupational status is viewed by theorists as a major component of a person's position in the social hierarchy; at least some social scientists hold that individual changes in socioeconomic status occur mainly through changes in the levels of occupations (Haller & Portes, 1973). Among youth, in particular, early occupational status is considered a predictor of long-term career potential (Kohen, 1973). Study participants were asked at age 19 to describe their current or most recent job and to specify the kind of work they would like to be doing "five to ten years from now." Their responses were assigned occupational status scores.[16]

---

[16]The scoring system was developed by Nam, LaRocque, Powers, and Holmberg (1975) and is based on ranking occupations in the 1970 Census in terms of the median educational and income levels of jobholders. This measure approaches occupational level as related to position in a social and economic hierarchy, rather than purely in terms of perceived prestige. Status scores were assigned through individual examination of each response; separate scales were used for males and females.

Table 12

EMPLOYMENT AND EARNINGS THROUGH AGE 19

Variable	Preschool (n = 58)	No-Preschool (n = 63)	p^a
Reporting they had never held a job	5%	9%	—
Working at time of interview	50%	32%	.031
Unemployed (i.e., not working and looking for work) at interview	38%	51%	—
Months without work since leaving school	4.9	10.3	.003
Months employed—			
age-19 calendar year	6.1	3.9	.015
age-18 calendar year	2.5	1.5	—
age-17 calendar year	1.4	.87	—
age-16 calendar year	.19	.40	—
Mean earnings, age-19 calendar year	$5,386	$4,347	—
Median earnings, age-19 calendar year	$2,772	$1,070	.061

[a]Tests employed are Fisher's exact test for the comparison of category frequencies, Student's t test for the comparison of means, and the median test for the comparison of median values. Two-tailed p-values are presented if lower than .100.

Unskilled, Unemployed, and Unhappy About It

Money exerts a major influence upon Dwight's thinking about life: "The greens, money. I like to have it, I like to spend it." Beginning with junior high school, Dwight has had a series of unskilled jobs— shoveling snow, cutting grass, washing dishes. And ever since graduating from high school two years ago, Dwight has usually been able to find employment at one job or another. However, he has generally waited for a job opportunity to present itself, rather than going out to seek employment on his own initiative. For example, Dwight has always liked auto mechanics but has relied upon friends and family to turn occasional jobs his way instead of turning his skills into a steady source of income. Dwight also "just kind of happened" upon his last job as a nurse's aide, a position he quit because he "couldn't deal with it." Today, Dwight is unemployed and unhappy with his status: "I am not really satisfied, living on social services." He would like to eventually open his own auto repair business, but he acknowledges that it will take capital to buy the necessary tools. Says Dwight: "I need to keep my mind on what I'm doing, you know, really start banking my money, instead of just———it off like I usually do, or otherwise I'll never get nowhere."

—from *Dwight Gaines: A Case Study*

Getting in There and Playing the Game

Gerald attended Michigan State University on a full athletic scholarship. He graduated with a major in criminal justice. Unable to find a good job, he has enlisted in the Army. While in the service, he plans to obtain his master's degree and then enter law school upon his discharge. Eventually, Gerald hopes to be a corporate lawyer or enter private practice. His college experience solidified for Gerald the importance of education as the means for economic advancement: "The economic and education, you can't separate them...Education, sacrifice, determination—it's going to be hard, but there are going to be sacrifices that one has to make. It has to start [when you are] a child; it's going to be a long process, but that's what it's going to take. Tough it out because the game is set, this is the system, this is how it's being played, education is a way. You can frustrate yourself or you can get in there and play the game."

—from *Gerald Daniels: A Case Study*

There were no differences between groups in either current-job or aspired-future occupational status. Considerable variation in status scores was evident within the groups, however. Aspired-future status was quite generally higher than current-job status. However, even the occupations aspired to were of fairly modest status; there were only eight persons (9 percent of respondents who could be coded) who anticipated occupations in the highest 10 percent of the status scores—engineer, doctor, attorney (four in each group). The most frequent job category aspired to for men was plant or factory work; for women, clerical or secretarial positions. The median status aspired to by males was 58, in the range of such occupations as retail salesman, sheriff, vehicle dispatcher, foreman, or office machine repairman. The median aspired status for females was 70, in the range of such occupations as biological technician, retail trade manager, real estate agent, and a group of occupations similar to those mentioned by men— foreman and sheriff.

Effects of Preschool on Economic Dependence and Self-Support

Preschool education led study participants to greater levels of economic independence. The age-19 Young Adult Interview included questions about current sources of support; the Michigan Department of Social Services, without identifying specific individuals, also provided information from their records that permitted us to make group comparisons of the use of public assistance by study subjects through September 1982. The results of analyses of these data are summarized in Table 13.

At the time of the age-19 Young Adult Interview, members of the group who had attended preschool were more likely to be supporting

Table 13

ECONOMIC INDEPENDENCE AND SOURCES OF SUPPORT

Variable	Preschool (n = 58)	No-Preschool (n = 63)	p[a]
From Age-19 Young Adult Interview			
Persons supporting themselves by their own (or spouses') earnings	45%	25%	.020
Persons receiving money from family or friends, other than for work	28%	35%	—
Persons receiving money from welfare[b] at time of interview (n = 120)	18%	32%	.044
Mean annualized welfare payment in 1981 dollars (n = 117)	$633	$1,509	.021
Persons receiving money from other sources (n = 119)	20%	22%	—
From official social service records			
Persons never receiving assistance	26%	22%	—
Persons ever assisted	74%	78%	—
Persons assisted only as dependents or minors	29%	22%	—
Persons assisted as adults or principal grantees	45%	56%	—
Type of assistance ever received by persons as adults or principal grantees			
Food stamps	40%	49%	—
Aid to Families with Dependent Children	17%	21%	—
Medicaid	33%	41%	—
General Assistance	19%	41%	.007
Most frequent patterns of combined services			
General Assistance and food stamps	17%	38%	.009
AFDC, Medicaid, and food stamps	16%	21%	—

[a]Statistical tests employed in this table are Fisher's exact test for the comparison of category frequencies and the F-test for the comparison of regression-adjusted group means (adjusted for gender differences). Two-tailed p-values are presented if lower than .100.

[b]*Welfare* as defined for the table excludes government payments such as unemployment compensation or social security. Data for the official records portion of this table was obtained with the assistance of staff from the Michigan Department of Social Services, who provided usage information without identifying specific individuals. The records reflect the usage of public assistance services through September 1982 within the state of Michigan. At that time study participants ranged between 20 and 24 years in age. Earlier cohort (older) members would have had more time during which to qualify for public assistance than younger ones. No significant group-by-cohort interactions appeared for these data. Information about the timing or duration of services was not available.

themselves on their own: 45 percent reported they were supporting themselves completely on their own or their spouses' earnings, while 25 percent of the group who had not attended preschool made this claim.[17] There was a complementary difference in the reported receipt of government public assistance funds, including unemployment compensation, social security, and various welfare sources: 18 percent of preschool attendees reported receiving money from public sources at the time of the interview, whereas for those who had not been to preschool the percentage was 32 percent. Excluding unemployment and social security payments, the mean annual amount of public assistance per person (in 1981 dollars) was $633 for the preschool group and $1,509 for the no-preschool group; mean annual amounts per recipient were $3,796 for those who had attended preschool and $6,014 for those who had not. There were no statistically significant differences between groups in the proportion of individuals who received money from family or friends or from other sources.

Official records of social services usage confirm that preschool led to reduced use of at least certain kinds of public assistance by study participants. Although the names of 92 study participants (just over three-quarters of the sample) were found in the Michigan Department of Social Services records,[18] only 61 (50 percent of the full sample) received assistance in their own right, as principal grantees or adults. A smaller percent of persons who had attended preschool received General Assistance funds (19 percent) as compared with 41 percent of those who had not gone to preschool. (General Assistance funds are given to persons who meet a needs test but fail to meet criteria for Aid to Families with Dependent Children [AFDC] program funds.) Public assistance from other sources—Medicaid, Aid to Families with Dependent Children, and food stamps—also showed differences in the same direction, but the differences between groups were smaller and might have occurred by chance.

The study subjects' most frequently occurring combined pattern of public assistance was General Assistance and food stamps to the same person; this occurred for 17 percent of the preschool group and 38 percent of the no-preschool group. Unfortunately, information about timing, support levels, or service duration for individual study participants was not available.

Effects of Preschool on Other Economic Activities

Study participants were queried in the age-19 Young Adult Interview about other aspects of their economic lives: whether they owned one or

[17]This claim may appear somewhat questionable in light of the reported low median income of the entire group; it should be interpreted in terms of the typical incomes of black 19-year-olds from disadvantaged environments. At this age, with few long-term commitments, a few thousand dollars amounts to a relatively large disposable income. Regardless of whether respondents are in fact self-supporting, the point to be made from the above findings is that the extent to which respondents perceive themselves as self-supporting differs by treatment group.

[18]Social services records in other states were not checked. The probable incidence of welfare usage outside Michigan is quite small.

Out of the Slums and Pushing All the Way

Gloria is in her third year of college at Eastern Michigan University. She plans on running a business when she graduates and eventually owning her own firm in computers, communications, or perhaps some area of biology. Even in high school, Gloria stated: "I don't want to be like those kids who dropped out. I want to get out of the slums so I can raise my own kids right." Being economically independent is very important to Gloria. She says of herself in comparison to those she grew up with: "They should be trying to better themselves, they shouldn't just settle. I would never settle, personally. I mean I think they should be trying to do something with their lives instead of being on ADC. . . . I have confidence and I have potential, so I'm not going to stop; I'm going to be pushing all the way."

—from *Gloria Henderson: A Case Study*

more items valued at over $100, whether they owned a car, whether they had made purchases on credit, and whether they owed money at the time they were interviewed.

A higher percent of persons who had attended preschool reported that they saved money with some regularity, as Table 14 shows. The difference between groups was significant at the .10 level, with 62 percent of preschool subjects reporting some money saved, compared with 48 percent of no-preschool subjects. No other statistically significant differences between groups were found regarding credit use, debts, or possessions. When the two groups are considered together, 12 percent of the total sample of study participants reported having purchased things on credit,

Table 14

OTHER ECONOMIC ACTIVITIES THROUGH AGE 19

Category	Preschool (n = 58)	No-Preschool (n = 62)	p^a
Reporting some money saved	62%	48%	.094
Reporting some credit purchases	10%	13%	—
Reporting some current debt	26%	24%	—
Own a car	31%	35%	—
Have a driver's license	69%	76%	—
Own one or more items worth over $100	57%	62%	—

[a]Statistical test in this table is Fisher's exact test; two-tailed p-values are presented if lower than .100.

and 25 percent—twice that number—reported some current debts; the difference is attributable to the fact that the question "Do you owe anybody money?" allowed respondents to include debts to other persons. Forty persons, one third of the study sample, reported owning a car at the time of the interview; while almost three fourths, 73 percent, reported they had a driver's license. Finally, 60 percent of the study sample reported ownership of one or more objects worth over $100.

Effects of Preschool on Attitudes Toward Work and Pay

Preschool education appeared related to study subjects' higher overall satisfaction with work at age 19. Seven items in the age-19 Young Adult Interview explored respondents' attitudes toward their current or former jobs and also toward the pay they received. Of the 121 study participants responding at age 19, all but 9 answered these questions; the 9 who did not respond were those who stated they had never worked in the past. The questions were part of a set developed by Freeberg to assess job satisfaction as part of an adolescent work-training program (Freeberg, 1974, 1976). Two scales were formed from these items: a 4-item scale related to satisfaction with work, and a 3-item scale related to satisfaction with pay.[19] Group comparisons based on aggregated categories for these scales are shown in Table 15. A greater proportion of the preschool group expressed high levels of satisfaction with work: 42 percent versus 26 percent of the no-preschool group. There were no differences between groups in satisfaction with pay.

Economic Analysis of Preschool's Effects on Early Socioeconomic Success

This section focuses on the cost-effectiveness of preschool on socioeconomic success. Specifically, we examine monetary benefits to society resulting from study subjects achieving higher and more regular earnings and reduced economic dependence. This is only a part of the total economic analysis; the complete economic analysis is presented in Chapter 5.

By age 19, the preschool group's employment experience was significantly better than the experience of the no-preschool group. Study participants who attended preschool were more likely to be employed at the time of the age-19 Young Adult Interview, and they were employed more

---

[19]The scales were developed through content analysis of the questions, and their structure was confirmed by factor analysis. They showed adequate internal consistency, with Cronbach alpha coefficients of .76 (4-item scale) and .74 (3-item scale). Two additional questions were asked but are not reported here, since they showed neither conceptual nor empirical consistency with the other 7 items.

Table 15

ATTITUDES TOWARD WORK AND PAY[a]

Scale	Scoring Range	Preschool	No-Preschool	p[b]
Satisfaction with Work				
Four items scored 4-12; α = .76[c]	10-12	42%	26%	
e.g., How close does your work come to the way you think a job should be?	4-9	58%	74%	.056
Satisfaction with pay				
Three items scored 3-9; α = .74	6-9	55%	53%	
e.g., How's your pay for the kind of work you do?	3-5	46%	47%	—

[a]n = 112.

[b]Test used is χ^2 statistic. Two-tailed p-values are presented if less than .100.

[c]Alpha is an index of internal consistency.

months of the calendar year in which they became 19. There appears to be a similar trend for months employed at 17 and 18 as well, although these differences could have occurred by chance (see Table 12, p. 47) at each year. The total effect of preschool on months employed between the ages of 16 and 19 is about 3.5 months; almost all of the difference occurs between ages 18 and 19, and most of it occurs at age 19.[20]

The findings regarding earnings are quite similar to those for employment: By age 19 the effects of preschool on earnings have just begun to be discernible, but the magnitude of the effect appears to increase over time. Table 12 shows that the preschool group had significantly higher median earnings at age 19 than the no-preschool group, though there is no significant difference between the means.

The employment and earnings data have strong substantive implications with regard to preschool's lasting effects. Despite the fact that the data are limited to a period that includes secondary school and the transition period from school to work, the evidence indicates a positive effect of preschool on labor market experience. The weight of evidence and the trends over time suggest that the effect will increase in succeeding years. Furthermore, there are theoretical reasons why one would expect earnings over this period to be *higher* for the control group, because of "foregone earnings" as experimental group members attend school and training programs instead of joining the workforce. That is to say, the preschool group's greater commitment to schooling might be expected to result in decreased labor market experience and, all other things being equal, in less employment and lower earnings. Economists commonly calculate the value of foregone earnings as part of the cost of increased educational

---

[20]Regressions on months employed that take into account differences by gender result in smaller estimates of the preschool effect, although the statistical significance of comparisons between groups is unchanged. Over the entire period of 16-19 years of age, the effect of preschool is to increase employment by 3.5 months (p = .032). The effect for 18 and 19 years is 3.2 months (p = .016), and for age 19 alone, 2.2 months (p = .010).

attainment. In the case of the study participants, however, preschool does not leave other things equal. Apparently, early education sufficiently affects other variables—for example, motivation and ability—to offset the effect of foregone earnings relative to the control group.

The earnings and employment findings contribute in several ways to the calculation of preschool's effect on lifetime earnings. First, these findings provide direct estimates of teenage earnings and indicate that preschool produces a net benefit rather than a cost (as one might expect) over this period.[21] Second, the findings remove a common objection to the conventional method of estimating lifetime earnings from cross-sectional survey data on educational attainment, earnings, and labor force participation.[22] Finally, they add an empirical justification to the theoretical rationale for estimating future earnings benefits. Preschool is not simply *predicted* to increase earnings on theoretical grounds; this earnings increase is *observed*.

Lifetime earnings, after age 19, were estimated for each study participant based on mortality rates for blacks (by gender) and on mean annual earnings of blacks (by gender and educational attainment). The result, shown in Table 16, is a "ball park" estimate of preschool's effect on lifetime earnings. Discounted at a 3 percent annual rate, the estimated present value of preschool's effect on lifetime earnings after age 19 is about

Table 16

PRESENT VALUE[a] OF PRESCHOOL'S EFFECT ON
LIFETIME EARNINGS

Benefit	Dollar Value
Earnings ages 16-19	$ 642
Earnings ages 20 +	18,318
Fringes ages 20 +	5,495
Total	$24,455

[a]Discounted at 3%; 1981 dollars.

---

[21]An alternative explanation for this finding is that the economic model predicting foregone earnings is incorrect for young blacks. Foregone earnings were assumed and estimated in our earlier economic analysis (Weber et al., 1978) before current data were available.

[22]Objections are commonly raised to the estimation of effects of educational interventions on the basis of the observed relation between educational attainment and earnings (or labor force participation). The most frequent objection is that the estimated relationship does not represent the effect of educational attainment alone on earnings. Instead, it represents the effects of other variables—for example, ability or motivation—associated with educational attainment, as well as attainment effects. If the intervention affects only attainment, and not the other variables associated with attainment in the population at large, this estimation procedure overstates the effect of the intervention. This objection would not apply to preschool, given that preschool affects the associated variables. Perhaps the most important objection is to the propriety of estimating a longitudinal effect from cross-sectional data. Since it is the difference between group earnings that is evaluated in the study, this objection may have less weight: although total estimates of lifetime earnings may be in error, age-specific patterns of education-earnings relations are likely to be closely estimated by cross-sectional data.

$18,000. This figure does not include fringe benefits or nonpecuniary benefits of employment. A reasonable estimate for the increment in these benefits is 30 percent of the earnings increase. Adding these additional benefits, and the observed earnings differences (from ages 16 to 19) to the estimated difference in earnings after age 19 yields an estimate of the total effect of preschool on lifetime earnings. The present value of this total effect is about $24,500. Under the conservative economic assumptions adopted for this analysis, this $24,500 reflects the person's increased economic productivity, and is considered a benefit to society as a whole.[23] From the more narrow perspective of the taxpayer, about 25 percent of the earnings effect, or $4,740 would be the present value of new tax revenue.

As young adults, study subjects who attended preschool are more economically independent than are those who did not. The evidence supporting this finding is presented in Table 13 on page 49. A higher proportion of the preschool group reported they were supporting themselves on their own (or their spouses') earnings. Interview data on welfare usage corroborate this finding: Fewer of the study participants who had attended preschool received welfare payments, and consequently the mean welfare payment was lower for the preschool group. Official records of social service usage extend this finding by providing information that differs in an important way from that provided by self-reports: The official records report status over a period of several years, a period that varies in length for different study subjects.[24] Self-report data are taken at one point in time—the moment of the interview. Information from official records does not reveal differences in overall levels of welfare received; it does, however, reveal a significant difference in the enrollment rate of one public assistance program, General Assistance.

---

[23]Two assumptions are required in order for the gains to society as a whole to be considered equal to the earnings gains of individuals. One is that a person's earnings tend to equal the value of that person's marginal product. The other is that increased employment and/or better jobs for some (as reflected in increased earnings) do not come at the expense of decreased employment or worse jobs for others. There are two alternatives to the first assumption, with opposite implications. On the one hand, if earnings are based on educational credentials alone, then increased earnings due to increased educational credentials do not reflect increased productivity and so must be a transfer payment. In this case, society's gain is less than that of the individuals. On the other hand, discrimination against blacks and women may depress earnings below the value of their marginal product, in which case society's gain is greater than that of the individuals.

The second assumption also has an alternative—that gains for some can only come with losses for others; if this were the case, the gain of society as a whole would be less than that of the individuals.

The assumptions adopted for this study are the most conventional among the alternatives and, we believe, the most appropriate. In particular, while acknowledging that discrimination probably lowers earnings and so introduces a downward bias to the estimated effect of preschool on lifetime earnings, the size of this bias is considered too small **in relation to the precision of our estimates** to warrant a correction. Moreover, since the bias lowers estimates of preschool's effects on earnings, ignoring the bias leads to a more conservative benefit-cost analysis than would otherwise be obtained.

[24]The length of time varied by wave, with the longest period (through age 24) for Wave Zero and the shortest (through age 19) for Wave Four. A variety of factors (among these the fact that data were made available by group but, because of agency restrictions aimed at protecting client confidentiality, without individual identification) complicated the interpretation of state social services usage records. The proportions of welfare recipients by group did not differ across waves. Self-report information, although less extensive, is simple to interpret.

The primary economic benefit to society from increased economic independence comes in reduced costs for social service programs. As with earnings, it is anticipated that the beneficial effects of early education will persist over a lifetime. Unlike earnings, however, there are no data relating the amount of welfare received to other variables affected by preschool, such as educational attainment. (The reason for this, again, is that welfare records were available to the study only on a group basis.) In this case it was necessary to perform some plausible extrapolation using the amount of welfare received at age 19 to examine the potential magnitude of lifetime welfare reductions. It seems plausible that the lifetime pattern of welfare use is one of increases during the primary childbearing years and of declines thereafter. On this basis, our extrapolation assumes that the amount of welfare received is double the age-19 level between the ages of 20 and 30, declining by 50 percent every 10 years thereafter. Corrections for group survival rates, inflation, and a 3 percent discount lead to the figures in Table 17.

The economic importance of reductions in welfare depends on the perspective adopted. From the viewpoint of society as a whole, welfare payments per se are not a cost, but a transfer from some members of society to others. Only the administrative expenses of welfare programs are a cost to society as a whole. Administrative costs are about 10 percent of the value of payments on average, so the estimated economic benefits to society from welfare reduction are relatively small—in the above extrapolation, their present value is about $1,500. From the taxpayer's vantage point, the view is quite different. Benefits include payments and administrative costs, and add up to about $16,415 for each person who attended preschool.

Putting together the benefits from increased lifetime earnings and from welfare reductions leads to the totals for the value of increased socioeconomic success shown in Table 18. The totals are quite similar, even though the relative importance of increased earnings and of welfare reductions are reversed.

Summary

Early education leads to increased employment and earnings at age 19, to increased economic independence, and to reduced dependence on welfare. This trend occurs in spite of increased school commitment and educational attainment, both of which would in theory be expected to lead to reduced employment and earnings. Other studies have shown that higher educational attainment and higher earnings in early jobs are strongly predictive of higher eventual earnings. To our knowledge, there are no studies with comparable predictions for reductions in welfare dependence.

Preschool appears to offer an opportunity for long-term socioeconomic improvement in a disadvantaged population. If corroborated by some of the other longitudinal studies of the outcomes of early education, this result has strong policy implications. It applies directly to the

Table 17

PRESENT VALUE[a] OF AVERAGE WELFARE REDUCTION
ATTRIBUTABLE TO PRESCHOOL

Benefit	Welfare Reduction	Administrative Cost Reduction	Taxpayer Cost Reduction
Age 19, per person	$ 546	$ 55	$ 600
Extrapolated	14,377	1,438	15,815
Estimated total	$14,923	$1,493	$16,415

[a]Discounted at 3%; 1981 dollars.

notion that there is a "cycle of poverty" that extends from one generation to the next, suggesting there might be some combination of policies that could break into that cycle and turn it into an upward spiral. This finding gainsays the general trend of conclusions from the major studies of the role of schooling in economic success (e.g., Jencks et al., 1972, 1979). Jencks et al. (1972, p. 8) offered the following two conclusions:

> There is no evidence that school reform can substantially reduce the extent of cognitive inequality, as measured by tests of verbal fluency, reading comprehension, or mathematical skill. Neither school resources nor segregation has an appreciable effect on either test scores or educational attainment.
> We cannot blame economic inequality on differences between schools, since differences between schools seem to have very little effect on any measurable attribute of those who attend them.

In other words, changing schools so that all are more like the best of the present schools would not in itself affect educational attainment or reduce economic inequities. This has been taken to mean that educational reform policies are useless per se; but, of course, not all possible educational reform policies were tested in Jencks's correlational analyses. Our study suggests that there is something that can be done with children prior to school (namely, early childhood education) that will help them to traverse the formal educational system more efficiently, with higher attainment, and with direct effects on early socioeconomic success.

Table 18

PRESENT VALUE[a] OF PRESCHOOL'S EFFECT ON SOCIOECONOMIC SUCCESS

Benefit	Benefit to Society	Benefit to Taxpayer
Increased lifetime earnings	$24,455	$ 4,740
Welfare reduction	1,493	16,415
Total	$25,948	$21,155

[a]Discounted at 3%; 1981 dollars.

58

We showed at the end of Chapter 2 that the present value[25] of reductions in educational system costs was more than enough to make one year of preschool a worthwhile investment by itself. If to these cost savings we add the benefits of increased lifetime earnings and reduced welfare dependence, we can show that on these grounds alone, even two years of the Perry Preschool Project's relatively expensive educational program more than pay for themselves; and there are cost reductions and benefits still to be considered. The complete calculation of costs and returns will be analyzed in Chapter 5.

From the Case Studies: Insights into Socioeconomic Success

The successful persons in our sample define success in terms of "who you are," while the less successful define success in terms of "what you have." Young adults who have achieved relative socioeconomic success view their achievement as the sign of something deeper, as a symbol of their independence or a sign that they have attained a status higher than that of their parents or peers. Those who have been less successful view material goods or money as ends in themselves. As our interviewer put it, "The successful kids overshoot their goals." They do not just aim for material goods; they set their sights on more abstract targets, such as an education, knowing that material success will be encompassed if they succeed. Those who are less successful remain concerned with the concrete goods per se: An immediate job with short-term gains appears more attractive to them than a prolonged education that will only pay off in the future.

This difference in attitudes between the successful and less successful is likely to be fostered at home; however, school experiences can certainly help to shape views about the meaning of success. Perseverance and patience are factors in school performance even in the earliest grades; these are characteristics that can be nurtured at the preschool level so their rewards are experienced as soon as the child starts in elementary school. The payoff—better performance as a result of long, hard work—becomes self-reinforcing and the behavior is perpetuated over succeeding school years. Successful children thus experience the fact that the rewards *will* come, and hence they have a basis for setting their sights higher than those who have not experienced such deferred gains.

---

[25]A definition of discounted present value is offered in footnote 13, Chapter 2, page 39.

Can It Be? A Path Out of Poverty?

There's startling news from a long, rigorous research project in Michigan. Yes, after all the years of experiment and disappointment American society does know one sure way to lead poor children out of a life of poverty.

It has different names — Project Headstart, developmental day care, nursery school — but the idea is the same: high-quality preschool education. And it works.

●

Why do poverty's children do so badly in school and life? People have long treated that as a mystery. There have been positive results, like those of Project Headstart, the mass preschool program of Lyndon Johnson's Great Society. But even then, people seemed determined to flyspeck the findings and hide behind the mystery of failed research.

Now, it will be harder to hide. For 20 years, a landmark study has followed the lives of 123 black children from the depth of deprivation, many from single-parent homes. Half of them were given high-quality preschool education beginning at age 3. The others followed the traditional path of schooling. Now, the participants are almost 20 years old and the contrasts are remarkable.

The report on the privately funded study is entitled "Changed Lives" and rightly so. Nearly twice as many in the preschool group have gone to work or gone on to college or post-high school vocational training. Some 20 percent fewer had dropped out of school or had brushes with the law. The High/Scope Educational Research Foundation in Ypsilanti, Mich., which conducted the study, estimates that because of the reductions in crime, society has saved about $3,100 on each person in the preschool group.

And that's just the most easily quantifiable saving, trivial compared with the long-term gains. For example, the preschool group required far less remediation in elementary and high school, and as a result gained the self-confidence essential to success in school and life.

Too much can be read into the "Changed Lives" results. The graveyard of American education experiments is filled with cut-rate imitations of successful pilot projects. The Michigan experiment worked because the preschool education it provided was of high quality.

Nor can the results be taken as a cure-all for poverty and deprivation. Early childhood education has improved the youngsters' prospects considerably — but not enough. It has only reduced the negative effects of a miserable environment. Not even the highest quality preschool education can substitute for reforms that reach beyond education.

But so what if this is not The Perfect Answer? For many youngsters, an early, caring start means an opportunity to escape from the cycle of poverty. It means defeatists are wrong when they lament that nothing works and that "research shows" compensatory education has failed. A 20-year study in the laboratory of life now shows there is good to be done. If society is willing to do it.

The New York Times
September 13, 1984
Copyright 1984 by the New York Times
Company. Reprinted by permission.

IV Preschool's Effects on Social Responsibility

In this chapter, we examine the subjects' relations with family and community—a theme encapsulated in the phrase "social responsibility." The study's conceptual framework, presented in Chapter 1, predicted that early education would lead persons to greater school success and, through school success, to increased early socioeconomic success and greater social responsibility. In Chapters 2 and 3 we presented effects of preschool in terms of group differences in educational success and early socioeconomic success. In this chapter we will describe the effects of preschool on social responsibility in the same way—comparing the behaviors and attributes of the group who attended preschool with the group, originally similar, who did not. We will consider the relation between school success and social responsibility in Chapter 5.

Preschool led study subjects to greater social responsibility. This finding to age 19 and beyond extends results obtained through age 15. The preschool group had lower crime rates and less delinquent behavior than the no-preschool group, as indicated by fewer arrests, fewer cases sent on to juvenile court, fewer months on probation, and fewer persons fined as adults. Fewer pregnancies and births through age 19 were reported by females in the study's preschool group. In the economic analysis, significant per-group cost savings have accrued because of reduced criminal justice system and victim costs resulting from reductions in crime.

The Components of Social Responsibility

As young people reach adulthood, they enter several arenas that require them to assume new roles and responsibilities. Forming permanent relationships and raising children, moving away or staying at home, becoming involved with local churches and associations, voting—these new arenas are important because they offer young adults opportunities to make choices that have significant and long-lasting consequences. Choices about school and work have been considered in previous chapters; in this chapter we consider choices that relate to family, community, and civic and legal systems.

Four aspects of social responsibility are examined: (1) involvement with the legal system; (2) formation of new family linkages and relations with the family of origin; (3) relations with neighbors and community groups; (4) other personal and social characteristics. Involvement with the legal system was assessed by examining participants' responses to interview questions on this subject and by examination of police and court records. The formation of new family linkages and relations with the family of origin were assessed by obtaining information on whether or not subjects were living at least part of the time at home; their attitudes toward the family, their family's attitudes toward them; their pregnancies and number of children, if any; and their marital status or living-together arrangements. Relations with neighbors and community groups were assessed by examining subjects' formal links with community institutions, organizations, and clubs; by analyzing subjects' responses to questions about involvement in activities "for others"; and by examining subjects'

62

voter registration and voting records. Other personal and social characteristics were assessed by examining the results of measures of self-esteem, subjects' perceptions of their health and illnesses, and their reported use of leisure time. The concluding section of this chapter examines the economic implications of the group differences.

Earlier Effects of Preschool on Social Responsibility

Evidence showing that preschool led to a reduction in antisocial behavior and misconduct is available from the elementary school years and also at age 15 (see Schweinhart & Weikart, 1980, Chapter 4). For example, elementary school teachers rated children who had attended preschool as having better classroom conduct and personal behavior than their no-preschool counterparts. Preschool was associated with a reduction in the frequency with which age-15 study participants reported being kept after class. Preschool also led to reductions in the frequency of self-reported misbehavior and delinquent behavior at age 15. The proportion of persons who had reported none or one offense was higher for the preschool group: 43 percent as compared with 25 percent for those with no preschool. There were fewer persons in the preschool group than in the no-preschool group with 5 or more offenses (25 percent vs. 52 percent). When delinquent behaviors involving violence or theft were weighted according to seriousness, a similar difference was found.

At age 15, differences between groups were not found in general self-concept, general parent-youth relations, and the use of youths' leisure time.

Involvement with the Legal System: Effects of Preschool on Delinquent Behavior and Misbehavior

The preschool group had fewer contacts with the criminal justice system than did the no-preschool group, including fewer arrests. This finding applies both when we look at each wave at age 19 and when we look at the complete sample through mid-1982, when the subjects ranged in age from 19 to 24 years.

Information in support of these claims was obtained from the examination of official police and court records on juveniles and adults, as well as from information provided by the subjects themselves (see Tables 3 and 4 on pp. 9-10). Juvenile court records were searched for all local courts at which cases involving study participants might have been heard and also for courts in other locations when participant interviews indicated there might be case information available. Juvenile police records were searched at all police departments in the local area, and also at other locations when necessary. Two kinds of searches were conducted: blind searches, on all study participants (organized into two lists by treatment group); and

name-specific searches, on subjects who had mentioned prior involvement with the law during an interview and had signed an authorization
for the release of information.[26] Adult police and court records were obtained through a search of the records of the Michigan Department of State
Police; this search was name-specific, and by mid-1982 every study participant who had been interviewed at age 19 had been covered. Adult
records data were obtained when the oldest study participants (those in
Wave Zero) had almost turned 25 and the youngest (in Wave Four) were a
few months under 20 years of age.

Early education led to fewer persons ever being arrested and also to
fewer arrests; Table 19 summarizes information obtained from both juvenile and adult records. Thirty-one percent of the preschool group were
arrested at least once through mid-1982, compared with 51 percent of the
no-preschool group. The total number of arrests was 73 for those who had
attended preschool (an average of 1.3 arrests per study participant) and
nearly double, 145, for those who had not (corresponding to an average of
2.3 arrests per study participant). Comparing groups on arrests through
age 19 (the oldest age-point for which there is information on everyone in
the study), in the preschool group 22 percent had been arrested and in the
no-preschool group 38 percent had been arrested ($p = .047$ by Fisher's
exact test). The total number of arrests through age 19 is, respectively, 50
(preschool group), an average of .9 arrests per person, and 82 (no-preschool group), an average of 1.3 arrests per person (for the comparison of
total numbers of arrests, $p = .021$ by χ^2 test with 1 degree of freedom).

Persons may be arrested for very different reasons. To compare offense
categories in some easily interpretable way, arrests were rescored in terms
of their relative seriousness. Seriousness scores were assigned to both
juvenile and adult arrest charges. The scoring procedure used a ranking of
offenses developed by Phillips and Votey (1981) on the basis of relative
seriousness scores in the work of Sellin and Wolfgang (1964). The basic
procedure was simple: Offenses involving violence or the threat of violence (ranked 1-11 in the Phillips and Votey scale) were each assigned a
score of 3; offenses involving the loss or destruction of property valued at
over $50.00 (ranked 12-26 in the Phillips and Votey scale) were each
assigned a score of 2; and less serious offenses (ranked 27-61 in the Phillips and Votey scale) were each assigned a score of 1. When multiple
charges were made at the time of a single arrest, the single most serious
charge was the one scored. Dismissed charges were ignored; when charges
were changed over the course of prosecution, the final charge was used.
There was no difference between groups on the mean seriousness score
across all scored offenses.

Youths who attended preschool came to the attention of juvenile court
authorities less frequently than their no-preschool counterparts. Table 20
summarizes the information available from juvenile records. It is important to note that juvenile police and court procedures are designed to

[26]A total of 55 study participants (20 preschool; 35 no-preschool) signed releases authorizing
access to police and court records (45 percent of 121 in the age-19 interview sample). Blind
searches of juvenile records produced additional information for four persons (with four
arrests) in the preschool group, and for five persons (with six arrests) in the no-preschool
group. Since individual identification was not available for these data, they were only used
in total event counts and not for counts of the number of individuals ever involved with the
legal system.

Table 19

SUMMARY OF POLICE AND COURT RECORDS

Variable	Preschool (n = 58)	No-Preschool (n = 63)	p^c
Persons ever arrested or charged (as juveniles or adults)	31%	51%	.021
Persons ever arrested as juveniles[a]	16%	25%	—
Persons ever charged or arrested as adults	25%	40%	.077
Total number of arrests per group	73	145	.0001[d]
Persons by number of arrests			
With no arrests	69%	50%	
With one or two arrests	19%	25%	.068[e]
With three or more arrests	12%	25%	
Mean arrests per 100 persons	126	230	
Seriousness Scores[b]			
Persons with arrests for crimes of property or violence	24%	38%	.073
Number of property/violence arrests	47	74	.005[d]
Mean seriousness score per person, property or violence arrests	6.71	5.75	—
Persons with seriousness scores greater than 3	19%	22%	—

[a]Records without individual identification were obtained for four persons in the preschool group (four arrests) and five persons in the no-preschool group (six arrests). These data are included in the arrest counts and in group means, but not in counts of persons ever arrested, since they could not be identified individually.

[b]Seriousness scores were derived from ordinal rankings developed by Phillips and Votey (1981). Arrest charges were used. Dismissed charges were ignored. In multiple-charge arrests, the most serious charge was scored. Where charges were changed, the final charge was used. For details of the scoring procedure, see text.

[c]Statistical analyses in this table are Fisher's exact test for the comparison of numbers of persons (e.g., number arrested or charged) between groups, and Student's t test for comparison of means, except as indicated. Two-tailed p-values are presented if less than .100.

[d]Statistical test is x^2 with 1 degree of freedom for comparison of event frequencies.

[e]Statistical test is x^2 with 2 degrees of freedom.

avoid bringing youngsters to court whenever possible. Before a case is heard formally by a juvenile court judge, for example, the juvenile authorities must request that a petition for a court hearing be issued, and the request must be accepted; each of these steps provides for alternative decisions. Although there is no significant difference between groups in the number of juvenile arrests, there is a significant difference in the number of petitions requested by juvenile police authorities: 25 in the group that did not attend preschool compared with 11 in the group that did. The numbers of arrests and of persons arrested show the same trend as do the data for adults, although differences between groups for juveniles did not reach the .100 significance level.

Persons in the preschool group had fewer offenses as adults than did those in the no-preschool group. Table 21 summarizes these findings.

Table 20

SUMMARY OF OFFICIAL JUVENILE DELINQUENCY RECORDS

Variable	Preschool (n = 58)	No-Preschool (n = 63)	p[b]
Persons ever arrested as juveniles[a]	16%	25%	—
Total number of arrests	30	44	—[c]
Mean arrests per 100 persons	52	70	
Number of petition requests submitted to juvenile court	11	25	.037[c]
Persons with petitions requested	7%	13%	—
Mean petition requests per 100 persons	19	40	
Number of sentences (adjudications)	2	5	—[c]
Persons with adjudications	3%	3%	—

[a]Records without individual identification were obtained for four persons in the preschool group (four arrests) and five persons in the no-preschool group (six arrests). These data are included in the arrest counts and in group means, but not in counts of persons ever arrested, since they could not be identified individually.

[b]Statistical analyses in this table are Fisher's exact test for the comparison of numbers of persons (e.g., persons ever arrested as juveniles) between groups, except as noted. Two-tailed p-values below .100 are presented.

[c]For comparison of event frequencies the statistical test is x^2 with 1 degree of freedom.

There was a notable difference in the number of minor offenses charged: 21 offenses for the no-preschool group as compared with 1 for the preschool group. There was also a notable difference in the number of persons charged with minor offenses: 10 (no-preschool) versus 1 (preschool). Minor offenses included such things as disturbing the peace and traffic violations. Arrests for more serious offenses showed the same pattern: The preschool group had 42 arrests, while the no-preschool group had 80. Although the number of persons sentenced did not differ by group, there were notable differences in both the average months spent on probation (12 months for the preschool group compared with 33 months for the no-preschool group) and in the percent of persons fined (3 percent for the preschool group vs. 14 percent for the no-preschool group). There was no difference between groups in the percent of persons sentenced to terms in jail. Lengths of confinement could not be compared, since sentences were extremely variable (for example, 2 to 20 years) and the actual time served on sentences often was not yet known.

Another perspective on the official records of delinquent behavior is offered in the summary of arrest frequencies in Figure 6. More preschool group members had no offenses, and fewer of them committed five or more offenses. The difference between groups is significant. Further breakdown indicates that of the offenders in the no-preschool group, 11 percent had offenses only as juveniles, 26 percent had offenses only as adults, and 14 percent were offenders both as juveniles and as adults. Offense figures for the Perry Preschool study can be compared to those found in other

Table 21

SUMMARY OF OFFICIAL ADULT CRIME RECORDS

Variable	Preschool (n = 58)	No-Preschool (n = 63)	p[b]
Minor			
Number of minor[a] arrests or charges	1	21	.0001[c]
Mean minor offenses per 100 persons	2	33	
Persons with minor offenses per group	2%	16%	.007
Nonminor			
Number of nonminor arrests	42	80	.028[c]
Mean nonminor offenses per 100 persons	72	127	
Convictions			
Number of convictions	20	24	—[c]
Persons convicted	16%	21%	—
Case disposition—probation: persons	7%	21%	—
Mean months on probation	12.0	33.0	.093
Case disposition—fines: persons	3%	14%	.037
Mean fines (in current dollars)	$168	$209	—
Case disposition—confinement: persons[d]	10%	13%	—

[a]Minor adult offenses included traffic violations and breaches of the peace.

[b]Statistical analyses in this table are Fisher's exact test for comparison of proportions of persons (e.g., those arrested or charged) between groups, and Student's t test for the comparison of mean values, except as indicated. Two-tailed p-values below .100 are presented.

[c]Statistical test is $\varkappa^2$ with 1 degree of freedom for comparison of event frequencies.

[d]Confinement terms were not compared because individual sentences do not have a single duration specified beforehand (e.g., 2 to 20 years), and terms actually served are not yet known.

studies. For example, Wolfgang, Figlio, and Sellin (1972, p. 66) report that 50 percent of nonwhite males had one or more offenses in their Philadelphia birth cohort, considering only the period up to their eighteenth birthday. In the Perry Preschool study's control group, 51 percent of males through age 17 had one or more offenses in the record.

The charges faced by study subjects were quite varied. Offenses most frequently recorded were burglary and larceny; assault charges were not uncommon. Serious charges included one murder, one manslaughter, and two charges of criminal sexual conduct. It should be noted that arrests themselves carry no presumption of guilt. We view them here as indications of the extent of group involvement with the criminal justice system.

In summary, data from official records say (a) that this was a population at significant risk of involvement with police and the court systems and (b) that early education reduced the extent of this involvement. The proportion of offenders (at least one time) in the preschool group was 31 percent—1 out of 3—whereas the proportion of offenders in the no-preschool group was 51 percent—1 out of 2. Chronic offenders, defined as persons with five or more offenses, comprised 17 percent of the no-preschool group, but only 7 percent of the preschool group. The overall number of arrests was only half as great in the preschool group. Though the average seriousness of crimes was the same for both groups, members

Figure 6

COMPARISON OF ARRESTS AND CHARGES BY GROUP

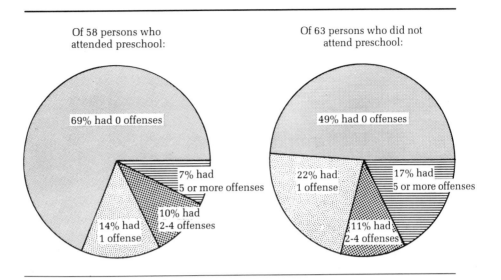

Of 58 persons who attended preschool:

69% had 0 offenses

7% had 5 or more offenses

10% had 2-4 offenses

14% had 1 offense

Of 63 persons who did not attend preschool:

49% had 0 offenses

22% had 1 offense

17% had 5 or more offenses

11% had 2-4 offenses

of the preschool group were given less probation and charged fewer fines.

Preschool also led to reductions in some types of delinquent behavior, as reported by the subjects themselves. Table 22 summarizes self-reported involvement with the police and in individual categories of misbehavior or delinquent behavior at the time of the age-19 interview. Those who had attended preschool reported 56 instances of involvement with the police per 100 persons; those who had not attended preschool reported 95 instances per 100 persons.[27] Significant differences were also reported in three individual offense categories; in all of these cases, the number of events reported was lower for the group that had attended preschool. For involvement in a serious fight, the rate per 100 persons was 45 for those who had attended preschool and 84 for those who had not; for involvement in a group or gang fight, the rate per 100 persons was 40 for those who had attended preschool, versus 92 for those who had not; and for causing someone an injury requiring bandages or a doctor, the rate per 100 persons was 36 for those who had attended preschool versus 68 for those who had not. Related analysis indicated that the proportion of individuals reporting two or more offenses involving violence or the destruction or removal of property is higher for those who did not attend preschool: 73 percent, compared with 59 percent for those who attended preschool ($p = .070$ by Fisher's exact test).

---

[27]The number of events reported by individuals is approximate. Interviewees were asked to respond in 1 of 5 categories for each behavior: never, once, twice, three or four times, and five or more times. To obtain a total count of events reported by each person, each response was multipled by the number of instances. Thus 1 remained 1; 2 remained 2; 3 or 4 was recoded as 3; and 5 or more was recoded as 5. The total number of events was then summed across behaviors. If anything, event estimates should be an undercount. This tends to underestimate the decrease in offense events resulting from intervention, given that individuals in the control group were more likely to use the "5 or more" reporting category. To permit comparisons across groups, event frequencies are reported in Table 22 and in the text in terms of rates per 100 persons.

Table 22

SELF-REPORT DATA AT AGE-19 INTERVIEW

Item[a]	Offense Rates per 100 Persons[b]		p[c]
	Preschool	No-Preschool	
Hit an instructor or supervisor	21	25	—
Were involved in a serious fight	45 ($n = 58$)	84 ($n = 62$)	.009
Were involved in a group or gang fight	40	92	.0005
Caused someone an injury requiring bandages or a doctor	36	68	.016
Threatened someone with a knife or gun	26	21	—
Took something worth under $50	107	89	—
Took something worth more than $50	64	70	—
Took something from a store	159	175	—
Took a car without permission, other than from a parent or relative	31	19	—
Took part of a car	33 ($n = 52$)	21 ($n = 57$)	—
Entered a place when they weren't supposed to be there	56 ($n = 52$)	40 ($n = 57$)	—
Set fire deliberately	13 ($n = 52$)	12 ($n = 57$)	—
Vandalized school property	46 ($n = 52$)	42 ($n = 57$)	—
Vandalized property at work	18 ($n = 51$)	9 ($n = 56$)	—
Smoked marijuana	312 ($n = 52$)	344 ($n = 57$)	—
Used other dangerous drugs	75 ($n = 52$)	51 ($n = 57$)	—
Were involved with police	56 ($n = 52$)	95 ($n = 57$)	.020
Mean number of offenses per 100 persons	676	754	—
Mean offenses per 100 persons, weighted by seriousness	1,236	1,525	—

[a]Items were taken from *The Monitoring the Future Questionnaire* (Bachman & Johnston, 1978).

[b]Number of respondents per group are preschool, 58, and no-preschool, 63, except as indicated.

[c]Statistical tests in this table are x^2 with 1 degree of freedom comparing group event frequencies, unadjusted; analysis of variance for means. Two-tailed p-values are presented if lower than .100.

Those who attended preschool scored lower on a serious delinquency scale ($p = .063$ by median test), in which self-reported property damage or theft and violent offenses were weighted by the offense's relative seriousness. Using a scoring procedure similar to that employed for official records data, we gave behavior involving violence or threats to persons a weight of 3, behavior involving property damage or theft of items with values in excess of $50.00 a weight of 2, and other property offenses a weight of 1. It should be noted that the relation between self-reported offense categories and legal system categories is imprecise and varies depending on circumstances. For instance, individuals were asked if they had ever "gone into some house or building when they weren't supposed to be there." Depending on the particular situation, this behavior could correspond to trespass, illegal entry, or even attempted or actual burglary.

Effects of Preschool on Family Linkages

Preschool education led study subjects to lower fertility rates, as reported by age 19. Female study participants were asked how many times they had been pregnant and how many children they had at the time of the interview. Seventeen pregnancies or births were reported by the 25 women who had attended preschool; 28 pregnancies or births were reported by the 24 women who had not attended preschool. The difference between groups is statistically significant ($\chi^2 = 3.16$ with 1 degree of freedom; $p = .076$); it corresponds to a pregnancy/birthrate of 68 per 100 women for those who attended preschool, and 117 per 100 women for those who had not. Men in the sample were also asked if they had fathered any children: 10 children were fathered by those who had attended preschool, and 15 by those who had not. This difference between groups for men was not statistically significant.

These figures complement the overall picture of study participants' relations with their families of origin and their formation of new family linkages. At age nineteen, 89 percent of the study sample were still single, and 69 percent were still living at home. Twelve persons (10 percent) had married or were living with someone (other than their family of origin) on a steady basis; one had married and divorced. Among individuals who were still single, most (71 percent) reported that they were looking forward to getting married eventually. Sixty-two children had been born to subjects or their spouses; one child had died soon after birth. Five women were pregnant at the time they were interviewed. Of the 40 persons who, at the time of the interview, reported having had or fathered children, 23 (19 percent of the total sample) reported one child; 14 (12 percent of the total sample) reported two; 2 reported three children; and 1 reported four. There were no differences between the groups in these areas.

A number of questions asked of study participants dealt with relations with the family of origin and perceptions of the individual by their family. To the question "How have you been getting along with the family you grew up in?" 97 percent of all respondents answered "Getting along great" or "Fair, getting by." When study participants were asked, "How does your family feel about how you're doing?", 90 percent of the respondents answered, "They think I'm getting by" or "They think I'm doing great." Seventy-four percent of respondents thought they had turned out as well or better than their families had expected them to. There were no differences between groups in these responses.

Effects of Preschool on Relations with Neighbors and the Community

In responses to the age-19 Young Adult Interview, subjects from the preschool group reported undertaking activities for family and friends more frequently than did no-preschool subjects. Respondents were asked whether they did certain things for themselves, for themselves as well as for others (such as friends or family), or not at all. The activities queried were these:

- repairing things around the house
- raising vegetables or a garden
- fixing cars
- making clothes
- building things
- cooking meals
- cutting the grass
- caring for children, babysitting
- house cleaning
- playing a musical instrument

Persons who had attended preschool were more likely to report they had done one or more of these things for themselves as well as others—60 percent, compared with 43 percent of those who had not attended preschool ($p = .041$ by Fisher's exact test).

The Making of an Involved Teacher

From her religious training, and the example set by her minister father, it is easy to see how Bonita came to believe in the value of helping others. Of his own school involvement, Mr. Emerson says: "I am not only concerned about my children, I am concerned about all of them when I go out there." Bonita is now fulfilling a lifelong ambition to be a teacher and help her community. She sees the educational system as an ideal organizing force for blacks helping themselves. Like her father, she sees parents' involvement in their children's education as a primary mechanism for bringing about lasting improvements. Bonita is therefore committed to reaching the parents and getting them involved in the schooling of their children: "They first have to know what's going on really, and I think everyone should put themselves on the same level—that nobody is better than anybody else. And I notice that when you talk to parents on the same level, they appreciate you more as a person."

—from *Bonita Emerson: A Case Study*

In contrast to doing things for family and friends, study participants who had attended preschool reported doing unpaid volunteer work less frequently: 14 percent of those in the preschool group had done unpaid volunteer work, compared with 33 percent of those in the no-preschool group. Both the sorts of activities and the organizations mentioned varied considerably. Included were social or fellowship organizations (such as the Fellowship of Christian Athletes); helping organizations (such as various local hospitals, charitable, and crisis organizations); and a variety of other services ranging from "yard work" and "babysitting" to distributing flyers for the school band and "pulling cars out of the ditch."

The relation between volunteer work and work done for others was not statistically significant. It seems quite possible that a group of persons could be more likely to do things for others such as friends or family and yet be less involved in volunteer work. The broad range of categories included under "volunteer work" makes interpretation of the difference between groups difficult. Almost the only common link across all the categories mentioned is that the services involved are unpaid.

There were no differences between groups in involvement in civic or other neighborhood organizations, or in voter registration or voting behavior. Sixteen percent of the entire study sample reported belonging to civic organizations or to local teams or clubs; slightly over one half of all study participants (52 percent) had belonged to some team, club, or organization in high school, and 12 percent of study participants had been elected to some position or office while in school. As of mid-1982, when voter registration and voting records were checked for the entire study sample, 31 percent of all participants had registered to vote, and 8 percent had voted at least once in a national, state, or local election. The majority of all voting activity occurred at the time of the 1980 national elections, with 7 percent of the sample voting. At that time 22 percent of the sample were registered to vote, although all but three study participants would have been old enough to register.

Effects of Preschool on Other Personal and Social Characteristics

There were no differences between groups on a number of variables dealing with general self-esteem, specific self-esteem, perceptions of health, and use of leisure time.

Ten questions in the age-19 Young Adult Interview dealt with general perceptions of self—that is, with persons' generalized self-esteem, as reported in Table 23. The questions themselves were slightly adapted from an instrument originally devised by Rosenberg (1965). Items were formed into a single scale by Guttman scaling, following the method used by the original scale developers; its validity is discussed by Wylie (1974). There were no differences between groups on the overall scale mean or for individual items.

Table 23

GENERAL SELF-ESTEEM BY GROUP

Level of Self-Esteem[a]	Preschool (n = 58)	No-Preschool (n = 63)	p[b]
High self-esteem (5-6)	79%	81%	
Medium self-esteem (4)	16%	19%	
Low self-esteem (2-3)	3%	0%	—

[a]Guttman scaling of 10 items, values 0-6. Sample item: I feel I have a number of good qualities (strongly agree, agree, disagree, strongly disagree).

[b]Statistical test for this table is x^2 with 2 degrees of freedom. Two-tailed p-values are presented if lower than .100.

Four age-19 Young Adult Interview questions (answered by 78 percent of the sample) asked subjects to select an area in which they did well and to compare their performance in that area with how they thought others might perform, as well as with how they thought others of their choice might perceive their performance. The intention of these items was to relate self-esteem directly to a specific area of life. Respondents chose a broad variety of interest areas, but school was the most frequently selected; 45 percent of respondents chose it. (School-specific self-esteem is discussed in Chapter 2.) Other areas selected by respondents included family (17 percent), friends (5 percent) and sports (11 percent); 21 percent of respondents chose disparate areas that could not be aggregated. There were no detectable differences between treatment groups on area-specific self-esteem, either when considered by interest area or when data were aggregated across areas.

Subjects were asked if they had any ailments or problems with their health; 11 percent responded that they had some problem. Excluding one health problem that was the need for glasses, the remainder of problems mentioned included symptoms related to infections (two cases), stomachaches and ulcers (three cases), joints or back problems (three cases), and an assortment of complaints including nerves, high blood pressure, and eye problems. One respondent stated she had health problems but refused to specify what they were. For 52 interview respondents who stated they had seen a doctor for some disorder in the previous year, the median number of visits was two. There were no differences between groups on problems mentioned.

The only difference between groups in the use of leisure time was for spending time at church. Persons with preschool were more likely to have spent time at church; 53 percent stated they attended at least sometimes, compared with 40 percent of those with no preschool (p = .074 by Fisher's exact test). Of the leisure-time activities queried, those most frequently engaged in by study participants were listening to music (98 percent of the sample) and watching television (86 percent of the sample). Hanging out with friends (reported by 69 percent of the sample) and sports (68 percent) were engaged in less frequently. Some amount of reading for pleasure was reported by nearly everyone in the study: 88 percent of the study sample reported reading a book, magazine, or newspaper "in the past few weeks." Differences between males and females occurred for two variables. Males less frequently reported watching television (80 percent, compared with 94 percent for females), and males more frequently engaged in sports (79 percent, compared with 53 percent for females).

Economic Implications of Preschool's Effects on Social Responsibility

Of the differences between groups in the area of social responsibility, the only one with clearly estimable cost implications is the preschool group's lower rates of crime and delinquency. The data available were used to estimate the economic benefits from reduced crime and delinquency through age 20 and to extrapolate this estimate beyond age 20. Each crime in the official records was assigned two costs: a victim cost and a criminal justice system cost. Victim costs were derived from national crime victimization survey data. Criminal justice system costs were estimated from local police and court costs (for juvenile offenses) and from national criminal justice system statistics (for adult crimes). Given that victim-based reports of crimes are much more frequent than arrests, cost estimates based on arrest rates are believed to considerably underestimate the costs of crime (Mallar, Kerachsky, Thornton, Long, Good, & Lapczynski, 1978).

As was the case in Chapter 3 with welfare data, a simple extrapolation was performed to infer the potential cost savings over participants' lifetimes. The base for the extrapolation is the average per-person costs of crime actually recorded over the years between ages 18 and 20. A simple procedure was developed to extrapolate to lifetime crime costs from these data, based on general trends in cross-sectional statistics for arrest frequencies and age in the FBI's *Uniform Crime Report* (U.S. Department of Justice, 1980, pp. 200-201). In this procedure the same crime costs are assigned for the period in which study participants are ages 21-25 as for the period in which they are ages 18-20 (in constant dollars); one half of this value is assigned for the period between 26 and 35 years of age, half again for ages 36-45, half again for ages 46-50, and half again for the rest of study participants' lives. Since these assumptions are based on cross-sectional data, no correction for mortality among study participants was carried out.

The estimated present value[28] of preschool's total benefit to society as a result of reduced crime is just over $3,100 per child. More detailed estimates separating observed from projected costs, and victim costs from criminal justice system costs are presented in Table 24. This present value estimate is quite probably low because it understates victim costs; more important, it is also quite likely to be low because noneconomic factors are not included. Much of the cost of crime to its victims is not expressible with any accuracy in dollars, since it also includes the factors of mental

---

[28]A definition of present value is provided in Chapter 2, footnote 13, page 39.

From the Case Studies: Insights into Social Responsibility

Successful individuals show a sense of responsibility that goes beyond themselves to encompass their families and their community. Those who have been less successful are primarily interested in themselves and often depend on others (their parents, the public assistance system, the prisons) to take care of them. This difference in attitudes might stem from relatively early experiences in which these individuals would have developed a sense of independence. We noted in the case studies that parents of preschoolers spoke of preschool as an important first step in their youngsters' "separation" from home; preschool further provided the children with an extra year or two before kindergarten in which to acquire social skills and the confidence that they could take care of themselves as well as help teachers and peers. These are the earliest manifestations of what we later call "citizenship."

The level of social responsibility also seems related to a range of orientations that goes from active to passive. Passive and nonsuccessful individuals seem to view themselves as victims or outsiders in relation to the rest of society. Seeing themselves as outside the mainstream, they feel less bound by the conventional rules that insiders accept. By contrast, those with more active orientations believe they can take on roles within the system and succeed in achieving their goals. This leads to a self-fulfilling prophecy: If you feel you belong in the system, you play by its rules; if you play by the rules, you are more likely to succeed; if you succeed you are accepted by, and hence feel you belong in, the system.

Where might early eduction fit? One of the first systems in which a child must be accepted is school. If preschool helps socialize children into the system so they feel a sense of belonging, they will play by its rules and fit in better. Further, fitting well into one system should make transitions into (and acceptance in) other mainstream systems much easier. By contrast, being outsiders in the school system will predispose children to become outsiders in other systems (such as the legal system). In this fashion, successful persons come to take control of their own destinies; the less successful come to feel that control is out of their hands.

Table 24

PRESENT VALUE[a] OF CRIME REDUCTION

Time of Benefit	Total Social Benefit[b]	Criminal Justice System Benefit
Observed through age 20	$1,233	$1,049
Projected from age 21 on	1,871	1,237
Total	$3,104	$2,286

Note. Table entries are in constant 1981 dollars. A definition of *discounted present value* or *present value* is offered on page 00, in footnote 13 of Chapter 2.

[a]Discounted at 3%; 1981 dollars.

[b]Total social benefit is equivalent to the reductions in victim costs and criminal justice system costs.

anguish, fear, and physical suffering; if monetary equivalents of these factors were to be provided, the benefit of reduction in crime would far exceed $3,100. There are also nonvictim benefits that are not included: The quality of life for persons who are not involved in crime (but might have been) has been improved. There is also a psychological benefit to people generally from reduced fear of crime, and there are reduced public and private crime prevention costs that accompany a general reduction in crime rates. Finally, even if all victim costs are excluded from consideration, the benefit to society simply from reductions in criminal justice system costs is almost $2,300.

V Reviewing and Interpreting Study Outcomes over Time

In the first section of this chapter we summarize the outcomes of the Perry Preschool program, presenting the findings that have been reported in previous volumes in this series as well as in earlier chapters of this book. The next section presents a causal model that illustrates how these preschool effects developed over two decades and how outcomes relate to each other. The final section offers a summary of the economic analysis of the program and its outcomes.

Summary of Group Differences

The Perry Preschool study is based on a program of early intervention in the lives of low-income children who were at risk of school failure and placement in special education. The treatment consisted of either one or two years of preschool education and weekly home visits. To evaluate the program's effects, participants were selected for the study on the basis of their similar background characteristics and were assigned at random to an experimental (preschool) group and a control (no-preschool) group. Follow-up of study participants has occurred regularly since the project began in 1962.

Immediate Effects of Preschool on School Success

During and at the end of preschool, early education improved the performance of study participants on IQ tests. The IQ difference between treatment groups diminished over time, however, and by second grade was no longer statistically significant. Similar trends were found for other measures of academic aptitude.[29] Nevertheless, early education led the subjects to increased academic achievement, as measured by standardized tests, throughout the elementary and middle-school grades. Teacher ratings of children's social and emotional maturity after kindergarten also showed significant overall trends favoring the group that had attended preschool (Weikart et al., 1978). By fourth grade, children who had attended preschool were less likely to have been placed in special education or retained in grade than those who had not attended preschool. Through the elementary years, preschool attendees also had fewer absences than their no-preschool counterparts. By age 15, youths who had attended preschool placed a higher value on schooling and had stronger commitments to school than did the no-preschool group (Schweinhart & Weikart, 1980).

Later Effects of Preschool on School Success

Through secondary school, youths who had attended preschool had fewer failing grades and better marks than the no-preschool subjects. Through-

---

[29]The Arthur Adaptation of the Leiter International Performance Scale (Arthur, 1952); the Peabody Picture Vocabulary Test (Dunn, 1965); and the Illinois Test of Psycholinguistic Abilities (McCarthy & Kirk, 1961). For details of findings, see Weikart et al., 1978.

out their entire period of formal schooling, compared to the no-preschool subjects, preschool attendees spent fewer years in special education, were less likely to be classified as mentally retarded, and more frequently were assigned to remedial education. At age 19, persons who had attended preschool had higher scores than those with no preschool on a measure of competence in skills of everyday life (the Adult Performance Level Survey). They also expressed more favorable attitudes toward high school than did the other group.

Preschool's Effects on Early Socioeconomic Success

Early education led subjects to higher levels of employment, less unemployment, and higher earnings by age 19. Study participants were more likely to be employed at the time of their interview if they had attended preschool; since leaving school, those who had attended preschool had spent fewer months unemployed. In the calendar year in which they were 19, preschool attendees had been employed longer and had higher median incomes than the no-preschool group; they also reported being more satisfied with their jobs.

Subjects who had attended preschool were more likely to be supporting themselves on their own (or their spouses') earnings at the time they were interviewed; they also reported receiving less public assistance than the no-preschool subjects. Examination of official records also showed that preschool led to reduced use of at least certain kinds of welfare: Persons who had attended preschool less frequently received General Assistance funds. Compared to the no-preschool subjects, a higher percentage of subjects who had attended preschool reported that they saved money with some regularity.

Preschool's Effects on Social Responsibility Through Early Adulthood

Fewer of the preschool subjects had ever been arrested, and that group also had a lower total number of arrests. Youths who had attended preschool were less likely to come to the attention of juvenile authorities. Those with preschool had fewer offenses as adults than did those without preschool: More of the preschool subjects had records of committing no offenses and fewer had records of five or more offenses. Preschool also led to reductions in some types of delinquent behavior as reported by the individuals themselves. Those who had attended preschool had lower median scores on a scale measuring delinquent-event frequencies weighted by seriousness.

Preschool education led the preschool group to fewer pregnancies and births than the no-preschool group as reported at age 19 by women in the study.

In their responses to the age-19 Young Adult Interview, persons who had attended preschool were more likely than their no-preschool counterparts to report "doing things to help" family and friends, but less likely to report doing volunteer work. Preschool subjects were also more likely than no-preschool subjects to report attending church sometimes or often.

This brief summary of group differences demonstrates that the children who attended the Perry Preschool were changed in ways that have had long-term, positive effects on their lives. To understand the role of early education in producing these long-term outcomes, however, we must move beyond the examination of group differences and look at the relations among study variables. We have developed a causal model for this purpose.

A Causal Model of Preschool's Effects

The Perry Preschool program has had long-term impact because the immediate program effects were the first links in a chain of cause and effects that permanently changed the lives of the preschool subjects. This chain of causes and effects is the basis of our causal model. Chapter 1 presented the conceptual framework for that model (p. 3). The statistical procedures of multiple regression analysis allow us to examine how well the model conforms to the data from the study. In what follows we present a causal model of the links connecting early childhood education to measures of adult success, in the context of some of the important effects of personal characteristics and family background. This is a rather modest attempt to elucidate the long-term effects of preschool, and not an effort to provide a complete explanation for differences among the study subjects in school and post-school success.

Figures 7 and 8 present a causal model of a dozen variables associated with the effects of preschool education, with Figure 7 isolating the chain of effects from preschool to adulthood. The variables in the model can be divided chronologically into three sets: variables in early childhood, school process variables in childhood and adolescence, and variables in early adulthood. The five early childhood variables are as follows: preschool, intellectual performance before preschool (as measured by Stanford-Binet IQ's), intellectual performance at school entry, family socioeconomic status, and gender. The four school process variables are as follows: social maturity and misbehavior[30] (representing commitment to schooling), number of years in special education (representing scholastic placement), and scholastic achievement. The three early adulthood variables are as follows: scholastic attainment (years of schooling completed), delinquency (arrests), and employment (months worked).

In Figures 7 and 8, each arrow indicates a hypothesized path from cause to effect. Arrows appear only when the association between variables is statistically significant (two-tailed $p < .100$). If an arrow does not join two variables, there is no direct causal connection between them,

---

[30]Social maturity is a factor based on eight items: appears generally happy; social relationship with classmates; [not] withdrawn and uncommunicative, friendly and well-received by other pupils; degree of trust of total environment (suspicious, trusting); [does not] appear depressed; level of emotional adjustment; direction of interest (introversion, extroversion); and [not] isolated with few or no friends. Misbehavior is a factor based on seven items: disobedient, influences others towards troublemaking, resistant to teacher, lying or cheating, resentful of criticism or discipline, easily led into trouble, and swears or uses obscene words.

80

Figure 7

A CAUSAL MODEL FOR EFFECTS OF THE PERRY PRESCHOOL PROGRAM

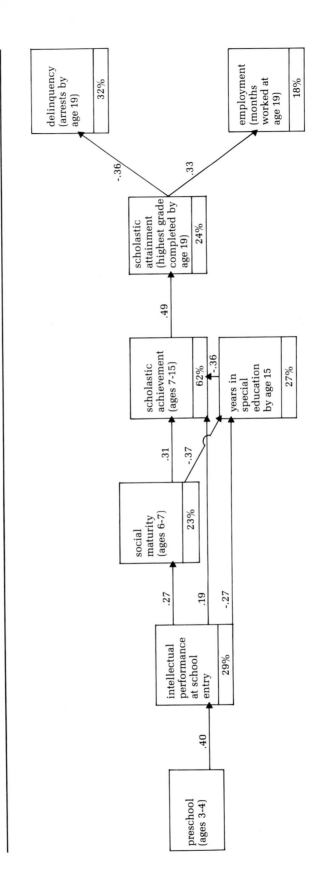

Note. Analyses are based on n = 112. Causal paths are indicated by arrows joining variables, with direction of the arrows from cause to effect. Path coefficients are beta weights in ordinary-least-squares regressions; arrows connect variables only if paths are significant (at p < .10, two-tailed). The directions of paths between variables measured at the same time points are dependent on the model's the-oretical framework and should be interpreted with caution. The percent presented at the bottom of each variable is the percent of variance in that variable accounted for by statistically significant predictors. Figures 7 and 8 are based on the same analyses; variables are excluded from Figure 7 only for purposes of clarity in presentation. The complete model resulting from analyses is presented in Figure 8.

Figure 8

A CAUSAL MODEL FOR EFFECTS OF THE PERRY PRESCHOOL PROGRAM IN THE CONTEXT OF IMPORTANT BACKGROUND VARIABLES AND INTERRELATIONS

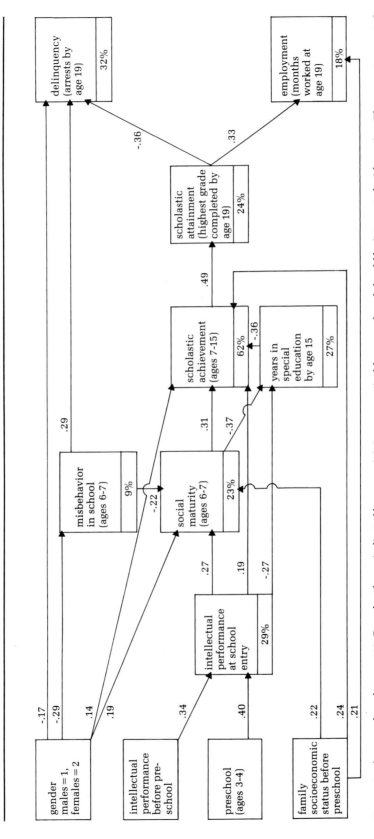

Note. Analyses are based on *n* = 112. Causal paths are indicated by arrows joining variables, with direction of the arrows from cause to effect. Path coefficients are beta weights in ordinary-least-squares regressions; arrows connect variables only if paths are significant (at *p* < .10, two-tailed). The directions of paths between variables measured at the same time points are dependent on the model's the- oretical framework and should be interpreted with caution. The percent presented at the bottom of each variable is the percent of variance in that variable accounted for by statistically significant predictors. Figures 7 and 8 are based on the same analyses; variables are excluded from Figure 7 only for purposes of clarity in presentation.

although there may be an indirect connection between them through other variables. The path coefficient next to each arrow is the beta weight derived from ordinary least squares regression analysis; this number indicates the degree of change in an effect, given one unit of change in the cause. The coefficient of determination appears below a variable and indicates the percentage of variance accounted for by the hypothesized variables appearing in the figure. The goal for any dependent variable is to account for 100% of its variance.

Turning first to Figure 7, we examine in isolation the links between preschool and adult success. Preschool had an immediate positive effect on intellectual performance measured immediately before school entry. This improvement in performance is hypothesized to affect initial transactions with teachers and the school environment, leading to greater school commitment and better scholastic placement. These hypotheses are supported by the finding of significant effects of intellectual performance on teacher ratings of social maturity (which implies school commitment), on placement in special education, and on achievement. Both social maturity and special education placement also had their own effects on scholastic achievement. Achievement, in turn, is the only significant direct predictor of scholastic attainment at age 19. Finally, scholastic attainment is the principal predictor of adult success as measured by number of arrests and months worked.

In Figure 8 the effects of preschool are shown in the context of the effects of other important early childhood background variables. An additional measure of commitment to schooling—misbehavior—is also introduced. The effects of the background variables are much as one would expect. Comparing genders (with other variables "held constant"), females are judged by their teachers to be better behaved and more mature. Females also have higher scholastic achievement and are less likely to be arrested than are males. Intellectual performance measured prior to preschool affects only intellectual performance measured at school entry. Family socioeconomic status has direct positive effects on social maturity, scholastic achievement, and employment at age 19. Lastly, although teacher ratings of misbehavior were neither directly nor indirectly affected by preschool, it is interesting that they are significantly related to the number of arrests through age 19.

Several of the intermediate connections in the causal model shown in Figure 8 are also revealing. Intellectual performance at school entry directly affected social maturity, special education placement, and scholastic achievement, and indirectly affected scholastic attainment. Intellectual performance did not affect delinquency or employment except through these scholastic variables. Scholastic achievement was the gateway to scholastic attainment; none of the other school process variables affected scholastic attainment except through their effects on scholastic achievement. Similarly, scholastic attainment served as the gateway to early employment for the other school process variables.

In summary, the causal model confirms that preschool education provides poor children with a "head start" both intellectually and socially. It suggests that the initial effect of preschool on intellectual performance generates long-term effects through its intermediate effects on scholastic achievement directly, and on commitment to schooling and scholastic placement, which indirectly affect scholastic achievement. These intermediate effects are important in their own right—increasing subjects' maturity, reducing their need for special education services, enhancing their scholastic achievement, and eventually helping them to stay in school longer. Finally, the effects of preschool have extended beyond school into the adult world as these young people have found more employment and have experienced less involvement in delinquent activities than their no-preschool counterparts.

A Summary of the Economic Analysis

This section presents the overall results of cost-benefit analysis and consolidates the economic implications of the findings presented in earlier chapters.

The Costs of Early Education

Of the immediate effects of the preschool program, the most obvious is program cost. Compared to program cost, other immediate effects of preschool are much more difficult to measure and to assign a monetary value; insofar as they can be measured, they appear to be of less economic significance. The first step in the calculation of program cost is the estimation of explicit costs. Basic cost data were obtained from Ypsilanti Public School reports of budget data, much of it collected earlier by Weber for her initial study (Weber et al., 1978), and from Ypsilanti Public School accounting records. Explicit program costs are categorized as follows: instruction, administration and support staff, overhead, supplies, and psychological screening.

Instruction costs include teacher salaries, fringe benefits, and the employer's share of social security taxes. Administration and support staff costs represent the contribution of nonteaching special education staff to the preschool program, including the program's management by the Director of Special Education. Overhead costs include a share of the costs of general administrative and nonteaching staff of the school system, as well as maintenance, utilities, and other general school system costs. Supply costs represent the equipment required each year for the classroom. This category includes the costs of food for daily snacks, as well as materials used by the children. Finally, screening accounts for the costs of testing and interviewing to select a sample that was economically disadvantaged, with a relatively poor prognosis of educational success.

There are also implicit program costs that must be estimated to measure the Perry Preschool program's full economic cost to society: imputed interest and depreciation on fixed capital. Imputed interest on fixed capital is calculated to account for the income foregone when fixed assets were employed in the preschool program. It is assumed, in other words, that if these assets had not been used in the preschool program they would have been used in some other way that benefited society. The loss of these other benefits is a cost of the preschool program and it is accounted for by imputing interest on the fixed capital. Depreciation on fixed capital is calculated to account for the decrease in value of fixed assets due to wear, age, and other causes.[31]

Costs by major category for a typical school year (1963-1964) are presented below:

Explicit Costs

Instruction	$26,251
Administration and support staff	1,100
Overhead	1,600
Supplies	480
Screening	115

Implicit Costs

Interest and Depreciation	2,236
Total Program Costs	**$31,782**
Cost Per Child	**$ 1,589**

These costs are in 1963-1964 dollars. Total program costs by year and wave are listed in Table 25, in dollars actually spent in 1962-1967 as well as in constant 1981 dollars both undiscounted and discounted at 3 percent. The average present value of per-child cost for one year of preschool is $4,818 and for two years it is $9,289. Average undiscounted costs for one year and two years are, respectively, $4,963 and $9,708. Year-to-year variations in costs per child result primarily from variation in the teacher-child ratio; the number of children varied from one year to another, while the number of teachers remained fixed.

The cost-per-child figures presented above indicate that the Perry Preschool program was relatively expensive. This is not surprising, since it was a program of high quality for children whose educational prognosis was poor. However, the expensiveness of the Perry Preschool program relative to other programs may easily be exaggerated unless other factors are taken into consideration. One factor is that the Perry Preschool program cost figures are not simply budgeted expenses but upper-bound estimates of the full economic cost of the program to society. For example, the preschool program did not pay anything for the physical facilities it used (many preschool programs use space that is donated or provided at a below-market price), but we imputed a cost for these facilities because there was an opportunity cost to society, since the facilities could have been used for something else. Another factor is that the figures represent the actual costs of the program rather than the minimum cost of producing the program's results. This minimum would have been reached only if the Perry Preschool program was the most efficient possible, but it was an experimental program dealing with many unknowns. There was little knowledge about what was efficient. In addition, there is some evidence from the program that it could have been made more efficient. The student/teacher ratio, a major determinant of program cost, varied between 5

---

[31]This way of estimating the facility costs of the Perry Preschool program, while appropriate in estimating costs to society as a whole, may not be typical of the way educational administrators think about program costs.

Table 25

PERRY PRESCHOOL TOTAL PROGRAM COSTS

Costs	School Year				
	1962-63 $n=21$	1963-64 $n=20$	1964-65 $n=25$	1965-66 $n=25$	1966-67 $n=12$
	Wave 0 $n=13$	Wave 1 $n=8$	Wave 2 $n=12$	Wave 3 $n=13$	Wave 4 $n=12$
Total costs, current	$19,632	$12,665	$16,583	$19,135	$20,425
Per-child costs, current	1,510	1,583	1,381	1,472	1,702
Per-child costs, 1981	5,223	5,287	4,501	4,624	5,044
Present value[a]	5,071	4,984	4,243	4,359	4,754
	Wave 1 $n=8$	Wave 2 $n=12$	Wave 3 $n=13$	Wave 4 $n=12$	
Total costs, current	$12,129	$19,117	$18,068	$17,783	
Per-child costs, current	1,516	1,593	1,389	1,482	
Per-child costs, 1981	5,172	5,320	4,527	4,655	
Present value[a]	5,021	5,165	4,395	4,519	

[a]Present value is discounted at 3% per year from the start of the program for each study cohort; thus the first year of preschool is discounted at 3% and the second at 3% compounded for two years, or 6.09%.

to 1 and 6.25 to 1 with no perceptible influence on program results. More important, one year of preschool produced the same effects as two.

In addition to the program costs borne by the general public, there were immediate costs and benefits to the children attending preschool and to their families. There were no fees and all school supplies were provided by the program, so that explicit costs can be set at zero. The only resource required of participants in the preschool program was their time, which therefore constitutes an implicit cost. For the children, the net immediate effect of early education was positive (a benefit) rather than negative (a cost). The program was designed to be enjoyable and enriching; the level of cognitive ability of participants surged substantially ahead of that of the children who did not attend preschool. Thus we may conclude that preschool attendance produced for the participating children substantial benefits that outweighed the opportunity cost of their time (considered as the satisfaction they would have received from their activities had they not attended preschool). Since it proved impossible to assign a monetary value to this net effect and it is assumed to be positive, we conservatively set it at zero.

The Perry Preschool program had two immediate effects on the parents of children attending preschool: It provided child care for part of the day and it involved home visits in which teachers worked with both children and parents. An exact value for child care (apart from any expected long-term benefits) cannot be determined; however, a lower-bound estimate can be derived from information on the amounts parents in similar populations paid for basically custodial child care. Our estimate is

$299 per child per year in constant 1981 dollars; the discounted present value is $290 for one year and $572 for two years. The home visits required parents to spend time—a cost—but also provided benefits. These benefits might include opportunities for positive social interactions with the teacher and their children during the home visit; services provided by the teacher in conjunction with the home visit (for example, providing information about social services and bringing educational materials to the home); and opportunities to generally interact more positively with their children and to better understand their children's development. Again, these kinds of benefits are nearly impossible to quantify and even more difficult to value monetarily. However, we can continue to assume that the net effect of the home visits was positive. Further, parents' participation in the home visits was voluntary; parents could, and sometimes did, choose not to receive a visitor. Parents' participation in home visits can therefore be interpreted as evidence that participation was (in the parents' own judgment) preferred to the best alternative use of their time.[32] The net effect of home visits for the parents is, for this reason, conservatively estimated to be zero, with immediate benefits left unquantified.

The immediate economic effects of the preschool program for the study are program costs (borne by the general public), opportunity costs of time for participating children and parents, child care and what can generally be described as a higher quality of life for both children and parents. Program costs are precisely estimated; a lower-bound estimate of the monetary value of child care is also produced. For the remaining effects, the value of benefits is determined to exceed time costs, but the amount of this positive net benefit is unknown. In summary, the net present value of the cost of one year of the preschool program is estimated at $4,818 (in 1981 dollars). The net present value of one year's part-time child care provided by the preschool program is $290. Comparable estimates for two years are $9,289 for program costs and $572 for part-time child care.

The Benefits Resulting from Program Outcomes

In previous chapters the effects of early education on school success, early socioeconomic success, and social responsibility have been extensively documented, and the economic consequences of these effects have been discussed. This section summarizes the effects noted above and takes a broader approach to the analysis of economic outcomes by exploring all of the significant costs and benefits, regardless of whether their monetary value can be estimated.

The economic consequences of increased school success can be divided into those accruing to program participants and those accruing to the general public. The general public receives benefits because costs of

---

[32] It can be questioned to what extent parents' willingness to participate in home visits results from the value placed on the immediate effects of the visits, as opposed to expectations of long-term benefits to the child. Here the question is not relevant, since we do not elsewhere measure benefits to the parents of assuring long-term benefits to their children. We would argue that the parents' concern for the long-term welfare of their children extends beyond, and is not substantially dependent on, the expectation of economic transfers from child to parent in the future.

elementary and secondary education are reduced; this cost reduction was discussed in Chapter 2, and its average value per student in the Perry Preschool study amounts to $7,082 (in 1981 dollars, undiscounted). The discounted (at 3 percent) present value is $5,113 for one year of preschool and $4,964 for two years. School success, paradoxically, also represents a cost to the general public, since students stay in school longer; this cost is already included in our calculations through grade 12. On the basis of age-19 interview data on college enrollment and national statistics on educational attainment, the preschool program's average effect on costs of higher education was estimated to be an increase of $1,168 (undiscounted) per person; discounted at 3 percent, the present value is a cost increase of $704 for one year of preschool and $684 for two years. Almost the entire cost is borne by the general public.[33]

Program participants benefit from increased school success by receiving an increased quantity (and possibly better quality) of education. These benefits can be categorized either as consumption benefits (yielding immediate satisfaction) or as investment benefits (yielding satisfaction over an entire lifetime). Some of the investment benefits of school success have been measured in the Perry Preschool study by age 19 and we discuss these when we consider social responsibility and early economic success. Other investment benefits can only be predicted from educational outcomes and will be considered later.

Immediate benefits raise participants' quality of life both in and out of school; there are several measures pointing to increased quality of life for persons who attended preschool: Their achievement scores were higher, as were their grades; they were less likely to be labelled as mentally retarded and placed in special education programs; and they had more positive attitudes toward high school. These results suggest that their school experiences were more worthwhile and enjoyable. Greater school success may also have increased the social status of preschool participants in their schools and communities. Finally, the experiences involved in attending college, apart from their longer-term implications, may themselves be considered benefits.

Investment benefits of school success were measured partially at age 19. Benefits in the area of social responsibility occur in the areas of reproductive events and of crime and delinquency. Women who attended preschool reported fewer pregnancies and births by age 19. This finding is consistent with evidence that the ability to obtain desired family size as well as desired timing and spacing of births increases with the level of education (Michael, 1975). We believe that delaying the onset of reproductive events for teen parents is of benefit both to the study participants and to the general public, but our data are too incomplete at this point to assign a monetary value.

---

[33] All study participants attending college were enrolled in public institutions; tuition at public institutions of higher education accounts for only about 13 percent of total revenues (National Center for Educational Statistics, 1980, p. 144). A number of students obtained subsidized loans for tuition payments, which shifts more of the costs to the general public; the same result occurs with scholarships offered to low-income students. There are unquestionably a number of private costs of school—books, supplies, and transportation, for instance. These are viewed as relatively minor and are not estimated here. Details of all calculations are provided in a technical report (Barnett, 1984).

88

Efforts to assign a monetary value to effects of preschool in reducing crime and delinquency were considerably more successful. Reasonably complete estimates could be obtained for criminal justice system costs. Costs to crime victims, however, could only be partially estimated.[34] Building on data for crime and its costs through age 20, an extrapolation for lifetime costs of crime was produced. The present value (discounted at 3 percent) of the preschool program's effect on crime costs through age 20 is $1,233 for one year of preschool and $1,197 for two years. Estimates of the effect beyond age 20 are presented later.

The final category in which effects were manifest by age 19 is that of economic success. Benefits were measured in these interrelated areas of economic success: employment, earnings, and economic independence. Compared to subjects with no preschool, those who attended preschool were more likely to be employed at the time of interview and had experienced fewer months unemployed since leaving high school. They had higher median annual earnings at age 19 and were more satisfied with their type of work. They were more likely to have some savings. In conjunction with their greater labor market success the preschool attendees were more likely to consider themselves self-supporting. In this regard they were also less likely to be receiving welfare and received lower payments, on average.

Even for these measures of economic success, we were not able to translate all benefits into monetary values. The benefits of labor market success are measured by the increase in earnings only, which through age 19 is $1,040 undiscounted, with a present value (discounted at 3 percent) of $642 for one year of preschool and $623 for two years. This earnings increase captures some of the benefits from increased employment, but not all of them, as there is some value beyond mere earnings to having more regular employment (and less uncertainty regarding income). In addition, we have no measure of the monetary value of the greater satisfaction with type of work reported. The primary beneficiaries of this labor market success are the preschool program participants and their families. However, a significant portion of earnings, about 25 percent, benefits the general public through increased tax payments. Turning to the participants' increased savings, we have no measure of the amount of increase and thus cannot estimate the monetary value to the participants or the general public. Likewise, the participants' increased economic self-sufficiency, though a widely held and highly prized goal, is a benefit for which we have no complete measure of monetary value. There is certainly some value to both participants and society from participants' avoiding the need for welfare payments. The cost of welfare payments to society as a whole is merely the administrative cost of these payments; the payment itself is not a cost but a transfer from the general public to welfare recipients. That is, although the general public benefits by the amount of the payment plus the administrative cost, the welfare recipients lose the amount of the payment (a loss offset by increased income). In Chapter 3 we found that the estimated decrease in annual payments was $876 undiscounted, with ad-

[34] No attempt was made to measure costs of crime and delinquency to those persons committing the acts, except insofar as costs of imprisonment or a criminal record are reflected in foregone earnings.

ministrative costs of 10 percent ($88). The present value (discounted at 3 percent) of the decrease in annual payments is $546 for one year of preschool and $530 for two years, with administrative costs of $55 and $53, respectively.

The effects of the preschool program are unlikely to have ended at the point of our last measurement. Indeed, theory and empirical evidence indicate that the effects observed through age 19 have permanently changed the lives of the preschool participants. These permanent changes can be predicted from the observed effects, and their benefits evaluated over the participants' lifetimes. Some of these changes can be predicted quantitatively, others only qualitatively. Where predictions are quantitative it is possible to estimate the monetary value of benefits. Where predictions are qualitative it is only possible to indicate that benefits are associated with the changes; dollar values cannot be estimated.

Changes in economic success, self-sufficiency, and social responsibility can be predicted quantitatively from observed effects at age 19. These changes have been partially measured at age 19, providing an empirical justification from the sample for their prediction beyond age 19. The benefits predicted are increased earnings, reduced crime costs, and reduced welfare costs. The estimation of monetary values for each of these benefits was described in earlier chapters. Increased earnings is the most important of these because of its magnitude. The present value (discounted at 3 percent) of increased earnings beyond age 19 (including wages, fringe benefits, and other employment-related benefits) is estimated to be $23,813 for one year of preschool, and $23,121 for two years. Reduced crime costs beyond age 20 are estimated to have a present value of $1,871 for one year of preschool and $1,816 for two years. Finally, the present value of reduced welfare costs (administrative costs only) is estimated to be $1,438 for one year of preschool and $1,396 for two years.

In addition to the benefits quantified above, there are a number of other benefits of early education that may be expected but have not been measured in the present study. These predicted benefits are based on the observed improvement in educational outcomes and the empirical relationship between educational attainment and other important social and economic variables. They are related to such areas as family formation, personal and family health care, the quality of leisure, and consumer activities. It would have been premature to attempt their measurement at age 19; since they have not been measured, there are insufficient grounds for any predictive estimation of their magnitude. They are not considered here.

Summation of Costs and Benefits

To summarize all of the costs and benefits identified, Table 26 lists measured and predicted costs and benefits and the estimated present value of each. As shown in that table, summation of costs and benefits yields a sizeable positive net present value for both one and two years of preschool. Thus, judged simply on its overall return, the Perry Preschool program was a good investment for society. This general conclusion depends to some extent on predictions of costs and benefits beyond age 19.

However, even if the analysis is limited to costs and benefits directly observed through age 19, the data support a very strong conclusion. By age 19 it is clear that there is a positive net present value generated by one year of preschool. In other words, by age 19, fifteen years after the initial investment, the data demonstrate that one year of preschool is a good investment for society.

The degree of confidence that can be placed in the conclusion that preschool is a good investment depends on the margin for error allowed by the results and on the strength of the underlying statistical evidence. From the ratios in Table 26 it can be seen that the size of benefits relative to costs allows considerable margin for error. The present value of benefits exceeds seven times the present value of cost for one year of preschool. In earlier chapters, for each of the variables yielding economic benefits, we presented measures of the statistical confidence with which preschool's effect has been estimated. We also have such measures for preschool's overall effect on measured economic benefits per se through age 19 (age 20 for crime). Table 27 presents our best estimate of preschool's total measured economic benefits for society, and for taxpayers only, together with the estimated standard deviations and p-values. Total benefits to society include benefits for participants, taxpayers, and potential crime victims.

Table 26

SUMMARY OF COSTS AND BENEFITS[a]

	Benefit or Cost[b] (in dollars)	
Type of Benefit (or Cost)	1-yr Preschool	2-yr Preschool
Measured		
Preschool program	-4,818	-9,289
Child care	290	572
Education, K-12	5,113	4,964
Earnings, ages 16-19	642	623
Welfare at age 19	55	53
Crime through age 20	1,233	1,197
Predicted		
College	-704	-684
Earnings after age 19	23,813	23,121
Crime after age 20	1,871	1,816
Welfare after age 19	1,438	1,396
Net benefit[c] (dollars)	28,933	23,769
Benefit-cost ratio	7.01	3.56

[a]Table entries are present values in constant 1981 dollars, discounted at 3% annually.

[b]Costs are indicated as negative amounts.

[c]Column sums differ from net benefits because of rounding.

The information presented in Table 27 indicates that we can be quite confident that preschool has significant economic benefits. We are somewhat less confident that preschool's measured economic benefits *through*

Table 27

PRESCHOOL'S EFFECT ON MEASURED ECONOMIC BENEFITS[a]

Type of Benefit	Effect	Standard Deviation	p[b]
Taxpayers' and potential crime victims' benefit[c]	$6,544	$3,874	.094
Total social benefit[c]	6,846	4,045	.093

[a]$n = 109$

[b]The statistical test used is Student's *t* test; p-values are reported if less than .100.

[c]Present values discounted at 3% for one year of preschool.

Table 28

DISTRIBUTION OF COSTS AND BENEFITS[a]

	Benefit or Cost[b] (in dollars)			
	For Preschool Participants		For Taxpayers and Potential Crime Victims	
Type of Benefit or Cost	1-yr Preschool	2-yr Preschool	1-yr Preschool	2-yr Preschool
Measured				
Preschool program	0	0	-4,818	-9,289
Child care	290	572	0	0
Education, K-12	0	0	5,113	4,964
Earnings, ages 16-19	482	467	161[c]	156[c]
Welfare at age 19	-546	-530	601	583
Crime through age 20	0	0	1,233	1,197
Predicted				
College[d]	0	0	-704	-684
Earnings after age 19	19,233	18,674	4,580	4,446
Welfare after age 19	-14,377	-13,959	15,815	15,355
Crime after age 20	0	0	1,871	1,816
Net benefit[e] (dollars)	5,082	5,224	23,852	18,544

[a]Table entries are present values in constant 1981 dollars, discounted at 3% annually.

[b]Costs are indicated as negative amounts.

[c]Assumes 25% of estimated earnings is paid in taxes.

[d]Some college costs are undoubtedly borne by the participants and their families, but we have no estimate for the amount. The most conservative assumption toward increasing the relative benefits of participants was to assign all college costs to the taxpayers.

[e]Column figures may not sum to net benefits due to rounding.

age 19 alone exceed costs, although this is our best estimate of the outcome. If we also consider the predicted benefits beyond age 19, we can have considerably more confidence. Even if actual benefits through age 19 had fallen 1 standard deviation below the mean, the addition of only one-tenth of predicted later benefits would be sufficient for benefits to exceed the costs for one year of preschool.

The preschool program can be judged by another criterion in addition to that of its returns to society—the fairness of its distribution of costs and benefits. Table 28 offers some perspective on this issue. The estimated present value of net benefit is positive for both taxpayers (especially potential crime victims) and program participants. No one loses; taxpayers and participants both are better off with early education than without it. It should be noted that the program costs of early education were not borne by the participants. Indeed, from our analysis, it is clear that they should not bear these costs. If families of study participants had to pay for even one year of preschool, their returns through age 19 would be considerably lower than their costs. There is little hope that they would recover the cost of two years of preschool even over the entire lifetime of their child. Since taxpayers are the primary beneficiaries, taxpayers should bear the primary burden of financing early education for children from low-income families.

VI Preschool's Long-Term Impact: Summary of the Evidence

The question of the effectiveness of early childhood education for children of low-income families has been investigated by dozens of social scientists over the past two decades. This chapter summarizes what is known about the effectiveness of early childhood education by analyzing the results of several of these longitudinal evaluations.

In the early 1960s many leading educators and social scientists suggested that preschool education for poor children was a way to break the cycle of poverty, assuming a chain of cause and effect that linked family poverty to children's scholastic failure and subsequent poverty as adults. Their suggestions eventually led to the establishment in the summer of 1965 of the national Head Start program. Speculation was that providing preschool education for poor children would enhance their intelligence. This theory received support from early reports that several experimental preschool programs were in fact raising IQ's (Klaus & Gray, 1968; Weikart, 1967).

However, in 1969 the oft-cited negative evaluation of Head Start by Westinghouse Learning Corporation and Ohio University was released. It diminished President Nixon's support for the program (Steiner, 1976, p. 32) and was also largely responsible for the widespread and incorrect belief, still held by some today, that Head Start was a failure. Henry Levin's 1977 statement is typical of the tone of the times: "Good [preschool] programs are able to produce salutary increases in IQ for disadvantaged children, but these improvements are not maintained when the children enter the primary grades."

As the years went by, however, evidence of preschool's effectiveness began to mount. Evidence from several evaluations demonstrated that good preschool programs have both short- and long-term positive effects on low-income subjects. In this chapter, seven of these evaluations are considered, including the Perry Preschool study. Two secondary analyses of multiple studies are also reviewed. There are many other studies that bear on these issues, but these are among the best; reviewing them will provide a clear picture of the long-term effectiveness of early childhood education and of some of the problems researchers face in conducting such studies.

The Seven Studies

The seven studies, taken together, have followed subjects at least to age 9 and at most to age 20. Three of the studies have followed children beyond 18, the age of expected high school graduation. Table 29 identifies each of these studies, the year it began, its location, and its most recent major report.

These seven studies are frequently associated with the research scientists, typically educational or developmental psychologists, who initiated them. Susan Gray's Early Training study and David Weikart's Perry Preschool study began in 1962. Phyllis Levenstein's Mother-Child Home study began in 1965. In 1966, Francis Palmer began the Harlem study. Also in 1966, Eleanor Monroe and M. S. McDonald of the Rome, Georgia,

Table 29

THE SEVEN STUDIES:
IDENTIFYING INFORMATION

Study	Year Study Began	Place	Child Age at Last Report	Recent Major Reference
Early Training	1962	Murfreesboro, TN	21	Gray, Ramsey, & Klaus, 1982
Perry Preschool	1962	Ypsilanti, MI	19	(this monograph)
Mother-Child Home	1965	Long Island, NY	9-13	Levenstein, O'Hara, & Madden, 1983
Harlem	1966	New York City, NY	13	Palmer, 1983
Rome Head Start	1966	Rome, GA	20	Monroe & McDonald, 1981
Milwaukee	1968	Milwaukee, WI	10	Garber & Heber, 1981
New York Pre-K	1975	New York State	9	Irvine, 1982

school system began that town's Head Start program on which they would conduct a follow-up study in 1981. Rick Heber and Howard Garber initiated the Milwaukee study in 1968. In 1975 the New York Department of Education began an evaluation of its Experimental Prekindergarten program under the direction of David Irvine. This statewide program was established by the New York State Legislature in 1966 and now receives about $10 million a year in state funding. This evaluation helped persuade New York Education Commissioner Gordon Ambach to make his widely reported statement in 1983 that children should begin school at age 4.

The seven studies have been conducted in the United States, east of the Mississippi River, in both northern and southern states; they are located in a cross-section of America's urban communities. Six of the seven studies evaluated programs that operated in only one location.

Design of the Seven Studies

As shown in Table 30, four of the seven studies were of experimental design; their treatment groups were selected from the same population by procedures designed to assure group equivalency. In the Early Training and the Milwaukee studies, groups were formed by random assignment of subjects. In the Harlem study, treatment groups were selected by applying the same sample selection procedures to children born in different months.[35] In our Perry Preschool study, children were paired on the basis of similar preprogram IQ's; then pairs were split randomly between two groups, with subsequent reassignment of some pairs to equate the two groups on other background factors.

---

[35]In the Harlem study, one of the two program groups had an average IQ at age 3 that was 6 points higher than the average IQ of the control group at age 2 years, 8 months; however, this group difference was controlled for in analyzing the statistical significance of group differences.

Table 30

THE SEVEN STUDIES:
DESIGN INFORMATION

Study	Procedure for Formation of Groups	Special Sample Characteristics[a]	Original Sample Size	% Found at Last Follow-up
Experimental design				
Early Training	random assignment	—	90	80%
Harlem	selections from same population	boys only	315	81%
Milwaukee	random assignment	mother IQ's 75 and below	40	80%
Perry Preschool	assignment of matched pairs	child IQ's 60-90	123	98%
Quasi-experimental design				
Mother-Child Home	assignment by site	—	250	74%
New York Pre-K	some assignment by site	42% white; 42% black; 16% other	2,058	75%
Rome Head Start	self-selection	black and white	218	71%

[a]All samples were selected on the basis of family poverty. Unless otherwise noted, 90% or more of the subjects are black.

Three of the seven studies were of quasi-experimental design; their treatment groups were selected from different populations. Two out of three report evidence that their control groups were demographically better-off than their experimental groups, thus biasing comparisons against finding program effects.

One quasi-experimental study, Rome Head Start, began in 1966 by identifying all first graders in Rome elementary schools who qualified for federal funds as economically disadvantaged. Some of these students had attended Head Start and some had not. In the absence of data to the contrary, the possibility cannot be ruled out that Head Start children and non-Head Start children in this study differed in important ways before the study began. There is no reason, however, to expect bias and, if bias occurred, it might even have operated against finding program effects.

The Mother-Child Home study, another quasi-experimental effort (during the period reviewed here), was offered to all willing participants within a given geographic area, who were then compared to a demographically similar group in a nearby geographic area. The groups thus selected were generally equivalent on important background factors, though there is some risk that uncontrolled preprogram group differences may affect study outcomes.

The New York Prekindergarten evaluation, the third quasi-experimental study, compared two control groups to an experimental group of approximately 1,800 youngsters who attended the program in 1966. The control group for comparisons of test scores consisted of 87 children on the program's waiting list. This group may or may not have differed from the program group, depending on the original procedures for selecting children from the list. For comparisons of scholastic placement, the control group consisted of both the waiting-list group and a group of 171 children of slightly higher demographic status from other school districts. For example, program-group mothers reported 10.9 years of schooling, while other-district mothers reported 12.0 years of schooling.

The Seven Samples

The research of the past two decades on the effects of early childhood education has focused on children living in poverty. As Americans emerged from the Second World War, their attention turned to the domestic issues of civil rights and poverty. Martin Luther King, Jr., and others focused the nation's attention on the plight of blacks in the U.S. President Lyndon Johnson declared a War on Poverty and led Congress to pass the Economic Opportunity Act of 1964, the law that initiated the national Head Start program.

The concern in the 1960s for righting the wrongs of poverty was closely tied to the struggle for black civil rights. Therefore, response to these concerns focused on the needs of the black population, combining new compensatory education programs with new policies of equal rights in voting, housing, employment, and education. It is not surprising, then, that most of the samples in the research reported here are predominantly black. In most of the studies reviewed here, 90 percent or more of the subjects are black.[36]

Table 31 lists special characteristics of the samples and sample sizes. The Perry Preschool study focused on children whose tested IQ's at age 3 were between 60 and 90. The Milwaukee study focused on children whose mothers had tested IQ's of 75 or below. The Harlem study focused exclusively on males. The New York Prekindergarten study was open to the public in selected school districts, so the sample more nearly represents the racial mix of low-income families. Sample sizes varied from 40 in the Milwaukee study to 2,058 in the Prekindergarten study. Excluding these two extremes, sample sizes varied from 90 (Early Training) to 315 (Harlem).

Attrition—loss of subjects—constitutes a major threat to the validity of longitudinal studies. As more subjects are lost, threats to both internal and external validity increase in seriousness and complexity; differential attrition by group can also pose grave problems. The scientists carrying out these seven studies fared well in finding subjects at their last follow-up: They all found at least 71 percent of their original subjects. The Perry Preschool Project ranked highest, with 100 percent of the original subjects found and 98 percent interviewed. The median proportion of subjects

---

[36]This focus on early childhood education for low-income blacks has left its mark: In 1980 for 3- and 4-year-olds in families with annual incomes under $15,000, the preschool enrollment figures were 37 percent for black children, but only 25 percent for white children (Kahn, 1982, p. 13).

Table 31

THE SEVEN STUDIES:
PROGRAM INFORMATION

Study[a]	Beginning Age of Child	Program Duration in Years	Program[b] for Children	Program for Parents
Milwaukee	3-6 mo	6	full-time year-round	educational/ vocational
Perry Preschool	3 or 4 yr	2 or 1	part-time	weekly home visits
New York Pre-K	4 yr	1	part-time	opportunities for classroom involvement
Rome Head Start	5 yr	1	part-time Jan-Aug	opportunities for classroom involvement
Early Training	3 or 4 yr	3 or 2	part-time in summer	weekly home visits during school year
Mother-Child Home	2 or 3 yr	2	twice-weekly home visits	twice-weekly home visits
Harlem	2 or 3 yr	1	twice-weekly 1:1 sessions	no separate program

[a]Studies are arranged in estimated order of program scope and cost, most extensive first.
[b]Unless otherwise noted, programs operated during the school year, approximately September through May.

found in these seven studies was 80 percent. Differential attrition across groups was not large enough to constitute a major problem.

The Seven Programs

Table 31 presents features of the programs evaluated in these seven studies, arranged in estimated order of program size and cost. The Milwaukee program was the most extensive, providing full-time, year-round developmental child care, as well as an educational and vocational program for mothers, for six years. The Perry Preschool program featured one home visit per week and a morning classroom program each day for two school years (one school year for Wave Zero). Its classroom component was equivalent in scope to the one-school-year programs of the New York Experimental Prekindergarten and the Rome Head Start programs; the latter two programs offered parents opportunities for involvement with the classroom program, as well as several home visits during the school year. The Early Training program offered part-time classroom experiences five days per week in the summer and weekly home visits during the school year for either two or three years.

Two projects offered sessions only twice a week. The Mother-Child Home program consisted of twice-weekly home visits to parent and child for one or two years. The Harlem study provided the least extensive program—one-to-one sessions between a tutor and a child twice weekly for eight months.

The Analyses of Multiple Studies

The two analyses of multiple studies reviewed in this section were conducted by the Consortium for Longitudinal Studies and the Head Start Synthesis Project.

The Consortium for Longitudinal Studies was an association of a dozen educators and psychologists, each of whom had initiated a longitudinal study of an early childhood program during the 1960s and agreed to collaborate in a follow-up assessment during the late 1970s. The Consortium was formed in 1975 by Irving Lazar of Cornell University and Edith Grotberg of the U.S. Administration for Children, Youth and Families. The Consortium was established to investigate the long-term effectiveness of the early childhood programs and to provide a better foundation for summarizing outcomes than is possible in the usual reviews of the scientific literature. The investigators of the Perry Preschool study belonged to the Consortium,[37] and this review profits from their experience with that group. A major benefit of the Consortium was that it based its conclusions on careful review of the methodology of each study; this report maintains that tradition.

Consortium staff carried out detailed analyses of attrition in the constituent studies and concluded that attrition for the data analyzed was not a problem for these studies. The results of each study were analyzed separately. Then separate hypothesis tests for a given variable were pooled across studies to determine if there was an average effect across all the programs studied.

The Head Start Synthesis Project is an ambitious project that is to be completed this year (1984). All Head Start studies conducted between 1965 and 1984 are being reviewed and a meta-analysis of these studies is being conducted. (A meta-analysis of studies converts program effects to the same units of measurement, then compares effects to each other and averages them across studies.) The U.S. Administration for Children, Youth and Families awarded a contract for this work to CSR, Inc., a Washington-based consulting firm.

Findings

The documented effects of early childhood education may be organized according to the major outcome or outcomes at each age-period of the participants. These outcomes and ages are the following:

---

[37]The Early Training, Harlem, and Mother-Child Home studies' investigators also belonged to the Consortium.

- Early childhood: improved intellectual performance

- Elementary school: better scholastic placement
improved scholastic achievement

- Adolescence: lower rate of delinquency
higher rate of high school graduation
higher rate of employment a year later

A review of the evidence follows.

Improved Intellectual Performance

The best-documented period of preschool effects is early childhood, and the best-documented preschool effect is an immediate improvement in intellectual performance as represented by intelligence test scores. Six of the studies reviewed here have such data; all six have documented the immediate positive effect of early childhood education on intellectual performance. Four of the studies reported a maximum effect of between ½ and 1 standard deviation (16 points on the Stanford-Binet); statistically significant group differences were gone by age 8. The intensive Milwaukee study had a maximum effect of 2 standard deviations (32 points), with an effect of over 1 standard deviation when children were last tested at age 10.

Two other studies in the Consortium for Longitudinal Studies reported effects on IQ of about ½ standard deviation, gone by age 8. Ramey, Bryant, and Suarez (1984) reviewed an additional 11 experimental studies with IQ data available on children between the ages of 1 and 6, eight of them having data on children between the ages of 1 and 3. In every study, the average IQ of children who participated in preschool was as good or better than the average IQ of children in the study's control group. IQ differences ranged from 0 (in two studies) to 21, with a median IQ difference of 6. In the eight studies with IQ data for children between the ages of 1 and 3, six had IQ differences between 0 and ½ standard deviation, and two had IQ differences between ½ and 1 standard deviation.

The Head Start Synthesis Project provides broad confirmation of the positive effect of Head Start on intellectual performance. One very encouraging finding of this review is that Head Start has improved over the years in this regard. In measuring the effect of Head Start on scholastic readiness, 21 studies that were conducted between 1965 and 1969 found an average effect of ⅓ standard deviation; 18 studies conducted between 1970 and 1980 found an average effect of over ⅔ standard deviation (Hubbell, 1983). Children's cognitive improvement was strongest at the end of the program, but improvement was found as long as three years afterwards.

Better Scholastic Placement

In the studies we have reviewed, as shown in Table 32, every single comparison of scholastic placement was favorable to the group that had received early childhood education. In four of the five studies with data on special education placement, such placements were usually reduced by

102

Table 32

THE SEVEN STUDIES:
FINDINGS FOR SCHOLASTIC PLACEMENT

Study	Program Group	Control Group	p[a]
Rome Head Start (age 20)			
Placed in special education	11%	25%	.019
Retained in grade	51%	63%	—
Dropped out of high school	50%	67%	.042
Early Training (age 18)			
Placed in special education	3%	29%	.004
Retained in grade	53%	69%	—
Dropped out of high school	22%	43%	.079
Perry Preschool (age 19)			
Placed in special education	37%	50%	—
Retained in grade	35%	40%	—
Dropped out of high school	33%	51%	.034
Harlem (age 13)			
Placed in special education	No data	No data	No data
Retained in grade	24%	45%	.006
Dropped out of high school	No data	No data	No data
New York Pre-K (age 9)			
Placed in special education	2%	5%	.006
Retained in grade	16%	21%	.019
Dropped out of high school	No data	No data	No data
Mother-Child Home (age 9)			
Placed in special education	14%	39%	.005
Retained in grade	13%	19%	—
Dropped out of high school	No data	No data	No data
Milwaukee	No data	No data	No data

[a]Two-tailed p-values are presented if less than .100.

half or more. In the Perry Preschool study, comparisons (presented in Chapter 2) show that the overall need for special education placement by student-years (rather than by students, as reported here) was reduced by half. Two studies report statistically significant reductions in grade retentions as well (the Harlem study could not obtain special education placement data).

Better scholastic placement (i.e., avoiding placement in special education programs) is a major contributor to the financial benefits of preschool education in the cost-benefit analysis of the Perry Preschool program, as detailed in earlier chapters. The strength and consistency of this finding in these other studies argue persuasively that the favorable cost-benefit ratio found for the Perry Preschool program applies as well to these and other early childhood programs.

One other study of the effects of early childhood program experience deserves mention here: the Cincinnati study (Nieman & Gastright, 1981). This study, similar in design to the Rome Head Start study, identified 551 children in one age-cohort in the city's schools as economically disadvantaged (that is, eligible for Title I programs) and compared the 410 who had attended full-day kindergarten (and preschool in most cases) to the 141 who had attended half-day kindergarten (and no preschool in most cases). The study found that those with full-day kindergarten experience had better scholastic placement. Only 5 percent of full-day children were placed in special education classes, as opposed to 11 percent of the half-day children; 9 percent of the full-day children were retained in grade, as opposed to 12 percent of the half-day children.

The central staff of the Consortium for Longitudinal Studies have reported similar findings on scholastic placement. Their technique of pooling probability estimates confirms that the likelihood of obtaining by chance all the findings listed in Table 32 is extremely remote (Lazar et al., 1982). The Head Start Synthesis Project has no additional data on scholastic placement.

Improved Scholastic Achievement

Most of the experimentally derived evidence of preschool's effects on scholastic achievement comes from the Perry Preschool study, with differences consistently favoring the preschool group over the no-preschool group at ages 7, 8, 9, 10, 11, 14, and 19. In terms of statistical significance, the strongest findings were at ages 14 and 19, the weakest at ages 10 and 11; these variations, however, may be due to varying difficulties of tests, with differences being more statistically significant for more difficult tests.

The only other study, of those reviewed here, with sufficient data on achievement tests (that is, for 70 percent or more of cases) is the Early Training study, which found some positive effects on reading at age 8, but no effects at 7, 10 or 11. The Cincinnati study, mentioned above, found statistically significant differences ($p < .05$) in scholastic achievement favoring the full-day kindergarten group over the half-day kindergarten group at age 7 (a difference of 19 percentile points), at age 11 (a difference of 12 percentile points, based on 70 percent of the original sample), and at age 14 (a difference of 6 percentile points, based on 50 percent of the original sample).

The Consortium for Longitudinal Studies analyzed achievement scores across seven of its studies. The pooled analysis found statistically significant positive effects on arithmetic scores at ages 10, 11, and 12, but not at age 13; and on reading scores at age 10, but not at ages 11, 12 or 13. Except for the Perry and Early Training studies, the studies had data for no more than 50 percent of the cases in their original samples, making any findings for individual studies suspect. However, the central staff of the Consortium conducted an examination of attrition and concluded, "Neither attrition nor differential rate of attrition directly introduce a bias into the results" (Lazar et al., 1982, p. 92).

The Head Start Synthesis Project reported virtually no achievement gains for the 16 Head Start studies conducted between 1965 and 1969, but found achievement gains averaging ⅓ standard deviation in the 15 Head Start studies conducted between 1970 and 1980.

Findings on Adolescent Behavior

The Perry Preschool study and the Rome Head Start study are the only studies, so far as we know, that have collected information on delinquency or crime, either from police and court records or from self-reports of study participants. Neither the Perry Preschool study nor the Rome study found a difference between groups in the number of persons referred to juvenile court. The Perry Preschool study did find that preschool education reduced delinquency—as recorded by self-report at age 15 (Schweinhart & Weikart, 1980, pp. 53-54) and by official records of either arrests or total number of juvenile court referrals to age 19 and beyond.

Both the Perry Preschool study and the Early Training study collected information on the teenage pregnancy rates of females in the studies. The Perry Preschool study reported a 64 per 100 pregnancy and live-birth rate for females who went to preschool, as opposed to 117 per 100 for females who did not go to preschool. The Early Training study found that 38 percent of the females in the study reported either a pregnancy or a live birth, with no difference between those who had gone to preschool and those who had not. The Early Training study did find that after pregnancy and childbirth, 88 percent of females who had gone to preschool were more likely to return and complete high school, as compared with 30 percent of females who had not gone to preschool.

Youngsters who had attended a preschool program were less likely to drop out of high school in three of the studies that we have reviewed. As shown in Table 32, high school dropout rates for those who had gone to preschool, when compared with those who had not, were 17 percent lower in the Rome Head Start study, 21 percent lower in the Early Training study, and 18 percent lower in the Perry Preschool study.

So far as we know, the Perry Preschool study is the only such study with data on the post-high-school employment of study participants, reporting an employment rate at age 19 of 50 percent in the preschool group and 32 percent in the no-preschool group.

Summary of Findings

On the basis of the evidence presented here, we draw the following conclusions about the effects of early childhood education on children living in poverty:

(1) Six of the seven studies show that early childhood education can have an immediate and positive effect on children's intellectual performance.

(2) Six of the studies show that early childhood education can reduce by half placement in special education classes.

(3) Three studies show that early childhood education can help prevent youngsters from dropping out of high school.

(4) There is mixed evidence from a few studies that early childhood education can increase scholastic achievement.

(5) The Perry Preschool study is the only study as yet to show that early childhood education can help prevent delinquency or teenage pregnancy or help improve the likelihood of employment during the year after high school. It can be added that although the Perry Preschool study is the only one of these studies to conduct a cost-benefit analysis, the strength of the findings about scholastic placement and high school dropout rates suggests that similar economic benefits would be found in the other studies.

VII The Lessons of Early Childhood Research

In this chapter we consider the lessons of early childhood research, including what we have learned of the nature and extent of preschool's effectiveness. We also consider the role of the research in policy formulation and the need to inform the public about the findings.

The Nature of Preschool's Effectiveness

What does the research tell us about the effectiveness of early childhood education? The most far-reaching lesson is that the impact of early childhood education can extend to adulthood. The difficulties of longitudinal research have caused some to doubt this fact. Some researchers have spoken resignedly of the "temporal erosion" of program effects. But we have found that the positive impact of programs of high quality endures; it is just the manifestations of this impact that change as people mature and move into new settings. This is not to say that a preschool program, by itself, can eliminate the effects of poverty. The case studies in Chapter 8 highlight the fact that a person's life is not transformed in some magical way by experience in a preschool program. But a successful preschool experience can permanently alter the success/failure trajectory of a person's life in significant and very positive ways.

Several stages of development converge to make the preschool age an opportune time for intervention. *Physically*, the young child has matured to the point that he or she has achieved both fine- and gross-motor coordination and is able to move about easily and freely. *Mentally*, the child has developed basic language capabilities and can use objects for self-chosen purposes. In the terms of Jean Piaget, the child has shifted from sensory-motor functioning to preoperational capacity. As Donaldson (1978, p.59) states, "from age four...the supposed gap between children and adults is less than many people have claimed." *Socially*, the child is able to move away from familiar adults and social contexts, into new settings. The fear of strangers, so common earlier, is gone, and the youngster welcomes relations with new peers and adults.

When we look at the basic accomplishments of early education, what stands out is that the child develops new competencies related to emerging social and physical skills and intellectual thought. Armed with these new competencies, the child learns to relate to new adults who respond to his or her performance very differently from the family. In short, the child learns to demonstrate new abilities in new settings and to trust new adults and peers enough to display these skills willingly. The child's willingness to try new things and develop new competencies is the seed that is transformed into later school and life success.

Are There Key Ingredients in Successful Programs?

Early childhood education does not always produce the dramatic effects described in this report. Are there certain elements that guarantee long-term effectiveness?

Program duration?   Among the studies reviewed in Chapter 6, programs with long-term beneficial effects ranged from six years of developmental child care and maternal training to one year of twice-weekly sessions for children alone. The typical effective program was a part-time preschool lasting a year or two with some degree of parent involvement, so the evidence supporting this type of program is the most extensive. But it appears that neither duration beyond two years nor unusual comprehensiveness of services are essential for program effectiveness.

Parent involvement?   Parent involvement, concluded Bronfenbrenner after reviewing many of the aforementioned studies a decade ago (1974), is the essential ingredient for program effectiveness. Later, the Consortium for Longitudinal Studies (1978) analyzed its constituent studies to see if parent involvement or some other program component was responsible for effectiveness; by its conservative analysis, no specific program component could be thus identified.

The strongest evidence against the parent involvement hypothesis comes from the Harlem study, in which parents were not involved. However, the Harlem program was not a typical, group-oriented preschool program, but rather a one-to-one tutorial program providing the child with sustained personal attention, if only for two hours per week. Such personal attention may indeed be what parents are providing their children as a result of parent involvement in a more typical program. While parent involvement may not be absolutely essential, the direct participation of the child in the program does appear to be necessary. None of the projects reviewed delivered services solely through third parties (from program to parent to child, for instance). Children were active participants in all of the programs in the reviewed studies, including the Mother-Child Home study, in which home visitors worked not only with the parent but also with the child. None of these studies considered parent education without child involvement, so they do not permit conclusions about this type of program. But, if child effects are the criteria of success, parent education must at least indirectly involve and affect children.

Curriculum?   Type of curriculum is another variable that appears to be unrelated to program effectiveness. This question motivated several studies during the 1970s, including carefully designed curriculum comparison studies by Karnes, Schwedel, and Williams (1983); Miller and Bizzell (1983); and Weikart, Epstein, Schweinhart, and Bond (1978); and larger studies such as Planned Variation Head Start (Bissell, 1971; Smith, 1973; Weisberg, 1974). It is difficult to find clear-cut differences in effects among the curriculum models employed. Rather, it appears that program effectiveness is much more dependent upon the overall quality of program operation than on a specific curriculum.

Competent leadership?   Most of the programs reviewed in this monograph were conducted by nationally prominent research scientists who in most cases were also experts in program development and implementation. But two of the programs—the Rome Head Start program and the New York Prekindergarten program—were not conducted by nationally prominent early childhood leaders, helping to allay the concern that only such leaders can operate effective programs. There is ample evidence, however, that competent leadership, provided by a supportive supervisor, is essential to overall program quality and effectiveness.

Costs?   In retrospect, we can say that the Perry Preschool program might well have had a higher benefit-cost ratio if certain efficiencies had been introduced. From our present perspective, though our sample size for this comparison was small, one program year at age 4 appears to have been as effective as two years, starting at age 3. The teacher-child ratio of 1 to 5 or 6 could have been as high as 1 to 8 or 9—the ratio employed in the Ypsilanti Preschool Curriculum Demonstration Project (Weikart et al., 1978) that achieved similar outcomes. However, considering the entire body of preschool evaluative research, we would not expect long-term benefits to result from a three-month summer program or from a program with a teacher-child ratio of 1 to 15 or 20.

These observations lead us to a basic conclusion about early childhood program operation: Program effectiveness cannot be guaranteed by inclusion of certain program features, such as the curriculum, staff-child ratio, facilities, or equipment. Instead, it appears that the best way to guarantee program effectiveness is to *operate* the program in such a way that a high level of program quality is assured.

Quality: The Key to Preschool's Long-Term Effectiveness

The development of programs of high quality is a priority for those dedicated to delivering on the promise of such child care and education projects as the Perry Preschool Project. It is not easy, however, to meet the challenge. It is entirely possible for staff to operate early education programs in such a manner that the outcomes described in this report are not achieved.

What are the elements necessary to produce a program of high quality? The National Association for the Education of Young Children (1983) has proposed a list of criteria, covering ten areas, deemed essential for program success. These areas are physical environment, health and safety, nutrition and food service, administration, staff qualifications and development, staff-parent interaction, staff-child interaction, child-child interaction, curriculum, and evaluation. These criteria—the consensus of expert opinion, practice, and research—provide a useful base for judging programs. In our opinion, however, programs could meet many of these criteria and still not be of high quality.

Such criteria are the basis for standards and licensing requirements in many states; they are necessary, but not sufficient, to maintain a high quality program. *Style of program operation* is the additional ingredient necessary to ensure high quality. The style in which a program is operated is manifested in the skillful blending of program elements, such as those described above. Elements of particular importance are as follows: curriculum implementation, parent involvement, staff supervision, inservice training provision, teacher planning time, staff relationships, ongoing evaluation, and administrative leadership. These elements are not rigidly tied to a "right" way of doing things; for example, it is not as important which curriculum is chosen, as *that* a curriculum model is chosen to guide program operations.

Who Profits Most from a Good Preschool Program?

The number of 3- and 4-year-olds enrolled in early childhood education programs, excluding custodial day care, increased from 1.5 to 2.3 million between 1970 and 1980. This means that the percent of all 3- and 4-year-olds enrolled increased from 20 to 37 percent. There are more early childhood educators as well. Membership in the National Association for the Education of Young Children has increased by 10,000 persons in the past six years, to a total of over 38,000 members in 1983.

Even as many parents are deciding that *their* children should receive early childhood education, we are compelled to ask, on the basis of the research reviewed here, Which children benefit most from early childhood programs? The research presented here applies directly to children who live in poverty and to handicapped children. In addition, we see a need to serve the children of women who work outside the home, particularly children in single-parent families whose mothers have low-paying jobs.

Children who live in poverty.   The risk of educational failure falls heavily on children who live in poverty. Their families are not able to pay for early education services. Of the 20.3 million youngsters aged 5 and under in this country in 1982, 22 percent lived in poverty—4.5 million children (U.S. Bureau of the Census, 1982b). In spite of our national efforts, including Head Start, the economically disadvantaged are underserved: 81 percent of 3-year-olds and 61 percent of 4-year-olds from families with incomes under $10,000 were not enrolled in an early childhood education program in 1980 (Chorvinsky, 1982).

Handicapped children.   There is evidence that early education helps children at risk of later placement in special education. The Perry Preschool study documented effects for youngsters who tested as borderline mentally retarded. Another study found that trainable mentally retarded children profited from at least two years of preschool (Moore, Fredericks, & Baldwin, 1981). Other studies have found short-term benefits for children with sensory impairments, language problems, and behavior disorders (U.S. Bureau of Education for the Handicapped, 1976); and Down's Syndrome (Ludlow & Allen, 1979; Maisto & German, 1979; Simeonsson, Cooper, & Scheiner, 1982).

Many believe that the handicapped, those who need special educational services, deserve priority in receiving early childhood services. In the 1981-82 school year there were nearly 228,000 children aged 3 to 5 receiving special education services through Public Law 94-142 (U.S. Office of Special Education and Rehabilitative Services, 1983), with 40,000 more served by Project Head Start (U.S. Administration for Children, Youth and Families, 1983). Altogether, these numbers represent only about half of all handicapped children in this age group. Twenty-seven states have no legislation mandating the provision of educational services for handicapped children aged 5 and under.

Children of women who work.   The number of women in the labor force has grown rapidly in past decades, reaching 45 million in 1980. Forty-three percent of children under age 5 in this country—some 8.7 million children—have mothers who work outside the home (U.S. Bureau of the Census, 1982b). A growing number of mothers head single-parent families; there were 3.1 million children under age 5 in such families in 1980. Many of these mothers have taken low-paying jobs that have not really removed them from the ranks of the poor. As these numbers grow, so does the need for preschool programs and child-care facilities. (In the mid-1970s, for example, there were 1.2 million licensed spaces in center- and home-based care for the 13 million children of mothers employed full-time outside the home.)

There appears to be little reason to distinguish between part-time preschool programs and full-time day care programs as far as their potential benefits to preschool-aged children. The Milwaukee Project (Garber & Heber, 1981) certainly demonstrated that a day care program can contribute to children's future scholastic success. Similar evidence on the benefits of a comprehensive program comes from Ramey's Abecedarian Project (Ramey & Haskins, 1981). Responsible child care program staff have a duty to meet the developmental needs of the children in their care.

Should Public Resources Be Allocated for Preschool Services?

The basic message of the Perry Preschool study is that early childhood education makes a major difference in the lives of disadvantaged children. The study was conducted with disadvantaged children at risk of special education placement and other special services. A frequently asked question is whether these positive results could also apply to middle-class children. In a general sense, the findings indicate the importance of early learning to all children's future success and adjustment in both school and the world at large. However, the study's findings apply primarily to children living in poverty. As a rule, children who do not live in poverty are not as much at risk for special education placement, school leaving, unemployment, welfare, and delinquency as those living in poverty situations. Thus, the specific benefits documented by the research reviewed in Chapter 6 can only apply to disadvantaged children.

Nevertheless, all children require developmental opportunities to thrive. Where do the resources come from to provide these opportunities and support? Families not living in poverty have more resources to share with their children; families that are poor and lack education have fewer resources to share with their children. According to a recent economic analysis (Espenshade, 1984), parents spend between $58,000 and $135,000 in raising a child to age 18. The amount goes up as family income goes up, though the proportion of income that families spend on children varies little as a function of family income. To some extent, depending on child and family characteristics, resources translate into developmental outcomes. Those children in families with enough resources to share are more likely to achieve and prosper than those in families with few resources to share. This correlation obviously is not perfect; nonetheless it is the basic model of many studies of intergenerational transmission of success, such as those reviewed by Jencks et al. (1972, 1979).

Assuming a strong positive correlation between amount of family resources to invest in a child and that child's developmental outcomes, the importance of investing public resources to help disadvantaged children succeed in school becomes evident, especially in light of the findings of the Perry Preschool study. While it is conceivable that similar advances could be demonstrated for middle-class children, evaluative studies have yet to provide definitive proof of this.

There is an implicit set of priorities operating here. If a family has very few resources for its children, these resources go to the necessities of survival, such as food, clothing, and shelter. Public resources for these families in need are similarly targeted, in such programs as Aid to Families with Dependent Children and food stamps. Once these basic needs are met, however, the child's other needs must be considered. This is the goal of early childhood education programs and of child care programs with an educational component. Many families purchase these services; but families that cannot afford them should be able to receive them at public expense through Head Start, child care funded by the Social Services Block Grant, and similar programs.

Federal, state, and local governments have always provided services for the public good. Public roads, parks, museums, zoos, and public television fall in this domain. The government affects the quality of life in many other ways as well—through police and fire protection, the national defense, economic policies, and welfare programs. We have shown that it is in the nation's interest to ensure that all children who cannot obtain early childhood education services because of lack of family resources receive public assistance to obtain such services. In addition to humanitarian concerns, a cogent argument in support of this goal is that preschool education is a sound economic investment that reduces community and social problems and their attendant costs to taxpayers.

Can This Research Be Used by Policymakers?

The body of research reported here has been used to support the preservation and expansion of the national Head Start program. It has also been used in various states to support the move toward providing public education at age 4, particularly for the poor or the handicapped. School districts and social service agencies have used the data to expand both education and child care facilities in local communities. The findings have also been published widely in both the professional and public press.

The Need to Reach the Public

Early childhood educators must communicate the importance of preschool education to the public. Most people are not opposed to providing early childhood education of high quality to those in need; they are simply unaware of its social and economic justifications.

The Case of *Young Children Grow Up*

In December 1980, the High/Scope Press published a monograph on the Perry Project titled *Young Children Grow Up: The Effects of the Perry Preschool Program on Youths Through Age 15*. Carnegie Corporation of New York, a major funding source for this study, helped to publicize the work, and summaries of the research were reported in most newsmagazines and newspapers throughout the United States. As a result, the provision of preschool for disadvantaged children was endorsed in a dozen editorials in major newspapers.

In the waning days of the Carter Administration, Stuart Eizenstat, Assistant to the President for domestic affairs and policy, sent a letter to the New York *Times* that began: "Your December 14 article on the beneficial effects of preschool programs renders a useful public service in improving knowledge about preschool services like Head Start and about the role of research in the design and execution of successful, cost-effective programs." Carter recommended a fiscal 1982 authorization of $950 million for Head Start—$130 million more than in the previous year.

More recently, President Reagan has declared to Congress and the nation, "There will be no cut in Project Head Start," and has numbered it among his social safety-net programs. The Administration increased funding for Head Start and re-authorized the program for three years. Reagan's controversial budget took most of the year to pass, but Head Start finally came out with $912 million for Fiscal 1982 and slight increases in the next three years of the Reagan Presidency.

—adapted from Schweinhart (1981), p. 187

In seeking to communicate with the public, early childhood advocates should start by contacting leaders who influence public opinion and public policy. Early childhood advocates can find leading citizens at meetings of various associations and organizations. Business leaders can be reached at meetings of such clubs as the Rotary, Lions, and Optimists, as well as the Chamber of Commerce. Educators gather together at school board meetings and various associations of principals and teachers. Church groups should also be approached, in part because they either provide or house in their churches the greatest number of child care facilities in the country (Lindner, Mattis, & Rogers, 1983) and in part because many of the community's opinion leaders attend these groups' meetings. Political leaders, of course, meet regularly in national and state capitals, and in county, township, and city halls. Professional associations of physicians (especially pediatricians), lawyers, and social workers also meet regularly. Once these persons are aware of the value to individuals and to society of early childhood education of high quality, they will be much more likely to support such efforts.

The widespread establishment of early childhood programs of high quality in the United States can only be accomplished with widespread public support. Certainly, key decisions, particularly about the national Head Start program, will continue to be made in Washington, D.C. We anticipate that other key decisions will be forthcoming in the next decade from state governments. In fact, state governments have the most to gain from the establishment of these programs, for it is state governments that now bear the vast costs of education (particularly for children from low-income families), of the legal system, and of the welfare system. Their initial financial outlays for provision of high quality early childhood programs for children from low-income families will, in the long run, result in savings in state budgets.

But there are thousands of decisions in thousands of other forums that will also affect the provision of high quality early childhood programs. Local school boards can commit local funds to such services whenever they choose to. One of the major expenditures, even now, of United Way and similar consolidated charities is for child care programs. Many corporations are now considering whether to provide early childhood programs for the children of their employees.

Most important of all, parents make decisions each day that directly affect the quality of life and the environment for learning and development of their young children. Parents must learn to accept only high quality early childhood programs. Those who are able to must be willing to pay for this program quality. We must all join with those who cannot afford to pay, to make sure that such programs are available to their children, because, in the end, the nation wins as well as the children and families served.

The Challenge to the Nation

It is time for the nation to recognize the importance of early childhood education to the healthy development of its children. The research does not indicate that all programs produce outcomes such as those reported in the Perry Preschool study, or that all children who participate in such programs will obtain the same strong outcomes. But it does indicate that such programs, on the whole, can produce outcomes of value to both families and society.

The research findings of the Perry Preschool study and the others reported in this volume, indicate that high quality early childhood programs for disadvantaged children produce long-term changes in their lives—changes that permit more education, training, and employment; less crime, delinquency, and welfare subsistence; and a lower birth rate for teenage mothers. These factors weave a pattern of life success that not only is more productive for children and their families but also produces substantial benefits to the society at large through reduction in taxpayer burden and improvement in the quality of community life.

Early childhood education is *not* a panacea, however. It does not solve the nation's unemployment problem. It does not solve the problem of how to deliver effective education in the elementary and high school years to the "graduates" of good early childhood programs. It does not solve the problem of inadequate housing. It does not solve the nation's crime problem. Early childhood education *does* give young children in need a firmer foundation on which to mature and prosper—an edge in opportunity and performance. It is *part* of the solution, not the *whole* solution.

The research demands prompt action to benefit the common good. We must get about the task.

VIII Growing Up in Ypsilanti: The Case Studies

Introduction

This chapter examines the lives of eight study subjects. This examination was undertaken to provide insights into the life circumstances of both the preschool and no-preschool subjects to better understand the group differences documented in earlier chapters. The causal model in Chapter 5 presents connections over time between variables at the group level; in this chapter we trace the ways in which these variables have taken expression for individual members of each of the treatment groups.

To do this, we look in detail at the growing years for eight subjects in our study sample. Equally represented are those who attended preschool (four subjects) and those who did not (four subjects); men and women; successes and failures (as judged by the educational, economic, and social outcomes considered in our study). The case narratives use the subjects' words whenever possible and include salient points as each case demands. The importance of six areas is examined for each case. The areas are as follows:

(1) Parental roles
  - discipline, rules, and limits
  - support and encouragement for education

(2) Attitudes toward money
  - degree of importance
  - why (un)important

(3) Role models
  - presence versus absence; identity
  - positive versus negative

(4) Church and religion
  - effect on family relationships
  - effect on attitudes and values

(5) Sense of responsibility
  - for oneself only
  - for others (siblings, cousins, children, community)

(6) Personality and goal orientation
  - active; internally motivated
  - passive; responding to external circumstances

In the last section of this chapter we consider how the effects of early education might have affected these variables.

The Case Studies

Case Study: Jerry Andrews

All names have been changed to protect the identities of the study's subjects.

The environment...the parents and the neighbors and the friends, to me, if they are right, if they want you to do right, then you should do all right. And I would say really it's the person that makes the difference....When you get to a point where you're out of high school, you got to wonder what you want to do. If you want to do it; you can set your mind to do it, you can do it.

Introduction

Jerry Andrews, aged 20, is currently enrolled in a pre-engineering program at a community college. Working half-time to finance his education, he plans eventually to enter the University of Michigan to obtain an engineering degree with a specialty in drafting. Jerry comes from a family in which the importance of education has been stressed for several generations. Although his parents were divorced when he was quite young, Jerry's uncles provided strong male role models for him while he was growing up and encouraged him to attend college. His mother attributes much of her son's current success to the help and support her extended family gave her as she was raising Jerry and his sisters. Jerry agrees but also sees important influences on his life from outside his family, notably from the friends who shared his academic interests and from the teachers and school counselors who encouraged him in his studies. Most striking, though, is the inner sense of determination and confidence that Jerry projects. One senses that, with his quiet yet forceful personality, Jerry Andrews has set his own course in life—drawing on the freedom and trust his family has given him to steadily fulfill his goals.

Case History

Jerry's preschool teacher described him as a "real nice, highly motivated little boy who was also very cooperative. Sometimes he was hesitant about trying new things, but for the most part he was really motivated." The importance of education in his family environment was also noted by Jerry's preschool teacher. Although neither Jerry nor his mother today remembers many specifics about preschool, it is clear that Mrs. Andrews' involvement in the program is still seen as having been of central importance. She says, "I liked it, you know. I thought, at the time, 'Why put your child in the preschool program if you can't get involved in it?'" Mrs.

Andrews not only was an active participant during home visits but further assisted as a classroom aide one year. She also describes Jerry's father as having been involved with the program and having played an important role in teaching things to his son during the preschool years.

In early elementary school, when Jerry was 6 or 7 years old, his parents divorced; Jerry continued to live with his mother and his three younger sisters. While Mrs. Andrews and the oldest of her daughters took this break very hard, Jerry seemed to adjust to this childhood crisis quite well. His test scores took a temporary drop at age 8, but other than that he encountered no problems at home or school. Of this period, Mrs. Andrews says: "You know he's been to four schools because we always moved around, which I thought maybe that wasn't good for him. But it didn't hurt him any. He did all right every school he went to, and the teachers liked him." In part, Mrs. Andrews believes Jerry came through the divorce because of his own quiet style of taking things as they came along. Says Jerry, too, of his father's leaving, "I accepted it."

But even more significant, especially in Mrs. Andrews' mind, is the role her extended family played in helping raise Jerry and his sisters: "He had a good life, you know, anyway." Mrs. Andrews' mother lived nearby and helped her a good deal: "She helped me raise the kids and they have a lot of respect for her. I don't think there's anything in the world [Jerry] wouldn't do for her, 'cause she wouldn't tell him anything wrong. I was one of the lucky ones that did have a family that helped, helped me with my kids, [helped me] teach them the right way."

If Mrs. Andrews' mother was instrumental in creating a generally positive atmosphere for the children, her four older brothers—Jerry's uncles—had the most important influence on her son's high educational aspirations. According to Mrs. Andrews, her brothers would always sit around and talk about everything—"life, politics, you name it." And Jerry would always sit with them, listening, and learning a great deal. Despite the economic hardship, three of these uncles had worked their way through college "and really did something; and that's why they encourage [Jerry] to keep on, you know. . . . So I had no problem as far as a male image; he really had them."

Although Mrs. Andrews sees her brothers as having provided Jerry's major role models, she acknowledges that even after the divorce Mr. Andrews continued to have an important influence on his son. Both Jerry's academic achievement and his motivation to prepare for a worthwhile career may be attributed to the varied influence of his father's characteristics. Mrs. Andrews says, "His dad is a very smart man. Very smart. Probably where [Jerry] got his knowledge from. And his father's worked everywhere—good jobs, responsibility. But he's just out there, hanging out. You know, [Jerry] don't do that."

Mrs. Andrews downplays her own intelligence and hence any direct effect she has had on Jerry's educational accomplishment. Yet it is obvious from many things she says and does that Jerry's high academic motivation stems quite directly from the importance his mother has always attached to education. Although Mrs. Andrews says the emotional impact of her divorce limited her direct participation in school activities and meetings after the preschool years, still she established a supportive environment at home. In elementary school, for example, she set the precedent that attendance was important: "I sent my kids to school everyday. Everyday. They won't miss school, nope." Doing homework was also something Mrs. Andrews stressed. Recalls Jerry, "They did pressure me a little bit when I got home. I had to do homework before I could go outside and play." But he sees this pressure positively, as a sign that his mother and her brothers cared about his education: "Through the years, if you put it in your mind that you don't have to do homework, later on, you just don't know anything. A lot of them drop out, a lot of them don't graduate; that's one of the big reasons why."

Jerry did not seem to require much outside pushing to take his school work seriously, however. Instead, he appears to have been internally motivated and to have approached school with his own quiet determination to succeed. All his academic records and reports, from kindergarten through high school, reflect a picture of a student who worked hard, did well, and was liked by teachers and peers. Says Mrs. Andrews: "All the teachers seemed to like Jerry." And Jerry recalls "liking every bit" of his school years: "I got along real good with my teachers. I just figured if I did all right with the teachers, they'd like me a lot. I didn't act up or nothing." Teacher ratings confirm this positive image; Jerry was seen as having a mature attitude toward school, as staying out of trouble, and getting along well with others.

Jerry's own impressions of the major influences on him as he was growing up confirm—but also add to—his mother's views. He acknowledges the importance of his family in instilling his positive attitude toward education. In addition, however, Jerry cites several forces outside his family as having affected his ambitions and further conveys the inner resources that, at least as much as these external factors, shaped the young man Jerry is today.

Jerry speaks warmly of the closeness of his extended family and of the pride that his uncles take in his going to college. Revealing the depth of his thinking, Jerry talks about the effect of poverty on his attitudes towards family relationships and education as he has grown up—attitudes one is not likely to find in his peers: "When you think about it, I guess I wouldn't take back everything. Being poor and all that stuff, I think I wouldn't have had it any other way, because I guess you're a little bit closer when you're in need." Of his grandmother's interest in her children's education, he says, "I believe she really stressed that being so poor, and with all those kids that there were, get some of them out and try to stress the meaning [of education]."

This set of values—that having money wasn't everything and that the road to economic advancement was through education—was passed down through the generations, particularly from Mrs. Andrews to her son. They both talk of simply accepting that there were many things the family couldn't buy: "I raised my kids like that. You know, if I can't buy it, I just can't buy it. And nothing bothers them. They don't go out and cry about it." Jerry says, "I really didn't have too much, money-wise, but I didn't want to buy anything anyways. We'd just go out and play with what [we] had. So, money wasn't too much back then." Although Jerry has always had jobs—beginning with neighborhood chores at age 10—there is no feeling that money per se has taken on extraordinary importance to him. Instead, he has saved what he has earned toward the purchase of small items that he takes pleasure in. These days, Jerry works 20 hours a week as a packer at a large thrift store. He has used the money to buy a used car and, above all, to finance his college education. If the lure of working and earning more money occasionally tempts Jerry, his mother reasserts the essential values that strengthen this family: "I mean, it's easy for him to say, 'Momma, I gotta work, I gotta get me a job, I'd rather get me a job than go to school,' and I say, '[Jerry] just keep on going, you know. Go to school.' Because I don't want him to quit school. I want him to keep on going."

Outside of his family, Jerry sees three major influences that have played a role in setting his goals: friends, teachers, and his high school guidance counselor. First and foremost, he repeatedly cites the importance of friends in his life, from elementary school through his current college friends. Jerry's friendships seem to have been based on shared academic interests, with the students reinforcing in one another the importance of learning and accomplishing something: "The friends I had were smart. There were a few of them that were really, really smart. I guess back in junior high, seventh or eighth grade, they helped me out a lot." These friends were chosen by Jerry regardless of color, and as a result, he had more white friends than many of his black peers. Remembering that her son was well liked by everyone in the neighborhood, Mrs. Andrews also recalls that Jerry nevertheless primarily chose his friends from school and hence had a racially mixed peer group. Although he was never explicitly forbidden from associating with the "tough" kids in the neighborhood, Jerry—through sensing his mother's preferences and/or exercising his own—"never went around in the wrong crowd."

Jerry claims that his teachers always rewarded and encouraged his academic accomplishments, especially in his elementary school years. He does not mention any specific teacher(s) as being more influential than others, but says of them as a group, "I guess the teachers helped a lot. Back then, I'd put them first." In high school, it was his senior counselor who became aware of Jerry's mathematical ability and encouraged him to go into engineering and drafting when he entered college. Without the influence of this counselor, says Jerry, "I would have ended up going to school, but not knowing what I was going for. I would have just been taking classes."

While these multiple and positive outside forces have undoubtedly done much to shape this young man, Jerry Andrews also strikes one as a person who has a strong inner core of self-sufficiency. Although his surface appearance is that of a quiet, well-behaved person who causes no trouble and is liked by everyone, underneath one finds a great reserve of determination and self-confidence. Because of Jerry's low-key style, even his mother admits that often "I couldn't figure him out." Yet she speaks of him with a combination of wonder and admiration. Talking of his latest accomplishments (designing a house for someone and pursuing an engineering career), she says, "I had to see for myself. I was just surprised. So he's doing what he wants to do now. So he's going to finish. I've got that much confidence in him; the boy's going to do all right."

All along, even if she didn't understand how or why Jerry accomplished something, Mrs. Andrews felt that because he was succeeding she had to give him the freedom to do things his own way. She cites as an example his late-night study habits: "I guess, well, that's the way he wanted to do it, so why not let him." This childrearing technique, a combination of freedom and trust, seems to have paid off. Jerry grew up projecting a sense of confidence in himself. Asked about what will have the greatest influence on him in the future, Jerry responds: "I guess, just me. If I want to do something, I should be able to do it." As a result, Jerry feels he is "pretty much in control of what happens to [him] in the future."

Yet Jerry is also a realist. He acknowledges that forces and events beyond his control will affect his fate to a certain degree. Beginning as early as his "acceptance" of his parents' divorce, Jerry seemed able to deal with these outer determinants and to temper them with his inner control and sense of direction. Jerry describes his style this way: "I just live...just let it come. Sometimes things don't happen the way you want them to. You really can't base your life on planning ahead all the time, if things don't work out. So I just let it go." At the same time he says of his career plans, "I knew what I was doing. While I'm in school, I know what I'm taking and I know what it's for and if that doesn't work out, you have to change it around and try to go this other way. Schoolwise, I just have to take it day by day." So, rather than having an inflexible plan, Jerry bases his life on options—always with the understanding that it is his own efforts that let him exercise these options.

The various influences in Jerry's life—his close family, his teachers' encouragement in school, and his own basic self-sufficiency—are apparent in the views this young man holds today. Asked about issues such as religion, or racial awareness and advancement, he gives well-considered answers with a consistent theme: People must decide for themselves what is important and then see things through. For example, religion was not an important part of growing up in Jerry's family, yet he has chosen to become a fairly regular churchgoer now. He says, "I believe if you get into it, you should stick with it. You shouldn't go into it just because somebody else is. You should wait until you are able to do it, just sit down and think about what you have started." Similarly, racial awareness was not emphasized in his upbringing, yet Jerry has raised his own consciousness in recent years and believes that more blacks must do the same. He sees this as important in their eventual determination to advance themselves through education: "I think black history ought to be taught back in elementary and up through high school. I guess they'll just learn more about their people. . . . [Then] maybe they'll really want to get their education and kind of change everything around."

In the same way that Jerry's family took responsibility for him and provided him with role models, Jerry now seems to be serving in this capacity for the next generation. He says of his younger sisters, "I figure that if I do all right, maybe it will rub off." Of friends coming up behind him in school, he says, "If I say I'm going to be in engineering, they say, 'Well, maybe I should try it.'" Mrs. Andrews also believes that, as the oldest, Jerry always felt a sense of responsibility for the rest of the family. She talks with obvious pride of one young nephew who wants to be like his cousin Jerry. Although this young man started out getting into trouble like others in his neighborhood, "He talks now, he wants to be like [Jerry]. He didn't used to talk like that. To him [Jerry's] all right, you know; this is the way he wants to be."

Assessing his own situation today, Jerry acknowledges the importance of his family in providing the environment and the role models that kept him from the pitfalls of poverty claiming many of his peers—dropping out of school and getting into trouble with the law. In turn, he sees the example he sets as being a critical influence in the lives of the children he himself hopes to have some day. But—in keeping with the way *he* had to set his own course—Jerry also says *his* children will have to make their own choices: "I will just have to trust them." If they set their own goals and pursue them with the same quiet determination as their father, Jerry Andrews' trust will be well justified.

Analysis

Jerry Andrews is a young man who has been fortunate in the combination of influences that have shaped his life. First and foremost, he has benefited from the support and encouragement of his extended family. This is a family which, for at least the last three generations, has valued education and seen it as the vehicle for rising above poverty. Jerry's grandmother instilled this attitude in her children, and through his mother and uncles, this respect for education was transmitted to Jerry. His uncles, in particular, seem to have been primary role models for Jerry, setting him an example of the rewards of going to college and making something of oneself.

Life has not been easy for Jerry and his family. His parents divorced when he was young and the experience seems to have greatly shaken his mother's confidence. Yet, here again, the extended family stepped in to provide the nurturing and support that Jerry and his sisters needed. Also, the family is not ashamed of being poor. Once more, however, we see how this family turned adversity into strength. Jerry's mother says she raised her children to accept this limitation and not to cry about things they couldn't have. Today, Jerry himself is eloquent in expressing the important lessons that he learned from the experience of being poor. He stresses that it gave him a perspective on what was really meaningful in life, with family closeness being at the top of his list. He is also aware that poverty attached a special significance to the value of education, particularly to the avenues opened up by college. For Jerry, as for his uncles, attending college means hard work and additional economic hardship to cover the expenses. Yet he is constantly reminded, again by this family that takes pride in his accomplishments, that the short-term sacrifice is worth the long-term advantage of obtaining his degree.

Supplementing this encouragement on the home front were the rewards for academic accomplishment that Jerry got from peers and from school staff. Though good luck always plays some part in determining the people who cross one's path, it is also clear that Jerry himself was responsible for seeking out and developing these supportive relationships. Yet Jerry made the effort to establish friendships at school with other serious students like himself, even though it meant breaking down some racial barriers. Similarly, Jerry made allies and supporters of his teachers. Even when he was very young, in elementary school, he made the conscious decision not to be a troublemaker like some of his peers. He wanted the teachers to like him, perhaps because he already sensed that academic accomplishment would be his access to personal rewards. Fortune again presented Jerry with an alert and sympathetic high school counselor who saw that this student possessed the necessary mathematical abilities to become an engineer. We will see contradictory instances (e.g., Bonita Emerson) in which a counselor was in a position to instead prevent a student from fulfilling his or her potential. Yet, even when a counselor is supportive, that stance alone is not sufficient to cause a student's success. The motivation to follow through, to turn the potential into reality, must come from within the student. This determination to see something through to its conclusion is a primary characteristic of Jerry Andrews.

The inner resolve of this young man is all the more striking because it is covered by such a quiet, low-key demeanor. Jerry Andrews is not an "obvious" person; even his mother, with whom he is close, admits to not understanding him much of the time. Yet she raised him with the freedom and trust to be himself. The confidence she had in his ability and good sense has been translated into Jerry's own sense of self-confidence. He projects an air of someone who knows he can succeed at what he set out to do. Jerry feels he is in control of his life. But he is, simultaneously, a realist; he doesn't count on good fortune to insure that his plans will always work out. Rather, he is willing to take what comes and rely on his own flexibility to temper whatever obstacles fate may present him with.

Jerry has drawn on his own experiences and his basic nature in formulating a set of world views about the society he lives in. He acknowledges the essential role that the support of family, friends, and community must play in advancing the development of poor black youths like himself. But he also clearly feels that there is no substitute for the resolve of the individual to make something of his or her life. For Jerry Andrews, "freedom" has been this optimal combination—the encouragement of others who trusted him enough to let him pursue his self-determined goals. Working at his own pace, and in his own style, this young man will follow his goals to their conclusion.

Case Study: Yvonne Barnes

All names have been changed to protect the identities of the study's subjects.

If I could, I would change a whole lot. I'd change everybody's personality and mine too. If I could change back the hands of time, I'd become a more better person than I am already, you know, 'cause there are a lot of things I want in life and I came at it the wrong way....For one thing, when I was coming up in school I should have knew what I wanted to do because now I kind of regret being bad in school and hanging out. I still ain't accomplished what I want in life...I wanted to become somebody and I haven't become that yet.

Introduction

Yvonne Barnes, age 20 and the youngest of eight children, lives with her parents in the same house she grew up in. Although she graduated from high school, Yvonne's school records are dotted with academic problems and disciplinary incidents from the time she entered kindergarten. Yvonne was seen as having trouble with her studies and as being very disruptive in the classroom; above all, she always resisted taking orders of any kind. Yvonne recalls her own school days as a time of "hanging out." She did just enough work to get by, but her greatest pleasure was when she skipped classes or hid out in the school building. Sports, particularly basketball, were all that Yvonne liked. But she destroyed her chances of playing on the high school team because of her pattern of getting into trouble and refusing to do her work. Looking back on her school history, Yvonne today voices the regret that she didn't do better. Yvonne wants to "be somebody" and acknowledges that her past hampers her now. Yet, along with the self-criticism, Yvonne has a great deal of self-pride; she believes that she can make something of her life as long as she wants to do it. Her current plans are vague and not totally realistic—she talks of getting a job, entering college, and enlisting in the Army, with no clear chronology or priorities. Regardless of the direction she takes, Yvonne is adamant about being ready to move on—leave home and leave Michigan. But as she herself admits, her attitude about life will have to change or she will find herself "hanging out" indefinitely.

Case History

Yvonne Barnes is the youngest of eight children, with five brothers and two sisters ranging in age from two to 12 years older than herself. Her father, a construction worker, has never had trouble finding employment. When Yvonne was about 5 years old, her family moved from Ypsilanti and bought a house in nearby Willow Run. Yvonne, having graduated from high school two years ago, still lives in this house today with her mother and father. Mr. and Mrs. Barnes recall that when they first moved in, they were one of only two black families in the area; about three years later, the neighborhood was mostly black, with families either renting or buying homes.

Mr. and Mrs. Barnes remember Yvonne's early childhood as being a trouble-free time. Says her mother, "Well, she was a pretty admirable baby. She never liked to play with girl things; she always liked to play with boys, trucks, cars, you know." Her father agrees that Yvonne was something of a "tomboy," but also admits to having gone along with it. "Yeah. She always wanted me to take her fishing when she was little; she always wanted to do what a boy done." Yvonne's transition to school posed no problems either. One of her brothers, exactly a year older than Yvonne, went to a Head Start preschool in the neighborhood. When Yvonne was three, she begged to go there too and was soon attending Head Start every day with her brother. Thus, when it was time for her to enter kindergarten, there was no major adjustment for Yvonne. Summing up her early elementary school years, Yvonne's mother says, "She did okay, yes she did okay."

Yvonne however, looking back, regrets that she did not make more out of her education. It is a theme that is repeated as she talks of her life in general: "I could've did better, I could've did better. I could've did a whole lot better. I could've did better all my life. In elementary, junior high through high school, I could've did better." As she recalls, her educational career did not start off too badly in elementary school: "Yeah, it was pretty nice." But she admits that even then it was hard for her to do her work; she would instead hang out and play. Yvonne remembers only one of her teachers at the time, in fourth grade, and says she liked this particular teacher because she *made* Yvonne get her work done: "Well, she helped me out a lot, made me 'sit down girl and do your work, quit being so bad.' She was nice though, she made you do your work. You wasn't coming in there to play or, you know, horse around or whatever. She made you do your work. She'd break out this paddle."

According to tester and teacher ratings from these days, however, Yvonne's academic and behavior problems in school were already quite severe. Testing showed consistently low scores and behavior ratings during test sessions showed Yvonne as being highly anxious and somewhat shy. In first grade, the examiner wrote: "High anxiety—afraid to make definite answers; some bizarre responses, poor psychomotor responses." By fourth grade, the tester underscored and double-checked "anxious" and added "hesitant about situation."

For Yvonne, the classroom setting was as problematic as the testing situation. She consistently received poor ratings in all areas of academic performance and socioemotional development. Academically, she was rated as not retaining learning, being hesitant to try, giving up easily, and having low motivation for success. On social and emotional variables, Yvonne was described as being isolated, withdrawn, and uncommunicative; having poor relationships with peers and teachers; being easily led into trouble and blaming others; being disruptive in the classroom and aggressive toward peers; impulsive, disobedient, and resentful of criticism or discipline. It is not surprising that Yvonne's prognosis for future academic success was seen as being very poor.

Mr. and Mrs. Barnes's attitude towards Yvonne's schooling is difficult to ascertain. Their own assessment is that they taught all their children that education was important, especially as a means for the economic advancement of blacks. Says Mrs. Barnes, "Well, one thing I really want them to do is get a good education, 'cause that was the main thing and whites didn't really want to see a black person ahead of them." Mr. Barnes states, "Education, the way they educate, you got to have education now in anything....If you can't read, you just left out." Although two of Yvonne's brothers did go to college, it is possible that education was stressed more for them than for Yvonne or her sisters. Asked, for example, about Yvonne's teachers, Mrs. Barnes says somewhat apologetically, "To tell you the truth, I about done forget 'em all. I shouldn't, but..." Yvonne's teachers consistently rated her mother low on dimensions such as "cooperation" and "participation in school activities." Yvonne claims her mother made her do homework—"It was either do your homework and then hang out, or get the whuppin' and still do your homework." But beyond this external constraint to meet school's basic requirements, there is no evidence that the value of learning and achievement for its own sake were reinforced for Yvonne at home.

This relaxed attitude toward education persisted for Yvonne and her parents into junior high and high school, despite the fact that Yvonne accumulated a history of disciplinary incidents. A series of offenses—smoking in the bathroom, fighting with peers, arguing with teachers—resulted in a total of three suspensions and two expulsions. Says Mrs. Barnes: "I think that's when she had her biggest problems, in the high school, in the junior high." But she goes on to minimize these problems, saying the teachers exaggerated the difficulties and that Yvonne was not an instigator, but only someone who hit back if attacked first. "They wasn't too bad to me, but you know, like teachers, they can make things worse than what they is. You gotta be there to know what's happening. Sometimes, teachers can see I could hit you, but teacher don't see when you hit me. Things happen like that and you can't explain because I'm over here saying you did, you saying you didn't, and she just only see one. [I] was the kind if you hit me, I'll hit you back. You don't start nothing, but if somebody hit you, you hit 'em back." Yvonne apparently would not tolerate being hit by anyone, including the school principal, who according to Yvonne, regularly doled out paddlings with a thick board. Says Yvonne proudly, "No, not me, she never hit me, I said, 'Kick me out.' She'd kick me out for two or three days. My mother said, 'You should have let her hit you, so you wouldn't get kicked out.' I said, 'No, no.'"

Academically, Yvonne continued to coast through junior and senior high school, doing a minimum of work and just getting by. Hanging out again seemed to be her favorite pastime: "I passed through, but I also did a lot of hanging out. I was skipping all the time. I'd do my work, I passed—that's one thing. You know, I do my work, and then after I got the grade for that one semester, or that week, then I knew it would be time to hang out." Her transcript for these years shows almost all C's and D's. In fact, when Yvonne was interviewed at the age of 14, she reported being only 50 percent certain that she would graduate from high school. Yvonne recalls having no favorite teachers back then, but she did like "a gym teacher cause she always let me come in, play basketball, and I stayed in gym, if I decided to miss a class or something. She would let me in, she was all right." It is interesting that by then Yvonne favored the teacher who let her hang out and skip classes; in elementary school it was the one teacher who forced her to work whom Yvonne remembers fondly.

Although she was always interested in sports, Yvonne found that for a girl, athletics wasn't available as an outlet in junior high, so instead she took up the clarinet. But even this effort was half-hearted and just "getting by"; "hanging out" was still Yvonne's major activity: "Well, really there wasn't too much sports for the girls back then; I had gym all the time, I played basketball. There wasn't really no sports. But I had band classes, so I played in the band. [I played] clarinet. I never really got down on it. I hit a few notes, but I was like, you know, like hanging out. I still got my clarinet. I play on it every now and then, you know, but hanging out was what was happening."

When Yvonne reached high school, athletics was more of an option for girls and she had an opportunity to play on the basketball team—her favorite sport. Again however, we hear Yvonne express regret for the fact that she wasted this chance: "Well, I messed up in high school when I had a chance to be on the basketball team and try to do something for myself or, you know, or make it to somebody's college or whatever. I was hanging out a lot, you know, just messing around, and I didn't accomplish what I wanted to, see, and I'm still mad at myself about that."

In all, one is struck by Yvonne's ambivalence in her feelings about school. On the one hand, she is honest about how much she enjoyed it as a place to hang out and socialize with her friends. On the other, she truly regrets that no one made her take her studies more seriously and that she herself let opportunities pass by. Her confusion is reflected in this fantasy she offered when asked how she would change the schools if given the power: "My school, if I had the power, I would make a castle out of my school. You come in, like the gates are closed. . . . Then lunch hour, the gates are open. I give people time for a little late lunch or what, hanging out. I give them time to come in, but I have it like a castle. You know, the high school is like a straight little hallway, a couple little turns and that's that. I would have a big old place [where] you can hide, skip, whatever. . . . It would be a good time, but people would still come to that school. It wouldn't be boring, there's always going to be something exciting about that school, you know, it's going to make everybody want to come. Even though you do hang out, it's especially that everybody [learn something]. Ain't going to pass no dummies, don't pass no dummies."

While Yvonne occasionally seems sorry that no outside force compelled her to study, she is basically a person who resists any attempts to control her. It is striking that when she is asked if there are any people in her life who have influenced her, Yvonne seems to equate influence with control and vehemently denies that anyone else has affected her. "Nobody really influenced me [except] I would say myself, really. . . . 'cause I don't listen to nobody. I mean, my mother she might tell me some stuff that's good for me. I listen to her, but really I look up to myself." Mr. and Mrs. Barnes cannot name anyone either who they think influenced or served as a model for their daughter. Instead, Yvonne seems to characterize herself as a leader, but interestingly, as a passive one—that is, she claims to make no attempt to "control" or influence others, they just follow her: " . . . you know, it seems like I might be a leader. It seems like everybody wants to follow in my little footsteps, all my friends, you know, if I do something crazy or weird, they might want to do that too. Well, I wouldn't be influencing them, they like [would follow]."

Although adamant that no one has influenced her, Yvonne does admit to admiring two of her siblings—the oldest sister and the oldest brother. She says of her sister, "I know I look up to my sister a lot. She don't influence me. She tries to help me out, but she don't influence me." And she says even more about her brother: "I liked my brother 'cause I always wanted to kind of be like him. He did pretty well in school. I wanted to go to college and that's pretty hard for me to get in there. He went to Eastern . . . and his wife is a school teacher. . . . I wanted to always be like him."

Toward the rest of her family, Yvonne has the same kind of mixed but relaxed and accepting attitude she expresses toward school and life in general. "Well, we seem like we argue all the time. Sometime we become a family and sometime we don't become a family." She reports getting along pretty well with her siblings, having the usual ups and downs. As the youngest, Yvonne occasionally got special treatment, but her parents agree she wasn't spoiled. Says Mrs. Barnes: "I don't think they spoiled her. Just being the baby, I mean, you know, a lot of things that she would want to do they would let her do by her being the baby, and she stayed the baby I guess till she got up big enough she want to try to change on her own." Yvonne and her parents have the same realistic attitude about their current relationships with one another. On living together in the family, says Yvonne, "I know I get on their nerves and, you know, they get on mine, but that's a family, you know, that's life. It's about the usual. I get along with them. We always have our misunderstandings between each other. We might be mad for a minute but then, you know, we don't have no long grudges going against each other. We be back family again in five minutes after we get through arguing."

This live-and-let-live attitude seems to have characterized all aspects of Yvonne's upbringing. We have seen that there was a general feeling that education was important, yet no real pressure to exert oneself in school. Analogously, the family's attitude toward religion was that it was important but not mandatory. Says Mrs. Barnes: "To me, the whole factor should be [religion]. But I know it hasn't been here, on the whole, but it has been some. I think it should play the biggest part. They used to go to church all the time until they got up big enough to make up their own minds. They don't go like I want them to go; they go when they want to go." Mr. Barnes agrees that letting his children make up their own minds is the only reasonable attitude. He adds that they have managed to learn and internalize the right set of values this way: "Young ones nowadays get wiser than we do. Not any more weaker, and wiser."

Respect for the individuality of each of their eight children has been translated, at least in Yvonne's case, into a certain kind of determination and self-pride. She's not completely happy with herself—she knows she could have done better—but she is not ready to give up because she believes she can get what she wants if she tries. Yvonne assesses her current life situation with this mixture of self-criticism, self-admiration, and hope: "I'm kind of satisfied but not really, because I could have been a better person, I could have been somebody. Everybody knows me, I'm a popular person. In school, I actually wanted to be a basketball player; that's what I really wanted to be. But I kind of messed up, but I'm still trying on it now, you know. I stay in my sports, I play softball too, but I'm still trying to get into playing basketball, that's what I want to do. My life, it's all right, it's so-so, it could have been better."

Looking toward the future, Yvonne's parents admit they have no idea what she might be doing in the short- or long-term future. Says Mr. Barnes, "I couldn't see in the future," and Mrs. Barnes, "I don't know. She says she wants to go to [business school] . . . so I hope that be part of her plans." Yvonne herself is indefinite about her next steps. She talks simultaneously about wanting to get into college, enter the Army, and find a job. These seem to be contingencies, in order of decreasing preference, yet none of these ideas is backed up by a realistic understanding of the requirements or opportunities involved.

Yvonne says, "I like to plan ahead. That's why I'm going to try to get into the service. But I'm going to try one more time to see if I can get into school. If I can't get into the school, I'm going to go ahead and, you know, make my plans to get into the service." In the next breath she says, "I'm going to stick around for a little bit to see if I can get me a job." Yvonne's plans for school seem more in the realm of fantasy. She wants to go but has had no success locally in being accepted. Instead, she believes from what she has heard that she would have no trouble being admitted to "some college" in California and has vague plans for moving there, staying with relatives of her parents, establishing residency, and going to school on a full scholarship: "I try to do good and I want to be somebody. If I keep living around here, I might not be able to get a chance to get into a college. I was thinking about even moving to California; both of my parents got relatives in California. They got a college down there for I think four years, the University of Cal or something they was telling me. This guy was telling me about it. He said you go down there and you can get in, and it wouldn't cost you nothing. You can take four years of college free, and that scholarship would pay for it. That's all I got to do is get there and make it."

Recognizing that getting to California will itself take money, Yvonne is seriously considering enlisting in the Army and accumulating some savings. Looking five years down the road, she shows her characteristic mixture of fantasy—dreaming about the star she wants to be—and determination—vowing to make it on her own terms and not letting others set her limits: "I'd like to be on the basketball court, but then again I might go into the service. That's what I really want to do, but people keep telling me, 'Naw, you don't want to do that.' But then I think I do, you know, I think I want to go there and see if I like it. I'm tired of people telling me, 'You're not going to like it so don't even waste your time. You don't like taking orders from home.' I don't really like too much taking orders from home, but it does depend on the kind of orders it is. But I think I can handle the Army if I want to do it."

Whatever future plan she pursues, Yvonne is certain about one thing—wanting to move out of her parents' home and see the world beyond Michigan: "If I can't get me no job, I'm going, I'm leaving. I got to get out of Michigan; I'm tired of being in Michigan. I've been there all my life, I want to see some of the world, I got to go somewhere, I want to move. I do want to move away from my family 'cause I think I'd probably be a better person, too." Yvonne states emphatically: "I want to get my life together," but she also admits, "I have to change my attitude. My attitude is really bad and that's the only influence I have is to change my attitude. If I'd change my attitude, I'd be a whole lot better."

Analysis

Yvonne Barnes is a young woman with vague prospects and no real sense of urgency to find a direction for her presently uneventful life. This lack of pressure—both internal and external—has characterized Yvonne's upbringing. Although both Mr. and Mrs. Barnes claim to value education, neither of them seem to have actively encouraged her to take her school work more seriously. They let Yvonne establish her own path, and she quickly took the easy route of skipping clases and doing the barest minimum of studying. Even when Yvonne built up a record of disciplinary troubles, Mrs. Barnes blamed it on the teachers' misperceptions as much as her daughter's misdeeds.

If no one in the family felt particularly responsible for Yvonne, she in turn has never seemed concerned about anyone but herself. As the youngest of eight children, Yvonne was not spoiled; nevertheless, it is not surprising that she didn't develop a sense of looking out for others, as we have seen in some of her peers who did have younger brothers and sisters to care for. Yvonne's individuality was not only tolerated but apparently encouraged in a family in which all the children were accorded the right to make up their own minds about things. Yvonne did not have to worry that her actions would hurt others; hence she was essentially free to do as she pleased.

Being free—without anyone else controlling or influencing her—is important to Yvonne. This attitude, however, results in several conflicts in her thinking. She states that she has no one but herself to blame for not having taken her studies more seriously, and yet she implies through her memories and fantasies that she would have done better if only her teachers had pushed her more or made their lessons more interesting. Similarly, she is almost defensive in her assertion that no one except herself has had any influence on her life. Yet she speaks wistfully of the older brother who has been to college and whose wife is a teacher, repeating how much she always wanted to be like him. Following her own rebellious course through school, Yvonne has severely limited her chances for entering college and being like this sibling—the only person, in fact, whom she speaks of with obvious respect.

By her own admission, Yvonne will continue hanging out in life unless she changes her attitude. Thus far, all her statements about the future begin with the word "if"—if I go to California, then I can get into school; if I decide to enter the service, then I know I can handle the Army; if I look around here, then I can find a job. Again, that sense of urgency is missing. Yvonne's tone does take on more animation and determination however, when she talks of her general need to move on and experience more out of life than Michigan has to offer. If nothing else, boredom with her present situation and curiosity about new places to "hang out" in the world, may provide Yvonne Barnes with the impetus to make some changes. Whether it is a change for the better, as she professes it will be, is up to her alone.

Case Study: Calvin Charles

I always liked to be the guy that called the shots. That's the way it was then, and it's the same way now—you get a little money, you can do that.

Introduction

Calvin Charles, age 23, is at the state penitentiary serving 18 months to 5 years for breaking and entering. A high school dropout, Calvin is someone the judicial system would call a "chronic offender." Articulate, particularly about his self-styled life of crime, Calvin relies on words primarily to justify his own actions. His actions, beginning with our earliest childhood documentation, reflect a consistent history of fighting with peers, and hostility and resistance toward adults. Calvin's course seemed set by third grade, when getting money became established as the dominant theme in his life. The conventional age-appropriate issues—education and later employment—neither concern nor motivate Calvin. Although an active and goal-oriented young man, his goals are in conflict with those of his society.

Case History

Although Calvin has few specific memories of his early school years, what he does remember is associated with getting into trouble. Asked what he would do when he got to school, Calvin replied, "Look for something to do wrong." Backing down a bit, he qualified his statement: "Well . . . not really something wrong, but it would always come out wrong." Pressed for details, Calvin recalls such incidents as accidentally dropping a block on another child's head in preschool (and deciding that the "victim" pretended to be hurt worse than he actually was), and ducking the kindergarten teacher whom he felt was being too strict with him. Such incidents illustrate Calvin's consistent, if minor, scuffles with peers and adults in the early school years.

Mrs. Charles, Calvin's mother, however, does not recall him having any such problems with people at that age. On the contrary, she says of his years at preschool, "He was always outgoing, you know, liked being around other kids. I think he liked it pretty much." The reason for the discrepancy in Calvin's and Mrs. Charles's reports is unclear. Calvin's tale may be as much a reflection of his current self-styled image—a young man who has chosen to be at variance with his society—as it is an accurate recollection of this period. His mother does acknowledge, though, that she could see Calvin, as early as age 3 or 4, having a "very strong personality . . . I think that's why he is the way he is today."

Reports from teachers and examiners during these early years suggest that the true picture lies somewhere in between the recollections of Calvin and Mrs. Charles. The preschool teacher wrote of Calvin: "He is curious, asks good questions, and is interested in many things. Likes to do his own choosing and reacts negatively to a limit or disappointment, if it is something he wants very much, and becomes stubborn and cannot be reasoned with, but he is learning self-control in this sort of situation." This negative reaction, rather than any control, predominated in testing situations; Calvin may have been responding to the structure of the setting or the frustration of not being able to perform many of the tasks requested of him by the examiner. Testers frequently noted that Calvin was overly active and easily distracted; he was very verbal but often about topics of his own interest rather than about the test questions. Calvin's hostility and resistance to performing appear in several comments. Those who tested Calvin at age 4½ and at the end of first grade stated that Calvin might have scored higher if he had been more willing to try the tasks required. Whether the problem was motivational or intellectual, however, Calvin's scores remained consistently below average.

This early pattern of resistance and poor intellectual performance proved predictive of the difficulties Calvin would encounter in the structured setting of the elementary school classroom. As recorded by teachers and supported by Calvin's own early memories, fighting with other children was characteristic of his behavior. For example, his first grade teacher rated Calvin as most like pupils who get into fights or quarrels with other pupils more often than others; have to be coaxed or forced to work or play with other pupils; have difficulty in learning school subjects; make unusual or inappropriate responses during normal school activities; and become upset or sick often, especially when faced with a difficult school problem or situation. Calvin's second grade teacher, while finding him less quarrelsome, reported that he had motivational problems regarding academic performance.

Interestingly, although Calvin and his mother disagree on whether he had early adjustment problems in school, they are in agreement that his major difficulties with authority began around the third grade. But they attribute the cause of the problem to very different sources. According to Calvin, money assumed a great deal of importance to him at this age and obtaining it became his major motivation in life: "About third [grade] . . . Yeah, I got to know where the money was, and I was always trying to think of something to do to get some money. That's the way it's been ever since." The implication is that acquiring money took precedence—in terms of time and effort—over school work. Calvin reports that he started out doing lots of little odd jobs (e.g., cutting the grass) to earn pocket money but quickly decided he could make more, and make it faster, by stealing. Even though, by his own admission, his parents were able to provide him with a reasonable amount of spending money, it was not enough for him: "Things wasn't too bad, but I always wanted more than I could get." He says of trying to get money to buy something like a basketball or football, "But that still ain't getting it, it's taking too long, actually, so you find out that

136

you can steal something and somebody will give you a reasonable amount for it. You do it two or three times and say, 'Well, this is it.' One thing leads to another."

Mrs. Charles, however, attributes her son's difficulties at this age to problems he was having with his school work. She says, "His marks weren't too good," and explains that he was specifically having problems with reading and math. Rather than being aware of any discipline problems, Mrs. Charles sees all of Calvin's difficulties at this age as stemming from academics. "Most of them were, I guess, like in his reading, things like that, he kind of fell behind. I think that's what kind of threw him off, you know. Then after a while he just stopped trying." Neither Mr. nor Mrs. Charles particularly remembers Calvin attempting to earn money through odd jobs at this age and, while acknowledging their son's desire for money, see it as emerging after the difficulties with school work first arose.

The school records at third grade corroborate Mrs. Charles's recollection about her son's academic difficulties. Calvin was referred for a psychological evaluation midway through the year, with the following entry by his teacher in his school records: "Slow in arithmetic and reading (below first grade level). Becomes frustrated and refuses to do work that is new to him. He has attempted to skip from school. Needs more help than I can give." Calvin was recommended for special education and repeated the third grade. During his second year in third grade, he also received tutorial help and teacher home visits. The consistent pattern of fighting with peers, evident in kindergarten and first grade, picked up and in fact continued throughout Calvin's school career until he dropped out in the eleventh grade.

Thus, even in early elementary school, Calvin appeared to be having two types of problems—one was keeping up with his grade level academically, and the other was repeatedly getting involved in disciplinary incidents. His parents' role in dealing with the former—taking an active interest in the learning aspects of Calvin's education—seems minimal. Although Mrs. Charles reports having attended PTA meetings and various conferences, she has no specific memories of any of Calvin's teachers, nor do she or Mr. Charles report ever having worked with their son at home on his schoolwork.

Calvin's parents have more to say about their involvement in disciplining their son. According to Mrs. Charles, the role of disciplinarian fell to her during Calvin's early years. She describes herself as not being permissive, but admits that Mr. Charles was "more strict, I guess." Still, Calvin's mother does not recall any particular problems with Calvin when he was young. She says of Calvin and his siblings, "I guess I tried to raise them all alike," but acknowledges in her son's case that "everybody has a different personality; with some it worked, some it doesn't, you know."

Mr. Charles attributes his own lack of involvement in his children's discipline to his time-consuming work schedule. He excuses himself: "You know, when you're a working man, you have little time . . . when you work in those plants. Sometimes I would have to work six days a week, sometimes twelve hours a day and, you know, you really don't have too much time with your wife or nobody else. And there are six, seven kids and they all have different personalities and you almost have to have a Ph.D. or a master's degree in psychology to relate sometimes."

However, Mr. Charles did begin to play a more active role in disciplining Calvin at about the age of 11 or 12, perhaps two years after his son began having serious problems in school. Of this period, Mr. Charles cannot recall any difficulties as disciplinarian: "I'd say, I think we understood each other quite well. That was most of the problem to me, what I expect from him and what he expected from me. That's about the way it went. I think we had a pretty good understanding." Calvin's father also does not recall using physical discipline very often, an impression that is sharply contradicted by his son's memories. Remembering the first time his parents caught him stealing something at age 9 or 10, Calvin says, "I got a whuppin', not a whuppin'—a killing. The first killing I ever got." Although he became more adept at hiding the evidence of his thefts, more such beatings followed for Calvin's various infractions. Calvin is particularly resentful of one beating his father gave him in fourth grade, allegedly for stealing 20 dollars from his aunt and uncle. Calvin admits to having stolen the money, but claims he got it elsewhere. The grudge, which he holds to this day, is that his father was in error over the source of the 20 dollars. Significantly, neither Mr. nor Mrs. Charles remembers this incident, still so vivid in Calvin's mind.

In contrast to the earlier days when Mr. Charles felt he and Calvin had a good understanding, Calvin's father believes that as his son grew older he just stopped listening. Concerned about the peer group Calvin was running around with, Mr. Charles tried to talk to his son. "I considered it a bad crowd. I talked to him, I met with him on it, and he'd hang out with them anyway. He seemed to understand what I was saying, but it didn't make any difference. . . . He always wanted to deny whatever I seen coming up, you know." His father also reports warning Calvin to stay in school, to no avail: "I was always on his case about staying in school, you know, I told him you need it, very bad. . . . But, I give up along the way. I just tell him, this is how it is, and I told you this is wrong. You don't want to go to school, you're kicked out of school, you don't want to do this, you're going to have to find a place to go. Especially when he got about 17, 18. And he was in and out of trouble."

Both Mr. and Mrs. Charles felt that Calvin was led into trouble by the friends he hung around with. Mrs. Charles is quite definite in believing that the root of the problem with these other children was parents who took no part in disciplining their sons: "This particular family, well I think their parents didn't really care what they did, and you know he [Calvin] got involved with them." Yet, despite their own involvement in disciplining Calvin, both Mr. and Mrs. Charles independently voiced the feeling that once he was outside the home, they had little control over Calvin's behavior. Says Mrs. Charles, "Discipline? Well, at home he wasn't no problem, but after they get out, you know . . . when they get out you don't know what they're doing." Mr. Charles echoes, "In my house here, that's where you have control, and that's all you have. Once they leave here, out in the street, what can you say?"

As Calvin got older, moving into junior high school, the influence of his home and early upbringing seemed to diminish even further. Not only were his parents' values ineffective in guiding Calvin's behavior, but other potential sources—such as religion or acceptable role models—were also absent. According to Calvin, his parents were not religious and (for reasons he doesn't explain) his mother would not allow him to attend church. He claims to have occasionally sneaked out of his own home to go to the church near his grandmother's house. But the impact of what he heard there was minimal. He went to church because "it just seemed like it was the thing to do. . . . I knew the things that I was doing was wrong, but I got into the habit." Similarly, Calvin can recall no family members or friends who influenced him in a "positive" direction. Instead, he claims to model himself after the fictional character Alexander Mundy from the television show "To Catch a Thief." Beginning around the age of 14, Calvin says he admired the style of this character—a distinctly "intellectual" one—and would try to apply it to himself: "I did the way he would go about planning, and I would like to do just about the same, and put it in this situation instead of the situation he was in."

Although Calvin fancied himself a "thinking man's thief," his school records continue to show a student with academic problems as well as disciplinary ones. As a result of having repeated third grade, Calvin entered junior high school one year older than his seventh grade peers. Initially enrolled in a regular academic program, Calvin was later referred to the Alternative Education Program and the services of a helping teacher. His history of fighting escalated, and in the eighth grade Calvin was suspended on an assault and battery charge involving another student. Although he claims, "I liked school all the way until I got to high school," school for Calvin seems to have been little more than a matter of attendance. If anything, it provided the necessary social contacts for furthering his illegal activities, which at that time were largely concerned with dealing drugs.

Outside of school, Calvin continued to have repeated brushes with the criminal justice system. His first official contact with the juvenile justice system came when he was 15 and charged with "deserting his home without sufficient cause." His adult criminal record is spotted with dismissed cases, convictions, and sentences; his activities and charges include possession of stolen guns, criminal sexual conduct, drug dealing, and larceny. In his own mind, Calvin saw no problem in balancing his criminal career with his responsibilities as a student. The school authorities obviously thought otherwise, and Calvin believes the high school principal was "out to get him" for having money and nice clothes: "He says, 'You come in here dressed nice all the time,' and he thinks, 'Where you getting the money from?' I told him it wasn't none of his concern, as long as I come to school and do what I'm supposed to do. It ain't your business actually. So he tells me, 'We're going to kick you out for the rest of the year because we don't want you in here.' . . . So I went back the next year and he was standing there." While not kicked out a final time, Calvin dropped out of school on his own in the eleventh grade.

Calvin's record of legal employment parallels his experiences with the school setting. Although his illegal activities provided him with adequate income, he nevertheless joined the CETA program at the age of 18. When asked why, Calvin responded that his CETA position was valuable in making the social contacts necessary for his other, criminal dealings: "The main thing is to do everything you can to find out everything you can about everything. . . . You don't know what information or what might come in handy where and what time, you know?" His job supervisor viewed Calvin in the same troublesome terms as did the school authorities, believing his employee neither put in a decent day's work nor got along with other workers on the job. He stated that Calvin's attitude toward the job needed improvement. Calvin's own statements regarding the world of work confirm his employer's evaluation; his attitude, even today, is that the value of a legitimate job is to provide a front, so that people will not wonder about the source of his income.

The job Calvin had at the time of his most recent arrest was apparently to serve this purpose. It was while working as a janitor at a large shopping mall that he was arrested for breaking and entering at one of the mall's shoe stores. He claims that this particular charge was false, but that because of his reputation—one he talks of with evident pride—the police were out to get him. Convicted, Calvin is now serving a term of 18 months to 5 years at the state penitentiary in Jackson, Michigan.

Although he has no specific plans for when he gets out of prison, Calvin talks vaguely of getting a legitimate job. His parents would like to see him change, but are realistic about his prospects. Says Mr. Charles, "I wish he would change and . . . try to get some free time in this free world and try to raise a family and get a good job. But they always say it's not gonna happen again, don't worry, don't worry. I'm not going back no more and all that." And Mrs. Charles says, "Well, if he don't change he'll be right back where he is." Calvin's own ambivalence about going "straight" is evident in the defiant attitude he expresses at the same time he talks of finding work: "When [my term] is up, like I said, I'm going to do what I want to." The shortage of jobs for young black men does not bother him. "Look here, as long as they make some money. . . . there's something I can do to get some." That has certainly been Calvin's history up to this point; the manner in which he comes by money in the future remains to be seen.

Analysis

Calvin Charles is a young man with a turbulent history. Beginning at an early age, his frustration in school appears to be associated with repeated disciplinary incidents and subsequent criminal activities. Although he fancies himself a "smart" thief, with an intellectual approach to crime, neither his test scores nor his school performance records corroborate this self-image.

Parent involvement, for Mr. and Mrs. Charles, was clearly weighted in favor of discipline over explicit educational concerns. Although giving lip service to the importance of learning and school, neither Mr. nor Mrs. Charles appears to have actively encouraged or helped Calvin in his schoolwork. As disciplinarians, first Mrs. Charles and later her husband believed that they were involved with Calvin. By their own account however, Calvin's disciplining was not always consistent; his parents differed in how strict they were, and when their methods didn't work they appeared to give up rather than search for more effective means of reaching Calvin. It is interesting that neither Mr. nor Mrs. Charles believed that Calvin internalized the rules and values they set down. Both voiced a philosophy that one could summarize as "out-of-sight, out-of-control." In Calvin's life, no other sources, such as the church or exemplary role models, substituted to provide an inner basis for decision making according to the accepted standards of society.

Calvin's orientation toward life is clearly an active one; he is a "doer" with a clear goal, and money is an obvious motivating force. Calvin's activity is directed toward his own gain—he feels and has no responsibilities toward others—and is always in the service of promoting his self-image as a bright criminal up against society. Money is valued for what it brings, again perpetuating a self-image reinforced by nice clothes, good cars, and other materialistic trappings.

For Calvin, having money—lots of it, obtained with a minimum of labor—is a primary source of self-esteem. Again, the dynamics are not completely clear, but the consistency of his history leads one to speculate. Academics, as a source of self-esteem, were closed off to Calvin early when it was evident he could not keep up with the demands of school. At the same time that his academic difficulties became obvious, around third grade, Calvin reports that money first assumed its subsequent life-long importance to him. It became, even at the age of 9, a substitute source for displaying his worth. The school system, however, did not just let Calvin's difficulties slide by. Several attempts—home visits, tutorials, alternative education programs—were made to help Calvin with his academic problems. Yet, for reasons that we cannot fully ascertain, these efforts did not succeed. Calvin seems to have determined early on to set himself apart from the mainstream.

Today, his criminal activities are still a source of pride for Calvin. Whether another source of self-esteem—one more acceptable to the general society—takes its place when Calvin is released from prison remains to be seen. Without adequate motivation and the necessary educational and job skills, however, Calvin Charles's prospects are not good.

Case Study: Gerald Daniels

All names have been changed to protect the identities of the study's subjects.

My earliest childhood memories are just daydreaming, you know, and I would daydream just what I wanted to be. I guess everyone thinks they are special, and I guess I thought there was something special for me to do, that was basically my whole little dream as a kid....To me, [the motivation] was simply within me. I just knew, growing up, there was something better. I felt that I didn't need nobody to tell me that, and I was just trying to find it myself, and I still am, still trying to find it.

Introduction

Gerald Daniels, age 24, attended Michigan State University on a full athletic scholarship. He graduated with a major in criminal justice. Unable to find a good job, he has enlisted in the Army. He plans to obtain his master's degree while in the service and then to enter law school upon his discharge. Eventually, Gerald hopes to be a corporate lawyer or enter private practice. Although sports were Gerald's door out of poverty and into a better world, he came to appreciate the academic side of education while in college. Today, his message to his five younger siblings, and to all blacks of the next generation, is that economics and education must go hand-in-hand. Gerald acknowledges that a youngster's success in the academic world takes hard work, determination, and sacrifice, but he believes anything worth having is worth this sacrifice. Above all, Gerald Daniels believes in the importance of the individual dream and the individual effort in making the dream come true. Although he was fortunate in having a supportive family as well as teachers, coaches, and counselors to encourage him in school, Gerald sees himself as the most important influence in his own life. He has faith in his own ability, and the resolve to work as hard as necessary to advance through the system.

Case History

Gerald Daniels is the oldest of six children. His parents never married, and although his father lives nearby, Gerald has had no contact with him since age 10. Gerald and his siblings were raised by their mother and stepfather, Mr. and Mrs. Mason, and also saw a great deal of Mrs. Mason's mother. The family was always a close one, and yet each person stood out as an individual; one can see here the roots of Gerald's later strong sense of selfhood.

Says Gerald of his family, "It's like a two-edged sword. I liked the close-ness about it, but we argued a lot. We all loved one another; it's just that we are all very independent, we each have our own way of thinking." Both Gerald and his mother remember that as the oldest, Gerald often took care of the younger ones. He recalls that when the fourth child was born, his first sister, "the idea of being the oldest, responsibility of looking out for the rest of them, really hit me. Up until that point, I was just happy to have some company."

In Gerald's memory, siblings and cousins—that is, family—were his only real friends until junior high school. Of himself as a young child, he says, "I was very introverted, I was very quiet. . . . In school I was not really meeting people because I was still basically shy." Mrs. Mason re-members that as the first and only child for a while, "he was a mama's boy" and stayed around home. However, she says Gerald adjusted rather well to being separated from her when kindergarten started, and contrary to his own recollection, Mrs. Mason remembers him as always having lots of friends: "He's the type of guy you can't help but like, because ever since Gerald has been in school there's always been kids coming to the house." Teacher reports confirm Mrs. Mason's version; Gerald was rated as socia-ble and outgoing with peers as well as teachers. He was seen as having no trouble making friends.

There is another interesting discrepancy: Whereas Gerald describes himself as quiet, both teacher and tester ratings throughout elementary school characterize him as impulsive. At age 4: "[Gerald] was somewhat difficult to test because he kept grabbing at test materials and was quite distractible." At age 5: "Large child; extremely hyper." And in the elemen-tary grades, "impulsive" and "distractible" were checked as being fre-quent behaviors. Mrs. Mason's memory is closer to her son's; she remembers Gerald as always being self-possessed, obedient, and well be-haved. It is not clear what the source of this discrepancy is, but one possible explanation is that Gerald's excess energy made it difficult for him to be still in traditional academic settings. This energy was bound up in sports from an early age. Says Mrs. Mason: "Well, [Gerald's] always been an athletic child, so he liked to play ball even when he was a little boy, you know, a baby, even before school." As we shall see, athletics have continued to be dominant in Gerald's life.

Despite this problem with impulsiveness, however, Gerald was a con-sistently good student throughout his elementary grades. Teachers gave him high ratings for showing initiative, being alert and interested in his school work, being motivated toward academic performance, and—even though easily distracted—still persisting and completing all his assign-ments. Gerald was seen as having an average to slightly above average chance for academic success at this point. His own memories of school in these early years are also very positive: "School was fun for me. I enjoyed it; I couldn't wait to go." He has many vivid and positive memories of his teachers. Strikingly, he says of several of them such things as, "I always felt she took a special interest in me," or "She spent a lot of personal time with me." Gerald's belief in his own specialness either caused, or was rein-forced by, many of his teachers responding to him on an individual basis.

Mrs. Mason also has positive memories of Gerald's school days:

"[Gerald] did fine. I never had any problems out of him going to school. He enjoyed going to school." His teachers saw Mrs. Mason as being very supportive of her son's education. She consistently received very high ratings on such variables as participating in activities, understanding teacher's goals, making efforts to aid her child's education, being cooperative, and maintaining a good relationship with the school. Gerald also feels that his mother was very supportive of him throughout his school years, although characteristically he feels that the primary impetus came from within himself: "Well, she sort of reinforced my self-motivation. And that self-motivation, that's something I thought about often and I just came to the conclusion that . . . I always had, and it was something that now that I'm older and I look back on it, it was something that my mother knew, and she encouraged it. She was always there in my corner. But she was a little weak in that if I wanted to fail, if I wanted to quit, she would have gone with that. That's why I have to rely on myself."

Yet, looking back on his elementary school days as well as the subsequent junior high school and high school years, Gerald today repeatedly voices the regret that he was not a more serious student. He recalls that in fifth grade, the first year he and other blacks were bussed across town, the disruptiveness of the classroom put an unfair burden on the teacher: "The stress and pressure which us kids put on her . . . really, I didn't learn nothing in that class that would help me in terms of my arithmetic and spelling. Basically, it was us kids' fault." Then, beginning in junior high school and especially in high school, sports took precedence over studying for Gerald: "I went out for sports. At that time, studying wasn't a really big thing to me. I never took the time; it was mainly the sports. It was the only thing I really knew I could do. . . . I did well in school, but I never took books home in order to study. I just did enough to get by; I didn't really try to do the best or better myself."

It is significant that just as Gerald takes much of the credit for his own success today, he believes he has no one but himself to blame for his "lazy" attitude toward academics. In fact, he reports that he actually had a great deal of encouragement from home, as well as from school personnel. Asked, for example, about his mother's attitude, Gerald replies, "Of course, my mother suggested many times [that I study more]. But, like I said, I'm the oldest and there are six of us now, and at that point in time there were five other people Mom had to give attention to. And being the oldest and being in that situation, if one doesn't have the personal drive to want to do it, he can find many reasons why not to do it. Basically, I was finding the reasons why not to do it."

In school, Gerald had encouragement from many sources—teachers, coaches, and counselors. Fortunately, these individuals were able to spark that personal drive in Gerald. He had at the time quiet aspirations of getting an athletic scholarship and believes his own determination, plus the direction others provided, was responsible for changing his attitudes about hard work and education. In junior high school, Gerald found his ninth grade history teacher understanding: "He was in sports too, and at that time I had problems with my study habits. After class, he would keep me and he would talk to me, give me pointers." His junior high school physical education teacher was also an inspiration: "Mr. W. taught me at an early age that everything in life worth having is worth sacrificing for, and that's really when I started sacrificing. I knew that football was something that could open some doors for me and at that point in time I just did what I could to get my dream." A young man, [Dan], with a background similar to Gerald's, also came to the junior high school as an athletic assistant. Gerald speaks of him as an important influence, again stressing the individuality of the attention he received: "[Dan] just let me know things, giving me that personalized instruction that I really couldn't get from my coach. It motivated me to work harder alone; it was basically a lot of lip services he gave us to keep us motivated, keep us striving." From [Dan], Gerald also learned about people "giving of themselves to help others, which is is a quality I admire, and it is something that I like to do, I like to give of myself."

Gerald's high school football coach "instilled in me the desire to work hard. He put that work ethic into me. He done a lot of things for me outside of football, such as spending time with me over at my house, explaining to me that it was more than just football, it was just that football could open doors for Gerald Daniels." Finally, Gerald's academic counselor reinforced the idea that more than football was necessary if he was to achieve his dream of going to college on an athletic scholarship. "Mr. R., my counselor, he took an interest in me academically. He found out . . . about my study habits and then he helped me a lot in that respect. I was still rebelling though. He was there day-in and day-out. Now that I look back on it, I appreciate it." At the time, this counselor rated Gerald as being very high in motivation and capable of making realistic plans about the future. With his encouragement, Gerald entered the Upward Bound program and received tutoring in college preparatory subjects.

Summing up the effects of his various role models during these secondary school years, however, Gerald again makes it clear how much he has his own good sense to thank for his ultimate success: "I have to say that Gerald Daniels himself was a positive influence in that I'm glad I listened to me a lot of times on important decisions that I had to make." Reflecting on what made it possible for him to advance, when most of his peers on Ypsilanti's south side have remained where they are, he again stresses that internal motivation plays a role at least equal in weight to any negative outside forces: "I mean, the real deal, blacks is the last to get hired and the first to get fired. That's just a fact, and it's tough, you could let that defeat you or you can just stick to it and keep plucking away. I choose to do the latter. I mean, it's an individual choice, you just learn it as a child. . . . That's why I guess I have to go back to saying that Gerald Daniels himself is a positive influence because I knew what I wanted and I just didn't give in to the negative; I always felt positive."

Gerald got what he wanted; he was able to enter Michigan State University with a full athletic scholarship in football. However, his lax study habits from high school caught up with him and Gerald realized that he would have to learn how to study if he wanted to make it through and graduate. Typically, he saw this as his own responsibility and gave academics the personal effort he had previously reserved for sports. "It kind of hit me when I went to college that the means to better oneself is there, but no one is going to take you there. I mean, you have to go about it yourself; I learned that. And once I did, I took the necessary steps. . . . I was studying for the first time in my life. I was fortunate enough that I was an athlete and we had a study hall program at Michigan State, and I was a part of that naturally, but I put in a lot of personal time, too. I was a step behind, and I had to catch up with my peers; once that was done I was fine."

His college experience solidified for Gerald the importance of education as the means for economic advancement. This new-found wisdom is something he feels obligated to pass on to his younger siblings: "Oh, I tell them all. I said that education is one step. I mean it's something that all kids have to do, so why not be the best? I wish it was something that I would have done as well as sports, but I didn't, but I've been through the system, still going through it, and I think, through my experiences that I've been through, I could help them out, . . . warn them basically about education." Gerald believes that not just for his siblings, but for all poor blacks, a better future lies in instilling a personal determination in young children to take their education seriously: "The economics and education, you can't separate them—education, sacrifice, determination. It's going to be hard, but there are going to be sacrifices that one has to make. It has to start [when you are] a child, it's going to be a long process, but that's what it's going to take. . . . Tough it out because the game is set, this is the system, this is how it's being played, education is a way. You can frustrate yourself, or you can get in there and play the game."

Gerald has a philosophy upon which he determines his own future as well. He believes in a combination of working toward long-range goals while simultaneously enjoying the day-to-day aspects of life: "I think it's good to plan, to plan down the road, five or ten years, whatever. But I also feel that one should live each day to the fullest. I think one should look at it in terms of future goals, but by the same token just get the most out of each day. But definitely, one should plan, have something to strive for, some goals, something to keep you going." Gerald has this same balanced perspective about himself and his satisfaction with his current life situation: "It could be better. I'm not satisfied; I'm still reaching, I'm living. I'm not content, but by the same token I'm not down on myself. I'm just having a little pause right now, but I'm still reaching."

Equipped with his college degree and a major in law and criminal justice, Gerald has been unable to find an appropriate job. "Right now, times are kind of hard. I haven't been fortunate in my search for jobs; either I'm overqualified or underqualified, or don't have any experience." Rather than being discouraged, Gerald has enlisted in the Army. He sees it as an excellent opportunity to continue his education. He hopes to pursue a master's degree in criminal justice while in the service and then use that as a route for entering law school when he gets out of the Army. Eventually, he hopes to be a corporate lawyer or enter private practice. In characteristic fashion, Gerald has this to say about his present situation: "The Army I went into mainly for the benefits, for the money; and it's just that right now I happen to believe personally that it's the best job a black man can get. The Army has this saying, 'Be All That You Can Be.' Well, I'm going to find out how much of it is real, because I think it's just like anything in life; you get out of it what you put into it. Right now it seems this is the best move for me."

Mrs. Mason sums up her son this way: "[Gerald] is a unique person. It might sound like a cliché, phony, or whatever, but after him I think they broke his mold, because he's got his ways, and you know, he has his funny ways, but [Gerald] is special. He's a unique person."

Analysis

Gerald Daniels is a young man with an active and positive orientation towards life. Although he grew up the oldest of six children in a large family, his sense of individuality seems to have been instilled there. It is hard to say where his sense of being someone special comes from, where he developed the sure knowledge that he was meant for something better in life. With characteristic self-congratulation, Gerald feels that it was a certainty he always had within him. He acknowledges that he was exposed to this optimistic attitude while growing up, yet he says the major credit for his strong internal motivation must be given to himself.

Though it is undoubtedly true that much of Gerald's stamina and ability are his and his alone, one must also acknowledge those other forces in his environment that saw to it that his basic strengths were not wasted. A primary and enduring influence in his development is Gerald's mother. Mrs. Mason has reinforced her son's self-motivation and has made it her business to become interested in his education from his earliest school days onward. While her direct efforts to help him were sometimes diverted by the need to attend to the other children, Mrs. Mason must have communicated to Gerald that she respected *his* ability to achieve what he set out to do.

Gerald was fortunate in having, in addition to his family, a succession of encouraging teachers, coaches, and counselors throughout his school years. Beginning in his elementary school days, Gerald can remember teachers who seemed to take a personal interest in him. When he became so involved in sports during junior high school and high school, the combined efforts of the academic and athletic staffs were responsible for helping him get sports and studies into a more balanced perspective. The message that these various role models finally communicated to Gerald was that sports were his entryway to the world, but that his ultimate success in making it to and through college depended on much broader efforts.

Gerald says it was his own discovery in college that he needed to take his studies seriously; the seeds for this insight had actually been planted by his mentors in high school. Nevertheless, it was with his characteristic brand of personal determination that Gerald tackled the academic challenge and, indeed, turned himself into a true student. Along with his self-admiration, Gerald also feels a calling to help others—perhaps inspired again by the models of those who helped him through school. Fulfilling this calling, Gerald is trying to steer his siblings and other black youngsters of his acquaintance along the right educational pathways. Gerald may be, above all else, responsible for himself—but his is not a totally selfish orientation. Coming from a close and supportive family, he has internalized the ethic of caring about others.

For the future, Gerald has been able to temper the disappointments of the current economic scene with his realistic and positive outlook. Unable to find a good job, he is using the Army as his access to furthering his education and eventually obtaining a law degree. Here again, Gerald's success will be a product of the interaction between his inner motivation and the opportunities that the outside system is making available to him. Alone, neither inner nor outer resources are sufficient. In combination, they can make the childhood dreams of a youngster like Gerald Daniels come true.

Case Study: Bonita Emerson

I have an aunt, who's teaching. She'd been teaching about ten years, when she lived with us for a while. I think she had a big influence...and my parents were always pushing me, too, to get a good education. They always pushed. They pushed us all.

Introduction

Bonita Emerson, age 21, has completed her bachelor's degree in special education and is planning to obtain her master's in this field. Teaching, particularly working with special needs children, seems to have been a lifelong calling for Bonita, beginning with her tutoring younger children as early as elementary school. Much of this young woman's sense of purpose and direction can be traced to her strong family background with its emphasis on mutual respect, education, and above all, religion. Junior high school was the period when Bonita's black consciousness was first raised, and the enduring importance of this consciousness in her life is reflected in her plans to open her own school for poor black youngsters, either here or in Nigeria. Her educational philosophy, about which she is quite vocal, stresses hard work on the part of children and active involvement on the part of parents. Bonita leaves one with little doubt that she will succeed in realizing the future she has planned.

Case History

By her own account, school has always been an avenue of success for Bonita Emerson. From as far back as kindergarten and first grade she recalls, "I know I was pretty bright. I was right on top of things." Mr. Emerson, Bonita's father, agrees, and her earliest school records confirm their reports. Said her preschool teacher, "She is obviously reasonably intelligent . . . pretty smart." Teacher ratings in elementary school were unanimous in predicting that she would succeed academically.

Mr. Emerson attributes at least some of Bonita's initial academic success to the early start she got through her preschool involvement: "I think it was the right help because she learned how to do a lot of the things when she got into kindergarten; see, they gave her a jump." However, it is clear that Mr. Emerson, a minister, believes it was the environment he and his family created at home, even more than outside influences, that affected Bonita and her siblings: "They got that base from home; the most important part is that home environment from their growing up until they are out." In fact, he admits that he sometimes found the intrusion of the preschool teacher into his home to be a nuisance. The preschool teacher herself sensed this defensiveness. She described the Emerson's home and values as being more middle class than that of the other families in the group and said, "They were a little bit more concerned about the preschool being for special kids or something like that and were not always cooperative, because I think that they felt like they were being put into a slot they didn't want to be in."

When Bonita was in kindergarten, her family moved to a predominantly white neighborhood on the edge of Ypsilanti, and hence she attended schools that, by her own reckoning, were no more than 2 percent black. Mr. Emerson says of the move, again reinforcing his position that parent involvement is the key to upbringing and education, "I didn't intend to stay in the [Perry] area because it was too crowded, there was too much disrespect from the children, so you know you couldn't profit too much because such involvement makes a whole lot of difference."

Bonita's memories of elementary school are positive. She remembers the names of all her teachers and can often recall small details or experiences from each grade. The roots of her calling to be a teacher are obvious even in these early school years. In sixth grade, she was one of the students selected to help out the kindergarten teachers and tutor first graders for three afternoons each week. About this time—age eleven—she began babysitting for mentally retarded children as a result of special training she received in the Girl Scouts. That Bonita's goal to teach and help others was present from the first is confirmed by Mr. Emerson's recollection of her elementary school years: "She had the desire to be a teacher and we encouraged her in every effort, brought her up in a Christian atmosphere, and the main thing that we always said that you have a goal in mind; that's the only way you will be successful. . . . She had ambitions from the beginning."

Academically, Bonita always did well. Within the school's tracking system—basic, middle, advanced—she was in the top group, beginning in elementary school and continuing on to the college prep classes in high school. Only one subject—mathematics—has consistently given her trouble. Even so, Bonita is not a person to give up. She says with determination,"But I still say I'm going to get better in that, in math; I'm always working on it."

In talking about school experiences, both Bonita and her father constantly return to the theme of parent involvement and its importance in a child's education. Says Mr. Emerson: "All of us were involved in the school from the beginning of day one until she completed it. . . . As the parents, we always stood behind [Bonita] and encouraged her. She was into books and things, and we would always buy the books and give her the ideas as much as we could read them. . . . If there was trouble, I was the man that solved the problem and we never had too many problems about that. . . . It's hard to get the black parents to get involved. If the parents don't seem to be interested in it and they don't even participate, well then they can say they don't care, but they couldn't say that about the [Emersons]; they know that I was there."

The only real problem Bonita remembers was having to overcome the reputation her three older brothers and two cousins had attached to the family name in school. As she describes them, they were athletes rather than students; they called themselves the "Rough Boys" and did "silly things to make the teachers angry." Upon entering junior high school, Bonita had to establish herself in her own right as someone who was a serious student and not a troublemaker. Here again, her father proved instrumental, coming to school to talk to the principal and to a teacher who Bonita felt was prejudiced against her because of her brothers and cousins. Says Bonita, "We talked and we got it straightened out."

But Bonita's home environment insured that all the children, including her brothers as well as her younger sister, never really got into serious trouble. Says Mr. Emerson, "As long as you are staying here, there is only one boss, that's me, that's it." And Bonita repeats that there was no point in trying any major wrongdoing at school because the children knew their father "would be up there in a minute . . . and they would be punished when they got home." Punishment at the Emerson household was occasionally being "whipped with a belt or a stick. And sometimes they'd make us work extra hard." Most often, discipline meant being deprived of a privilege, such as going to a basketball game. Before a punishment was meted out, Mr. Emerson always discussed what the children had done wrong and "allowed them to defend themselves." For Bonita, the usual infraction was "talking back—that's a bad habit." But by her own account as well as her father's, "I didn't really present any problems to them."

More often than punishing for bad behavior, the Emerson household rewarded its children for doing well. Again, this is most obvious in the area of educational accomplishment. The children were given a dollar for every A they got and Mr. Emerson says of Bonita, "She got a lot of money from me in school." Parental influence was also felt when Bonita and her siblings chose friends. Bonita says, "I knew who I could bring home and who I couldn't." Acceptable friends were those who respected their parents and were serious about their school work. While not explicitly forbidding Bonita to have friends in the "fast crowd," her parents would apply what she called "little scare tactics" if she brought one of them home: "They'd say, 'Where did that little fast girl come from? What's wrong with you—the next thing you know you'll be pregnant or something.'"

It is clear that Bonita's family instilled in her a sense that it was important to do something worthwhile with her life. From her religious training and the example set by her minister father, it is easy to see how she came to believe in the value of helping others. Even of his school involvement, Mr. Emerson says: "I am not only concerned about my children, I am concerned about all of them when I go out there. I don't go out there to defend just mine, I got to defend all of them on the same road."

That Bonita's personal ambition took the form of being a special education teacher was very likely influenced by her aunt—an important role model in Bonita's life. This aunt, also a special education teacher, came from Alabama when Bonita was 9, and she lived with the Emerson family for three years; she continues to live and teach in the local area today. Recalls Bonita: "I think she was a big influence. I was always watching her and I would go help her do things. I really enjoyed her." Mr. Emerson reports that Bonita still has a close relationship with her aunt.

Bonita's aunt was still living with them when Bonita entered junior high school, and this period of Bonita's education seems to have been an important one in setting her future course. Both Mr. Emerson and Bonita recall that she was very active and involved during these years. She remembers, "I was student senator, and I was in the choir and different clubs and organizations." Significantly, junior high was the period when Bonita's black consciousness was first raised. "There was one special teacher, Mrs. G., that I liked. She would always help us with black history, so I really like her." Bonita says that junior high school was also the time when she became self-conscious about her minority status, being one of the few blacks in the school: "I never liked that."

At home, although Bonita heard about being black down South from her grandfather and his brothers, there was no emphasis on the special problems people encounter as a result of race. On the contrary, Mr. Emerson says he is different from many of his people in not attributing hard times to blackness per se. He believes people of any color, particularly if they are poor, can encounter difficulties, and he holds firmly that it is the individual, leading a Christian life, who can improve his or her station. This is the attitude Mr. Emerson imparted to his children when they encountered any prejudice upon first moving into their nearly all-white neighborhood. They were taught to look after themselves; as Bonita puts it, "They just told us, 'Don't take anything from anybody.'"

Bonita, like her father, believes that blacks must take responsibility for advancing their own situation. Mr. Emerson believes the church must play a major role in this: "Well, religion as far as I'm concerned is the only thing in this world that lets you go ahead in life. If you put God in your life, you reaffirm the best of your abilities, set the same opportunities, and set the same priorities." Although acknowledging the importance of religion in her own upbringing, Bonita is cautious about its role in advancing the black cause: "[Blacks] have to have unity first of all; there's too many different sections and religion is one that can split up a lot of black folks, and there should be just some type of organization where their religion has nothing to do with it, and also that we support our own organization."

Bonita sees the educational system as an ideal organizing force for blacks to help themselves. Like her father, she sees parents' involvement in their children's education as a primary mechanism for bringing about lasting improvements. One can hear echoes of her father's position in Bonita's philosophy, to which she adds her own plea for instilling more racial awareness than she had growing up in a white neighborhood: "If these parents are up on things and know what's happening, it's a whole different story. . . . I also think they [blacks] should try to educate their own, and they just have to push more and more, and the way the whole system is set up, it's not really set up to give you any self-awareness."

But, although Bonita and Mr. Emerson both criticize the lack of involvement of black parents in their children's education, they diverge on where they lay the blame. Mr. Emerson confines his fault-finding to the parents themselves: "Well they just don't care, that's the only thing I can see." Bonita, on the contrary, believes that parents and the school system must share the responsibility when black children receive an inadequate education. On one side, she criticizes parents for assuming the schools are doing an adequate job rather than finding out for themselves what kind of eduction their children are really getting: "The parents just don't get involved. They say, "[She] is a good teacher, that's all I care about; [my child's] getting A's and B's on her report card," and they don't know what the child is doing to get those A's and B's—they may be just giving them out free. . . . They might treat the students differently if they find out the parents are watching them." On the other side, Bonita criticizes the schools for not encouraging parents, particularly the less educated ones, to become more involved: "The parents can only ask so many questions, because they don't know the questions to ask. And [the schools] give them any answer to get them off their backs."

Bonita's philosophy about black education appears to have been further developed during her participation in the summer Outward Bound program after tenth grade and then cemented by her encounters with high school counselors. Basically, she feels there is discrimination against black students in the form of counseling them into junior colleges and vocational fields, rather than acknowledging that they can succeed alongside whites in four-year colleges and the professions. The Outward Bound program challenged her and convinced her that the schools must challenge all black students instead of channeling them into the easiest track. Bonita acknowledges that she was fortunate in having her own parents monitor her courses, making sure that she followed the college prep track. But after her high school counselor tried to discourage her—telling her to set her sights no higher than being a Licensed Practical Nurse because she could never make it beyond junior college—Bonita lost all confidence in the public school system: "The bad thing about it is that so many people believed it. They [the other black students] never challenged him. And now every time something positive happens, I make sure he hears about it."

With her family's encouragement, Bonita was quite sure that she could make it through a four-year university. Having today received her bachelor's degree in special education from Eastern Michigan University, she would like to go even further and obtain a master's degree in learning disabilities. In the future, Bonita plans to teach black children locally for awhile and then set up her own school either here or in Nigeria (a good friend of hers is from there). Because of her own experiences and what she has observed she says, "I don't see myself working in the public schools too long just because of the way the system runs. I don't feel they're challenging students enough."

Instead, Bonita has very definite ideas about how she would structure the school that she plans to establish: "I think it would be good if the kids were on a more independent level; it's like you have this wide range of students, and some of them are way ahead, but they have to stay at the same level with the rest of the kids. And then you have those who are really extremely slow, and perhaps if the children were put on individual tasks more instead of a whole-class effort—I know it's a lot of work and it's much harder, but I think maybe they would get more out of their education." Bonita is also committed to reaching the parents and getting them involved in the schooling of their children: "They first have to know what's going on really, and I think everyone should put themselves on the same level—that nobody is better than anybody else. And I notice that when you talk to parents on the same level, they appreciate you more as a person."

Finally, Bonita's racial awareness and educational philosophy extend to how she plans to raise her own children some day: "Well, first I want them to know who they are, how our people got over here, and to understand—well, at least in this area, in this world—that black people are definitely treated differently. But I want them to have some self-respect, and I don't want them to take whatever the teacher says for granted. I want them to research things and know for themselves whether or not it's right or wrong, don't go taking everything they say, and to challenge their teachers. So hopefully at a very young age I'll have them involved in different things and will help them, educate them about their people."

Analysis

The themes and influences running through the life of Bonita Emerson are clear and positive. Her parents and her home environment have done much to shape this young woman; she has also established an identity and a set of convictions of her own.

It is obvious that Mr. and Mrs. Emerson placed a high value on education from the beginning and did whatever they could to encourage and support their daughter's school activities. Bonita's father cannot overstate the importance he attaches to parents' becoming actively involved in their children's schooling. Whether regarding the quality of learning or disciplinary incidents, Mr. Emerson was visible and vocal on behalf of Bonita and her siblings at the school office. Listening to Bonita today as she espouses her own philosophy of what will improve the quality of education for young blacks, one hears echoes of her father's beliefs. "Parent involvement" is the key phrase that springs from both their lips.

In addition to enjoying the closeness and support of her immediate family, Bonita benefited from the role model provided by the young aunt who lived with them from Bonita's ninth through twelfth years. With her strong religious upbringing, Bonita learned early that a worthwhile life lay in helping others. The presence of this aunt, a special education teacher, seems to have crystallized for Bonita the direction that she too would take in being of service to others. Bonita set this goal for herself early. Then, with characteristic determination, she pursued her course throughout junior and senior high school. She refused to let the discouragement of her high school counselor deter her. Believing his downgrading of her and other black students' abilities was racially based, Bonita went on to prove that he and the public schools were wrong. Bonita met the challenge of completing her college education; she believes others can do the same if it is expected that they will succeed.

The significance that Bonita attaches to her identity as a black woman is one important area of divergence from her father's strong influence. Mr. Emerson downplays race per se as a determining factor in an individual's life. Although Bonita's own racial consciousness did not really emerge until she reached junior high school, once she had achieved this awareness it became a guiding force in her life. While earlier home and school experiences taught her to fit into the white mainstream that she found herself a part of, a seventh grade teacher sparked in Bonita a sense of pride in her difference. Perhaps in the same way that Bonita's aunt focused her niece's altruism on teaching the learning disabled, this teacher further channeled her student's motivation toward helping people of her own race.

Religion, as well as education, has been another dominant force in Bonita's life. Yet here too she has thoughtfully worked out her differences from her parents', particularly her father's, set of beliefs. To Mr. Emerson, a minister, the church is the single most important factor in any life; without it even the most advanced degrees become meaningless. Bonita acknowledges the value of religion in providing a firm foundation for an individual. But she also sees that religious factions have the potential for destroying black unity. Her priority is to find that strength in numbers, letting people go their own way regarding faith, if need be.

It is a mark of the Emersons' family strength that they take pride in Bonita's having lived up to their values and yet feel comfortable with her distinct, albeit small, divergences. Although still young and single, Bonita Emerson has clearly internalized a sense of responsibility for others and is actively pursuing a career that she believes will make her dreams for young black children a reality.

Case Study: Marlene Franklin

I hope that I will be sitting back with a lot of money in my pocket and raising my kids to the best of my abilities, and with a new mate that is going to better my life. I am not going to look for no one that's going to make me look bad financial-wise. When I go out there to look for a new partner, I am going to look for a much better man than I had, and I am quite sure that I can get one—so I am going to try my best to go out there and get it, you know.

Introduction

Marlene Franklin, age 22, is being divorced after three years of marriage. She has two children, aged 1 and 2, and is receiving AFDC and food stamps. Marlene attributes the break-up of her marriage to her husband's dissatisfaction with her use of "weed," or marijuana, a problem that she feels he exaggerates. The youngest of five children, Marlene is the only one in her family to have graduated from high school. She was enrolled in a secretarial program for one year at the local community college but dropped out because, she says, she did not like one of her teachers. However, according to Marlene's mother, a strict disciplinarian, Marlene dropped out because she started dating and eventually met and married her husband. Marlene has plans for the future, but they are vague. She says she would like to enroll in another secretarial course, although her mother does not see any likelihood of her daughter's returning to school. Marlene is adamant about wanting to do a good job of raising her children, either alone or with a new mate. She talks about wanting to find a job, although she blames lack of transportation and child care for the fact that she has as yet taken no concrete steps in this direction. With her divorce pending, Marlene Franklin's emotional energy seems to be tied up in the process of waiting.

Case History

Marlene Burke Franklin is the youngest of five children in a family of four girls and one boy. Her father died when she was only 6 months old; Marlene's mother, Mrs. Burke, raised the children herself, although partially handicapped by being blind in one eye. Marlene herself does not recall much of her early years, but Mrs. Burke remembers: "She was just a momma's child. I mean she always wanted to be near, close to me." Although Marlene had some trouble separating from her mother to attend preschool, eventually "she learned to really like it." Mrs. Burke also has positive memories of the preschool experience and remembers that, she "went with them on different little trips." She agreed with the interviewer that preschool helped get Marlene ready for entering elementary school.

In elementary school, says her mother, Marlene continued to be "a momma's girl. She never ran around that much, she played at home near me; she wanted to be mostly close to me." It is interesting that the only person Marlene can remember from elementary school is her third grade teacher "because she treated me as though I was the pet of the class. I liked her a lot." Apparently, Marlene's need to have special adult attention carried over from the home to the school setting.

Both Mrs. Burke and her daughter remember Marlene as being a good, well-behaved student throughout her elementary school years. Says Mrs. Burke, "She liked school real good, all the way through; I had no problem out of her." And Marlene says, "I tried to be a good student, yes, and I would do all my work everyday." Marlene's teachers, from kindergarten through sixth grade, echo this picture of a well-behaved and hard-working student. Here are some sample statements: "She is a quiet, pleasant girl, always finishing her work correctly and on time"; "[Marlene] is very quiet, willing to do assignments given, agreeable disposition." There is also an indication, as Mrs. Burke noted, that Marlene was somewhat shy around her peers. Said her fifth grade teacher, "She has a slight degree of trouble interacting with others." And academically Marlene seemed to be at, or just below, average. Her sixth grade teacher summed up Marlene's elementary school history with this assessment: "Good worker but low in academic ability. She is well-behaved and has a good personality."

This pattern of a well-mannered but academically marginal student was consistent throughout Marlene's school career. She maintained average grades through eighth grade, after which her typical grades fell to D and remained at this level right through her graduation from high school. There was only one disciplinary incident in high school, a fight, for which Marlene got suspended. According to Mrs. Burke, however, "They found out that it really wasn't the ones that they sent home that fought," and so Marlene's reputation as a well-behaved student can be considered intact. However, this isolated incident does seem to have colored Marlene's way of looking back upon her school years. Even remembering her earliest days, she says, "When I got up to the first grade and second, kids wanted to fight, so I didn't really enjoy school as much as I did when I was going to kindergarten, but it was still fun." Of later years, she says, "I didn't like too much this junior high school because when you get there you are talking about more and more fighting, . . . and it was just a hassle for me."

More than anything however, and contrary to the "momma's girl" image, Marlene seems to have seen school positively, as a chance to escape from home. As early as preschool and kindergarten she recalls, "I did like going a lot, that I was getting away from my mother, and I enjoyed that part you know, getting away from home for a couple of hours." In junior high school, Marlene loved sports like basketball and volleyball: "I was on the teams and I enjoyed that a lot because I didn't have to come home from school and I was practicing everyday after school." High school too seems to have been valued primarily as a place *away* from home: "I loved doing my school work, . . . I am not going to say that I am an A student, but I liked it, you know, being there on time, being there as many days as I could, without missing; I enjoyed it, being in school."

Marlene's need to escape, a theme that we will see repeated in her current situation as well, can be traced to the strictness with which Mrs. Burke raised her children. She describes her philosophy of childrearing this way: "The best thing I think to make a good parent is sit down and tell your child the most important things about life, and what to do and how to do it. The first important thing I think a child should be told is to go to Sunday school and learn the truth about the Church and the Lord. And then to obey their parents, and obey older people; you know, don't be talking back at older people. And then run with or try to associate with the right type of children and people . . . A bad parent don't care about what the child do." These two themes—the importance of the church and the need for parents to be strict in disciplining their children—run through all of Mrs. Burke's comments about raising Marlene and her other children.

Mrs. Burke admits that she was strict with Marlene, whipping her with a switch up until the age of 16 for staying out too late. Marlene "didn't get the attitude of running away [but] she did pout." However, according to Mrs. Burke, she was more lenient with Marlene than with her older siblings: "I wasn't as strict on [her] as I was with them, but I had rules and regulations." Marlene also remembers that as the youngest, she received special treatment from her mother. Yet, in spite of—or because of—Mrs. Burke's stricter discipline with Marlene's older sisters, two of them have a long history of serious trouble. One has been a heroin addict for 10 years, has been involved in several robberies, and has four children—including a 12-year-old whom Mrs. Burke is raising. The second, also a mother of four, has a record of violence (beginning at the age of 14 with the stabbing of a fellow student) and is on probation for two years due to another knifing incident. Mrs. Burke believes that these older sisters did serve as reverse role models for Marlene, however, because she could see that she didn't want to be like them. Marlene's concern with the amount of fighting she felt was going on in school may also have stemmed from her fear of what she witnessed in her siblings.

Marlene's own reactions to her upbringing—her mother's strictness and its effect on her and her siblings—reflect a great deal of ambivalence. She constantly returns to the theme that she will not raise her children as strictly as she was raised, and yet in the next breath she says that she is grateful for her strict upbringing. In a long reflection on the subject, Marlene vacillates: "When I was coming up, my mother was kind of strict on me as far as company-wise. I am not going to be as strict on my kids as I was treated, but other than that I can raise them just about equal to the way I was raised, because I was raised okay as far as having the right mind to do some of the things that I have been doing. But yes I think I am going to raise them different; I was raised kind of like the old-fashioned way. As far as me going out and having a good time, [my mother] didn't want to trust him, didn't trust me, she was always thinking that we were going to go out and get pregnant. After I grew up and seeing that things are not as good as I expected them to be out there in the street, I really appreciate it the way she did keep me in the house, because I might have gotten pregnant before

I did (when I was 20) but I am glad she did do what she did. I am not going to be as strict on my kids as she was on me, but I am going to give them some restrictions so that they won't be coming up getting pregnant quick, and doing other things quick as far as using drugs, but she was pretty well strict on me, but I loved it."

Examining the above statement, and comparing it to the events in Marlene's life, points up some of the confusions this young woman faces. For example, Marlene says it was her mother's influence that kept her from getting pregnant in high school. "Just about all of my friends got pregnant." She reports that her mother made her want to be a serious student in school: "That's why I was always hanging out with people who want to go to school and want to learn. I didn't mess around with the ones who was out there just doing what they wanted." And yet, after high school, Marlene seems to have abandoned her studies in favor of her social life. She enrolled in a secretarial course at a community college for one year, but dropped out because, she says, "I had this one teacher—everything he said was a cuss and I got sick of it." Mrs. Burke, however, feels strongly that "[Marlene] would have continued in college if she hadn't messed around and dated. She ran into Mr. [Franklin] and that got her everything she has." Married at 19, Marlene became pregnant with her first child within a year and abandoned her educational career. Today she says she wouldn't mind going to another college but has no specific plans. Her mother says, "I don't believe that she would go back to school, no."

Similarly, Marlene's ideas about using marijuana show unresolved conflicts in her thinking. As she says, she wants to follow her mother's strict lead to make sure her own children avoid drugs, yet she will "let them smoke weed when they get at least 17 or 18 years old, but I am not going to encourage them." Marlene believes that the only reason her husband is divorcing her is because of her own smoking: "The marriage was okay, and it was a great marriage for me, except that my husband is divorcing me because I smoke weed; that's the only problem we had, other than that, it was perfect." Sometimes she reports that she has stopped smoking because it bothered him, yet she also complains that "you can't stop doing everything that you like to do for nobody, you just can't change your life completely for no one else. . . . You cannot stop a person from doing everything they want to do for their pleasure, because I was never going anywhere hardly—all I was doing was just sitting at home keeping my kids—so I have to have something to do." So, although Marlene acknowledges that she was rightly brought up to see drugs as wrong, she also seems to feel that smoking marijuana can be justified, in her case, as yet another form of escape from the restrictiveness of her parental responsibilities.

Marlene's life and attitudes today reflect this same mixture of determination to succeed on her own terms, counteracted by excuses and escapes. She is obviously distraught about her divorce, and yet she feels she cannot compromise herself any more to make her husband happy. Marlene mentions two types of support—legal and religious—which she has considered turning to as a means of coping with her present difficulties. Yet again, we see a pattern of plans not realized and excuses offered: "I even made this appointment at this professional legal center, because I really want to sit down and have someone tell me all the procedures of a divorce, and I couldn't make that appointment because I didn't have the money [$15] to pay them." And regarding the church: "If I was religious now I don't think I would be having these problems with my husband. I am willing to get into religion; he don't want to get involved, . . . [but] I have been thinking about that, you know, really I have been thinking about that. Yes, it is possible, yes, very much possible." Although getting involved would not seem to require too much effort on Marlene's part—her older brother is a preacher, and her mother and one sister are both very religious—we see once more an idea without any concrete action to follow it up.

Marlene also talks about looking for a job—in the next breath saying why she cannot, or has not, done so: "I am going to try and find me a job, then I have to try and find me a babysitter. If I could get a job, but I haven't really had no transportation to go out there and look because our cars broke down on us. But as soon as I can get that opportunity to go look for a job, I will, because . . . I need to get away from home to get my mind off things that are at home." The theme of escape from her troubles, even more than financial need, seems to be Marlene's primary motivation for wanting a job. Similarly, she sees finding a new mate as a means of rescue from her current situation. "There is someone out there that will be better to me than he was, and I am sure of that. I am going to find me one better than him, so that's what I am going to be trying."

As she talks somewhat vaguely of these future plans, there is nevertheless an appealing tone of determination and self-respect in Marlene's voice. Although her ability to accomplish these plans is open to doubt, there is one area—raising her children—for which her sense of resolve is convincing. "I am going to have to raise my kids by myself now, and it is going to be hard on me. . . . When a father splits, that can affect a child a lot, but I am going to try and not have that happen to my kids; I am just going to have them hold their heads up high. So I am just going to try to raise my kids to the best of my ability, so they won't be having no problems in school, you know. That's about all I can say about it."

Marlene Franklin is a person of competing characteristics—a passive escapism into a world of excuses vies with an active determination to create a better life for herself and her children.

Analysis

Marlene Franklin is a young woman in a bad situation with a poor prognosis. In the middle of a divorce, she will soon be a 22-year-old single mother with two young children to raise. Although she has a high school diploma, Marlene has no marketable skills. There is evidence that if she chose to, she could complete a two-year secretarial course and improve her chances of employment. However, as with much of her life, Marlene is full of excuses about the people or circumstances that hold her back from realizing any educational or career plans.

Studying the pattern of Marlene's life that has led to her current situation, one finds clear and consistent elements. Much of her personality may be traced to the strictness with which her mother, Mrs. Burke, raised Marlene and her four older siblings. Parental involvement in this home was largely centered on issues of discipline—rules and regulations about whom one went out with, where one went, and when one returned home. Although education and schooling were said to be important, it is not evident that anything beyond lip service was given to learning. Marlene was the only child in the family to graduate from high school, and although her behavior record was nearly unblemished, her academic record was barely passing.

Reactions to the strict discipline in the Burke home took several forms. For Marlene's older brother and one of her sisters, embracing the church as their mother had done seemed to be the result. At the other extreme, two of Marlene's sisters set out on a path of open rebellion and serious trouble at an early age—one addicted to heroin and another involved in repeated incidents of violence. Marlene seems to have been the most passive of the children; she settled into—rather than going after—a middle course. She gave up the church but nevertheless remained a conscientious, if not outstanding, student. School to Marlene was primarily an escape—a place to be that was away from the restrictiveness of home. When a more permanent means of escape presented itself to her however, Marlene went along with it. Thus, she quickly found herself married with two young children to raise. Even smoking marijuana—which she claims to be the cause of her divorce—was a pleasure she indulged in as her sole release from the daily restrictions of being a mother.

Marlene's future plans have these same elements of escape and excuse. She dreams about finding a new mate who will treat her better and of having a lot of money in her pocket. More immediately, she talks about going out and getting a job—as much to get away from her troubling home situation as to provide a better income than the AFDC and food stamps she now receives. But here too, Marlene claims that lack of transportation and child care have thus far made it impossible for her to fill out even a single job application.

The one condition that might motivate Marlene to improve her situation is the fact that she takes her responsibility for her children very seriously. She is adamant in her resolve to raise them in a manner that encourages self-respect and to see to it that their schooling does not suffer because they don't have a father. Although being a single parent is yet another circumstance that Marlene "finds" herself in, the responsibility that has been thrust on her may at last be sufficient to translate her basic sense of determination into action. If so, it will mark a turning point in Marlene Franklin's lifetime pattern of waiting for opportunities to present themselves.

Case Study: Dwight Gaines

It's just money, you know, it's money, that main influence. Get out and have a nice life 'cause you only live once, so you might as well make the best of it and do what you can do. If you can't do what you want, it wouldn't really be worth it. I know everybody can't do everything that they want to do in their life, but as long as you can do some of the things, what you want to do at the time, I think that's all.

Introduction

Dwight Gaines, age 21, graduated from high school after receiving a great deal of individualized academic help and spending four years in special education. Today, Dwight is unemployed and depends upon social services—a status he is very unhappy about. Dwight would rather be working, and in fact, his history shows that he has continually had jobs ever since his junior high school days. Bored and frustrated with school, Dwight was always more interested in earning money. He would work shoveling snow, cutting grass, washing dishes, or in the kitchen of a fast-food chain. Dwight's main interest was mechanics, and he took automotive repair courses in high school. Although he has not used this skill to generate a steady income, Dwight has consistently obtained various automotive maintenance and repair jobs during the past few years. However, it is characteristic of his employment record that Dwight waits for jobs to come to him. Family and friends refer people needing car work to Dwight; he does not seek such positions. Nevertheless, Dwight is sincere in his desire to find steady work and earn good money. After several years of spending all his earnings on cars and entertainment, Dwight says he is finally going to start saving it so he can buy the tools he needs to establish his own auto repair and body work business. But, in the meantime, Dwight Gaines continues to wait passively for job opportunities to come his way.

Case History

Dwight Gaines grew up as the next-to-youngest of six children. He had two older brothers (one of whom died when Dwight was 8 years old), two older sisters and one younger sister. His parents were separated, although his father, an alcoholic, occasionally spent time living at home. For much of his early childhood, Dwight was raised by members of his extended family. He lived with an aunt during part of elementary school, and after she

162

died, Dwight moved in with an uncle during his junior high school years. In the years just before and after entering kindergarten, Dwight lived with his mother, siblings, grandmother, and aunt. Both his grandmother and aunt were semi-invalids. His mother was on welfare, although she found occasional unskilled employment, for example, as a dishwasher.

Dwight has positive feelings about his family: "It was tight; we are still tight, you know, everybody's looking out for each other." In his earliest years, as noted, it was primarily the extended family that looked out for Dwight. Asked about this period, Mrs. Gaines admits she doesn't know too much about her son: "I mean, I wasn't too close to him but I do know some of the things he did. Mostly his auntie and his grandma, if there's anything to be asked you might ask them." These two individuals were mostly responsible for Dwight's day-to-day discipline and his religious training. Discipline was quite strict in the Gaines's household. Although Mrs. Gaines attributes much of this to Dwight's grandmother and aunt, her son recalls that his mother herself took a very active role. Recalls Dwight about the whippings she gave him, "That was her job—look like she took pleasure in it, seems like."

Religion was also very important in this household, and both Dwight and Mrs. Gaines agree that it was his grandmother who endorsed it. Commenting upon how much emphasis religion received as Dwight was growing up, Mrs. Gaines says, "Quite a bit. You know why? 'Cause their grandma made them go. From childhood on up, says you gonna attend church. Couldn't get around it, no type of way." And Dwight concurs: "Like my grandmother, she had us all in church every Sunday. You had to be there, you know, unless you was sick and that was your only excuse; you can read the Bible then. If you sick at home, you can read the Bible at least. My grandmother she would bring prayers home with her, she would take a tape recorder and record whatever he done said for the whole day. You either get the message or it's going to be brought to you, you know, so you'll hear it." Dwight not only went to church but also was in the choir for two years. However, when he was 17 years old, he "dropped out of church. I just didn't feel like going any more." Like several other young adults we are studying, Dwight is now thinking of returning to the church: "I think I might get back off into it, you know, going to church."

Although she is admittedly vague on details, Mrs. Gaines characterizes her son at the time of school entry this way: "He loved watching cartoons, he was interested in TV. And he loved to eat. But he was all right, a good boy. He wasn't no rowdy kid, I didn't have no rowdiness from him. He was okay." She also remembers that Dwight did not have many friends as a youngster: "He didn't associate with kids after he come out of school. He was at home watching TV." Dwight's memory is the same: "My mother, she started teaching me early in life that I would have to adjust when I got into school and learn from other people. It was a lot harder for me because I was shy. I was a big fellow, but I was really shy. And I couldn't get along with a lot of people in school."

Despite his shyness, Dwight recalls liking school—from kindergarten all the way up through high school: "I did, I liked school. I sort of wish I was back in high school now, you know. I really liked school; I wish I could go back. [Elementary school was] a ball, hey like I always went. The only time that I really missed was like I was sick and that was the only time that I really missed school, but a lot of days I went to school I was hungry, you know, like it was hard to adjust, to read, stuff like that." Mrs. Gaines recalls little about Dwight's school experiences. She says only, "He was average. You know, average child. I didn't have too much complaints about him at all."

School records paint a picture somewhat at odds with the Gaines's recollections. Instead of a socially troubled boy with average ability, Dwight is portrayed as a sociable child with academic difficulties. Tester ratings contain comments such as these: "Will get far on social skills but lacks reasoning ability," or "Poor achievement but may get by on social skills." Similarly, teacher ratings are high on social and personality variables—Dwight is characterized as being friendly and happy. But Dwight is rated very low on academic ability, even though he is credited with "trying very hard to learn."

By the middle of elementary school however, his academic difficulties became overwhelming and eventually affected his social behavior as well. Dwight's fourth grade teacher described him as being depressed and withdrawn. She also noted that problems at home contributed to those at school. Referring to the fact that Dwight was expected to help take care of his semi-invalid grandmother and aunt, she wrote, "I feel that the responsibility he encounters probably causes some of his frustration, in fact, much of it." As we have seen, Dwight's mother provided little support or encouragement for her son in his school work. From kindergarten through the elementary grades, Mrs. Gaines received consistently low ratings from teachers on school participation, understanding of educational goals, and involvement in her son's education.

In fifth grade, Dwight was certified as learning disabled and spent the next four years (grades 5 through 8) in special education. Fortunately for him, being in the Learning Center at least reversed the social problems that had cropped up the previous year. Said his fifth grade teacher: "There is no nicer child than this boy." Dwight was described as being "open" and "talkative" with teachers. He himself has very positive things to say about his experiences with the special education teachers in elementary school: "Mr. S., he was a special ed teacher. I used to like going down to his class because he was easy, he take his time, you know, he teach you individually. He would teach it to you at your own rate."

Dwight also improved academically with this individual attention, although it was clear to teachers that he would always encounter difficulties. At the end of sixth grade, the special education teacher described Dwight as having made "fine growth this year. [He] needs improvement in seeing himself as an individual capable of achievement academically. His motivation at this time is very inconsistent, varying from day to day. He needs lots of praise and encouragement to continue the progress he has made so far this year." His regular sixth grade teacher, summing up, comments, "[Dwight] is a good person and no discipline problem. He just needs a lot of encouragement and individual help."

Entering junior high school, Dwight continued to receive this help in the special education program. Again, he has good things to say about his teachers during those years: "I had special ed teachers. They take their time, show me what I had to do. It was hard for a while. Then I got my act together, started hitting the books, doing my homework and getting a lot better grades. Because I wanted to get out of school so bad then... and like now I kind of wish I was back in."

Mostly, however, junior and then senior high school were times of minimal school work for Dwight. He was more interested in doing odd jobs and acquiring spending money. About junior high school he says: "I didn't take my homework home like I should have. After school, Mr. C. [a teacher], he put me to work in his yard; he was really easy to get along with." Dwight also found he had no interest in school: "It was boring to me and I would skip school. I skipped school once, I go to the arcade and have me a ball, shoot pinball, be down there all day. Or out there shoveling snow, trying to make me some money." Dwight recalls being "busted" by one of the junior high school counselors who caught him shoveling snow during the day when he should have been in school.

Dwight undertook a series of jobs during these years—cutting grass, washing dishes. "I was out mainly making some money. I had a Taco Bell job after the tenth grade; I got in, I got a job. I got a break and I got into Taco Bell. I was working there for a long time; it was hard cutting back and they laid me off. They tell me they'd call me back, but I never been called back, so I went right back to what I was doing."

What Dwight was doing was hanging around at school and making money selling marijuana. It is the only period in his history when he made money by anything other than legal means. "I always had my little hustle. I sold weed in high school; I sold a lot of weed in high school. I had me a lot of money in my pocket." However, at this point in her son's life, Mrs. Gaines appears to have become more involved and to have had a positive influence on his behavior. Dwight credits her with stopping him from selling drugs: "Mama, she's cool. She was the stable type. Like one time she found the joints in my pockets and she really scolded me. She had a lot of influence on me. She said, 'Stop selling this stuff,' so I told her okay. And like the next day I had some more. She went and flushed them down the toilet. I didn't have any choice. She really got on me a lot."

The strongest words of praise Mrs. Gaines has for her son, during high school and up to the present time, are that he did not get involved in stealing like others of his peers. "No, I didn't have no trouble on that. About stealing or nothing like that—he was not that type." Instead, Mrs. Gaines is pleased that the work ethic she tried to instill in him has taken hold. Looking five years into the future, she says Dwight will be "working! Cause I have it embedded in his mind, if you want something you have to go out there and work for it. You don't go out there and steal it. You work for it. And that's it. I mean work. And ever since he come out of school, he gonna find him some type of job. I told him you work for it, you don't come out here stealing."

Indeed, ever since graduating from high school, Dwight has usually been able to find employment at one job or another, although not usually through his own initiative. For example, Dwight has always liked mechanics and studied it in school: "My cousin told a few people that I could do mechanics, that I took mechanics in high school, and whatever really needs to be done to a car, I can do it." Although Dwight has not turned this skill into a steady source of income, he has gotten various auto maintenance and repair jobs in the last two years through recommendations from family and friends. Dwight was also a nurse's aide at a convalescent center for a while, a job he hadn't planned on but one that "just kind of happened. Only I couldn't deal with it." He feels he could handle this job better now and says he is going to apply at another place he just heard is hiring aides. Unemployed at the moment, Dwight is unhappy with this atypical status: "[I am] not really satisfied, living on social services."

In five years, Dwight hopes to be "working everyday. I really want to find a nice job. I'm going to try to go to college off of one of these grants—a grant, you know, they usually send people to school." In light of his past academic difficulties, Dwight's plans for college do not sound realistic. However, his long-term goals are at least more in keeping with his skills than with his initiative: "Twenty years from now, being a businessman. I want to be in hydraulic or refrigeration repair. I know I'm going to be making a lot of money off my other field; I do body work. That'll be my sidelined thing, you know. To make me some money I'll do body work, be a good mechanic, change a transmission for you if you need one." For the first time, says Dwight, he is saving his money to start buying the tools he needs to establish himself in the auto repair business: "I'm fixing up on my tools now, I got me half a box. I need to keep my mind on what I'm doing, you know. Really start banking my money instead of just jacking it off like I usually do, or otherwise I'll never get nowhere."

As in the past, money continues to exert a major influence upon Dwight's thinking about life: "The greens, money. I like to have it, I like to spend it." Whether or not he is successful in obtaining the money he wants will depend upon Dwight Gaines's future employment record.

Analysis

In characterizing Dwight Gaines, a mixture of adjectives comes to mind. On the one hand, he impresses the observer as being honest and, in a quiet way, determined to succeed in achieving his own modest goals. As even his earliest teachers commented, Dwight is a "nice" person. On the other hand, however, this young man is noticeably passive; there is a lack of energy in the way he moves through life, waiting for things to happen to him and accepting, without too much fuss, whatever comes his way.

Both his school history and his employment record typify Dwight's capacity for putting up with life's frustrations as long as they do not exceed his rather high tolerance levels. Academically, Dwight was identified early as a child with learning difficulties. Yet, teachers also noted that in spite of his obvious limitations, Dwight tried very hard to learn. Only at one point—in fourth grade—did the combination of repeated school failure plus lack of support at home surpass Dwight's ability to deal with his problems. Fortunately for him, Dwight was a case where special education helped to avert more serious problems. The individualized attention he received helped him academically. Probably because of Dwight's basic good nature, he responded well to the personal concerns of the special education teachers. Unlike other youngsters in our sample (such as Calvin Charles or Yvonne Barnes), Dwight did not translate his academic problems into behavioral and disciplinary problems at school.

Dwight's work history is also filled with incidents of potential frustration, none of which has evoked a strong reaction on his part. When he got laid off from his Taco Bell job in tenth grade, Dwight was disappointed but just went back to selling marijuana to temporarily bolster his income. Although he describes getting the Taco Bell job as a "break," Dwight does not voice a correspondingly negative feeling about having lost it. Unemployed today, Dwight describes himself as not really satisfied. Yet, one does not sense any urgency on his part to reverse this situation. Dwight talks only vaguely of applying for a position similar to the one he recently left. Although he couldn't deal the first time with the responsibilities of being a nurse's aide, and although he does not offer any reasons why his attitude would have changed, he just says complacently that he thinks he could handle this type of job now.

Complacency is also a word that applies to Dwight's behavior regarding the one type of work he possesses both interest and skill in—auto mechanics. In spite of his proven ability, Dwight cannot depend upon this work for a guaranteed income because he does not generate any business. He waits for others to obtain referrals for him. Although he hopes to establish his own business some day, Dwight is only now starting to think about the need to save money so that he can buy his repair and body work tools. He says he has to save his money instead of wasting it as in the past—but again one senses no great self-disappointment that he has not looked after himself better so far.

Like other young adults, Dwight has his dreams. But at the moment he feels no frustration that these dreams have not yet come true, and he exhibits no drive that would help him to make them come true in the future. Unless something occurs to change his basic pattern, Dwight Gaines will continue to wait for and meekly accept whatever life happens to offer.

Case Study: Gloria Henderson

All names have been changed to protect the identities of the study's subjects.

I would probably tell [my daughter], give her the same advice my mother gave me and I would probably stress even more how hard it was for me and how even harder it's going to be for her and that it's a rough world out there. And you can't depend on nobody but yourself, so it's your life. I can't make you do anything, but if you want to be on ADC or whatever all your life, that's your business, but I'm not. I've worked hard, you know. You can't make anybody do nothing; all you can do is give them advice and hope they take it, if it's good. And I would just be there for her whenever she needed me.

Introduction

Gloria Henderson, age 20, is in her third year of college at Eastern Michigan University. She plans on running a business when she graduates and eventually owning her own business in computers, communications, or perhaps some area of biology. A single parent, Gloria lives in her own apartment with the daughter she had when she was a senior in high school. Although she lives on her own, Gloria continues to maintain her lifelong closeness to her mother. Mrs. Henderson has served as a role model and inspiration for Gloria, and they have mutually helped and supported one another through many difficult times. Mrs. Henderson went through two divorces as Gloria was growing up, both of which she now attributes to her own growth and the fact that her husbands could not change along with her. Mrs. Henderson began to take a very active role in her labor union, and when Gloria was in junior high school, her mother returned to school, where she is gradually completing her degree in industrial social work. Although these transitions caused some temporary declines in Gloria's school work, in the long run she has internalized the conviction that people should not settle for being anything less than they can be. Again, taking the lead primarily from her mother, Gloria sees education as the most promising means for a young black woman like herself to achieve her goals. With her mother behind her and her small daughter providing added incentive for the future, Gloria Henderson is on the way to success.

Case History

Gloria Henderson is the oldest of three children, spaced far apart. Her brother is five years younger and her sister seventeen years younger. As the oldest and only child for several years, Gloria developed a very special relationship with her mother—one that influenced her thinking about life as she grew up and that continues to affect her today. Because Mrs. Henderson was employed, Gloria also spent a great deal of time with both of her grandmothers who took care of her while her mother worked. Gloria's parents were divorced when she was in elementary school. Her mother remarried and Gloria took her stepfather's last name. This second marriage eventually ended in divorce, when Gloria was about 12 years old. Although Gloria remembers her growing-up years in very positive terms, she does say, "I can't really think when my mother and father split up and how it all happened, but that was the only thing that really hit me psychologically."

Going all the way back to the earliest years, Gloria and Mrs. Henderson speak very lovingly of one another. When asked about people who influenced her life, Gloria responds that both of her grandmothers and her mother were important and then goes on to praise especially her mother's qualities: "My mother, and my grandmother, and my other grandmother, were major people in my life, I can remember that. Because they were always there for me, no matter what. . . . It's kind of hard to explain, but things that most mothers wouldn't or couldn't deal with, my mother could deal with. My mother's different, she's very different. I know no mother can be compared to my mother; she's just very special to me. It's just that so many things have happened and you can't help to love certain people if they are always there for you and always understanding and willing to talk to you about things, like some mothers tend to just come to conclusions, don't even give their children time to explain or listen to their side. I never had that problem, I always got a chance to explain."

Mrs. Henderson has this to say in turn about her daughter as a child: "She appeared to be a very creative and warm child, not overly active, but active. I think we spent a lot of time together for those first five years, and I had always been into a lot of reading and things like that, so we did a lot of things together. There was a lot of time spent with her and myself." Although Gloria remembers always having lots of material things and getting money from her parents whenever she wanted something, Mrs. Henderson emphasizes that Gloria was not a selfish child: "And she was the type of child who always shared everything. She had a lot of nieces and nephews who were not well off, you know, as we were, and so she got a lot of things and she was always willing to share everything she had with them. And so she was that kind of a child."

It is also obvious from both of their early recollections that education and learning have always been stressed in Gloria's upbringing. Speaking of the three women who brought her up, Gloria recalls them in terms of strictness and how much emphasis they placed on educational matters: "Well, with my grandmother on my father's side, she used to always make us watch the news and stuff like that and we would count. She would make us count and try to read our ABC's and we would have to take naps and stuff like that. My other grandmother, she was more free, she would let us run and do anything we wanted to—watch cartoons, tear up the house. My mother, Mama pretty much let us do what we want, especially me, because I was the only child for a long time. She used to buy me books. I used to always read, or try to read and count."

Mrs. Henderson also recalls the importance Gloria's paternal grand-mother placed on education: "She got the discipline from that side. But always, you know, in the teaching sense, particularly her grandmother on her father's side." Mrs. Henderson herself actively fostered reading and arithmetic skills at home; she attributes the fact that Gloria immediately adjusted well to school to the positive attitude fostered at home: "She didn't have any problem. I hear a lot of people say that the first time in school is traumatic. But she was prepared for it; we had talked about it, and this was the means of achieving the gains of things in life, so I never had a problem with her in school. She was a good student; she got along well with the children, with the teachers; she always ended up maybe being the teacher's pet. . . . And it was also a matter of one of the things that I do even to this day with [Gloria's brother]. I make them read it to me. Tell me what that means to you. Taking them to the store, and saying, Okay, you've got 25 cents and this costs this, and this costs that, so what are you going to buy with the amount of money that you have? I keep telling them that it's very important that they be able to add, subtract, multiply, divide, read, write, and speak. And all these things go together and one's not good without the other." Mrs. Henderson sums up Gloria's early school days: "She did great. She was an above average student from the very beginning."

Tester and teacher ratings from the elementary school years confirm that Gloria was basically a bright and responsive student. Testers noted that she was outgoing, involved, cooperative, and very talkative; Gloria began using complex language at an early age. Teachers' descriptions are similar, although Gloria did experience some mood changes in fifth grade that her understanding teacher attributed to her parents' concurrent di-vorce. Occasionally, one comes across statements that Gloria could have done better if she had tried harder, that she lacked self-motivation. These are balanced, however, by observations that when Gloria did have a prob-lem, for example, with arithmetic in grades 3 and 4, she worked on it at her own pace. Most strikingly, every teacher in Gloria's early grades com-ments on what a good reader she was; apparently Mrs. Henderson's per-sonal attention and encouragement in this area had a positive effect. It is not surprising that Mrs. Henderson herself was given very high ratings by the teachers on such dimensions as aiding her daughter's education and participating in school conferences and activities. And Gloria knew she could count on her mother's involvement. Says Mrs. Henderson, "[She was] always volunteering me to cook something, 'My mama will bring this, my mama will bring that.' I think that's very important for children to be able to say that."

Gloria's own recollections of her early school days are vague, yet positive. As with her grandmothers, she recalls her teachers in terms of strictness versus leniency, obviously preferring the latter. Although her mother's memory and teachers' ratings indicate that Gloria had no trouble with peers, Gloria herself remembers a period in about fourth or fifth grade when she didn't run with any particular clique of girls and was often picked on as an outsider. However, even as Gloria talks of this time, one gets the feeling that it was not very significant. She follows the recol-lection with, "I really didn't have too many problems." One reason Gloria did not feel the lack of friends was that she had a large extended family for company and, as her mother remembers, "It just tended to stay that way until she got older."

In junior high school, too, Gloria held herself somewhat apart from the other girls. However, she learned how to present herself so that she was no longer bothered by peers just "because I didn't never hang with nobody. I just turned over a new leaf and I wasn't going to take no mess off nobody and that's how I carried myself." By her own assessment, Gloria was cute and well-dressed and this caused a certain amount of jealousy, but it was all in the form of talking behind her back; "I never got into fights or anything like that." Mostly, however, junior high school was the time when Gloria discovered boys; her remarks indicate that boys and sex became a long-term preoccupation for her: "[Junior high school] was when I first started getting into boys really. My first kiss, my first holding of the hands, thing like that; I started dressing more lady-like, I guess." What Gloria liked best about junior high was "walking home after school. Everybody used to always walk home and there was this pass and everybody would go through it and meet with their boyfriends." Even remembering her teachers during these years, Gloria talks especially about the men and the ones she had crushes on.

At this point, academics held little interest for Gloria. She enjoyed basketball and cheerleading, and studies were just something to be gotten through. Homework was best done in school during the day so that when she got home she could "talk on the phone a lot." Yet even in describing her lack of interest, Gloria implies that there would be a change of attitude toward education in the future: "School was all right but I didn't really like it too much. I couldn't really get into school; it was fine, I passed, and that was all I was concerned with. To be honest, school didn't really interest me, and it didn't for a long time. I mean I had B's and C's and an A now and then, but it didn't mean much, I just wanted to pass, that's all I was concerned with—passing and hurrying up and getting out."

School records from junior and senior high school indicate that Gloria's grades were even lower than she recalls, almost all C's. Only sports were important, and Gloria was motivated enough to get all A's in physical education. The discrepancy between her ability and her achievement makes one hark back to the notes in her elementary school records that Gloria was not performing up to her potential, that she lacked self-motivation and could do better if she tried harder. When Gloria's mother was interviewed during her daughter's high school freshman year, she too felt that Gloria could have done better academically. Mrs. Henderson also stated that she felt partly responsible for her daughter's low grades and guilty about the fact that she was not more available to help Gloria with her homework and encourage her more actively in her studies.

The reason Mrs. Henderson was not as visible as she had been earlier in supporting her daughter's education is that she herself was making major transitions in her career and educational level. Mrs. Henderson was becoming extremely active in her union, assuming the position of union steward and being responsible for handling labor-employee relations. In addition, she went back to college when Gloria was in junior high school and has since been gradually working towards her bachelor's degree. Today, Mrs. Henderson is enrolled at Eastern Michigan University and needs to complete about one more year of coursework for her degree in industrial social work. These transitions, occurring over a period of several years while Gloria was growing up, inevitably affected her home life and family relationships. Although they were difficult years, Mrs. Henderson believes that she—and from her example, Gloria—learned some important lessons. Mrs. Henderson describes the changes and their impacts this way: "When you start turning around and you start career-focusing your energies, it sometimes causes a little rockiness in the marriage and that's what happened in mine. I became a union activist and started getting involved in a union, so my household got shaky and ultimately it ended in divorce, you know, the first time. And it was because of that that I always explained to her that a man has to accept you as you are and your dreams and your goals and be supportive of that, and you in turn have to be supportive of what he does. That's the kind of person that you look for, the kind of person who is growing and changing and challenging things. You don't need all negative kind of thinking. So [Gloria] went through that struggle with me and she saw me make a decision that I wanted to go back to school, I loved the union, and you know that was good for her [to see]. And I was willing to give that [marriage] up to reach my goal, so I think she'll be very selective when she decides. When she gets a man, he'll have to have equal footing, I don't think she's going to settle for anything less."

Although in the short run Gloria paid a price academically for her mother's growth, in the long run the model Mrs. Henderson provided has proven to be Gloria's greatest inspiration for achievement. Says Gloria, "What [my mother] says, her opinion, matters a lot; she's number one. I'll just use what she taught me and think of some of the things that we went through. I doubt very seriously if I will go to outsiders for advice." Significantly, too, those years were a time when Gloria could begin giving something back to her mother. Mrs. Henderson reports that Gloria took on major responsibility for helping to raise her baby sister when her mother needed to travel for the union and when she went through a long illness. Gloria says, "[As the oldest child] I would help my mother a whole lot. You may not believe it, but parents need to talk about things sometimes too, and we just have this kind of relationship, we can sit down and talk to each other."

While Gloria's grades did not improve in high school, we can see a change in her attitude at this time. Junior high school was a place to pass through and get out; but in senior high school Gloria stated: "I don't want to be like those kids who dropped out." She said she planned to work hard in college, that she wanted to be a medical technician and "get out of the slums so I can raise my own kids right." Her attitude stemmed not only from the positive role model her mother was providing, but also from the reverse role model presented by some of her mother's friends and less well-off members of the extended family. As Mrs. Henderson describes it, Gloria saw her mother helping these women and their families living on welfare and was able to determine that she wanted something better for herself: "[Gloria] was able to see what happens when you have a lot of babies and you're not married; so she was able to see that, but she was able to say, 'Well, I think now I don't want to be on welfare, I don't want to have a houseful of kids.' But she also heard me saying, you know, 'That's the situation so I'll help,' so she saw healthy things, but she also saw things she didn't want for herself."

Nevertheless, Gloria's attitudes and behavior were still not consistent, and in her senior year of high school Gloria herself had a baby daughter. Regardless of the psychological dynamics involved, the birth of Gloria's baby is not talked about by either woman as having presented any particular problems; life went on. Mrs. Henderson says: "Sure, she had a baby. She had a baby at the end of her senior year. It was not a problem for us because it didn't stop her. She went on to school and we made the arrangements. She didn't fall behind when she had the baby; she went on and graduated so there was not time lost and she went on to college that September. We worked it out." Gloria talks—or doesn't talk—of it in the same way; the child's father is never mentioned. Instead, Gloria sees something very positive about the impact upon herself of having had a daughter: "Kids are beautiful, but they kind of hold you back a little bit, a little; they can hold you back period if you let them, or they can give you incentive to go on, and that's what mine has done."

Paradoxically, what ends up limiting many other poor black teenagers was for Gloria the impetus that finally made her behavior consistent with the motivation she had until then only given voice to. Gloria describes this motivation to get an education and make her way into a better life as again originating with her mother's lesson: "My mother always used to tell me that it's rough. I can remember she used to always stress that being black you have one strike against you and being a woman you have two strikes. Without the diploma, without the college degree, there was no way I was going to get over." Mrs. Henderson puts it this way: "I told her that particularly being a black woman in America was a painful experience but I believe I always told them I don't let them say, 'I can't.' And I'd tell them, 'you can do, don't say you can't, you can do anything you want to.'"

Gloria has now internalized her mother's teaching. For herself, and for all blacks, she does not believe in settling for anything less than achieving one's full potential: "They should be trying to better themselves; they shouldn't just settle; I would never settle, personally. I mean, I think they should be trying to do something with their lives instead of on ADC. They can go to school, almost anybody can go to school now, they can get a grant. Well, I'm not going to never settle. I'm not, they can think whatever they want to, I'm not. It might take me twenty years to get out of school, but I bet you I have what I want." Gloria adds that to get to where she is now, it is important to have someone behind you: "If they don't have a good education or job, it could be a poor background, nobody behind them pushing them. Just having nobody that cares—that has a lot to do with it, you have to have somebody to care, somebody to be there when times get hard. A lot of people don't have that, and that's a very important part."

Fortunately, Gloria had someone behind her—her mother. As a result, she is today in her third year of college at Eastern Michigan University, living in her own apartment with her daughter. Asked about the future, Gloria replies: "Well, I plan to have my own business or be running one. I hope to be in a much better financial state than I am in now. I know in five years a lot's going to happen, but right when you get out of college, nine times out of ten you don't get placed right away. But I plan on getting placed right away. I have confidence and I have potential, so I'm not going to stop; I'm going to be pushing all the way." Consistent with her own philosophy that you can't plan too far ahead, Gloria has not yet decided what the specific nature of her business will be. Allowing for fluctuations in the economy as well as changes in her own interests, Gloria says at this point only that her marketing will be in one of three fields: computers, communications, or biology. Her long-range goals include having her own house, but marriage is not necessarily in the picture: "Me and marriage don't make it. If the right person comes along and he can get me up on the altar, I'll marry him, but I doubt it very seriously. But in twenty years, who knows!" Gloria is clearly her mother's daughter as she voices these sentiments—she aims to achieve her goals on her own terms, as a successful individual in her own right. As Gloria's mother puts it: "I think she'll get married but [not] until after age 30. I think that she will do all the things that she wants to do and she realizes that a union of that sort cannot give her freedom. Because I tell her, marriage is fine, but there's so many things out there that you need to see, you need to experience, and you should do them now."

Mrs. Henderson's predictions for her daughter's future closely parallel Gloria's own. She adds, however, a note she has struck before, that is, about Gloria's generosity to others: "Well, I think that five years from now she will have, number one, reached her goal; she's going to be a hell of a businesswoman. . . . I see her standing behind that desk taking care of business and making some money. And also doing some good. I see her also being a very community-minded person. I think she will understand that once she reaches her goal you can, in fact, never go back to the ghetto but you can help. I see her pulling and helping and encouraging kids and working at another angle, I see her doing that. I see her following right in her mama's footsteps."

Analysis

The events and experiences in the background of Gloria Henderson could have resulted in a life of wasted potential. That they did not is largely to the credit of Mrs. Henderson, Gloria's mother, a woman who provided a model of strength in adversity and of confidence that a black woman can advance as far as she is willing to push herself. As a role model, Mrs. Henderson taught Gloria to look to herself for a sense of worth, rather than to depend on others. In particular, the flirtatious, adolescent Gloria matured into a young woman who understood that she had to accomplish the goals she set out for herself on her own; she could not depend on a man to give her that sense of achievement.

Her mother's message, however, was not that one should be cut off from human support. On the contrary, people—male or female—had to care for one another, providing encouragement and mutual assistance in difficult times. This Gloria and her mother did for each other through several family crises—Mrs. Henderson's divorces and a serious illness and Gloria's unplanned and early parenthood. Gloria learned that with support behind you, any problem can be surmounted. In turn, Mrs. Henderson set the example for her daughter that one must help others. Although Gloria is better off financially than most of those around her, she has grown up with a generous spirit. A lifetime of seeing her mother help family, friends, and others in the community who are less fortunate has instilled this sense of responsibility in Gloria as well.

Perhaps the most striking feature of Gloria's life is that becoming a mother while a senior in high school has *not* in any way slowed her educational and career progress. It has become a cliché that teenage parenthood writes one's life script, that it is tantamount to a truncated education and a lifetime of dependence on welfare. Gloria's case emphasizes what serious researchers in the field of adolescent parenthood are now discovering: The causes of early motherhood are complex; no stereotypical set of antecedent conditions exists. Similarly, the consequences are by no means predetermined. Crucial to the teenager's ultimate adjustment is a strong family support system—the kind Gloria found in her mother. Also crucial is the value system internalized during the teen's lifetime preceding childbirth. As we saw in Gloria's case, the assumption that education would play a significant and valuable role in her life was shared by her extended family long before she even entered school. Finally, the outcome of teenage motherhood rests on the individual herself—whether she has an internally motivated drive for life or assumes the passive victim's stance. In Gloria's case, her responsibility for a child increased her incentive rather than held her back.

A constellation of forces—both external and internal—has shaped the person Gloria Henderson is today. She is a young woman who leaves no doubt that she not only will follow in her mother's footsteps but also will travel on pathways of her own.

Case Study Conclusions

What is the role of preschool education in affecting, or interacting with, the variables that make a difference in the success of the young lives just described? Some members of the sample who attended preschool have not been successful, just as some without the preschool experience have done quite well so far. But the fact remains that when judged by mainstream standards, more of those who attended preschool have been successful, in terms of the educational, economic, and social outcomes we have examined. The case studies give us insights into the lives of selected individuals in the sample and permit us to consider, in eight specific cases, how the presence or absence of preschool education affected the subsequent course of life events and circumstances. We emphasize that scientifically valid conclusions cannot be drawn from these eight case studies. Rather, the cases are useful for suggesting hypotheses for future study and for providing a "real-life" context to enhance the formal presentations of earlier chapters.

Table 33 summarizes comparisons across the eight cases in each of six areas of study outlined at the beginning of this chapter. Four factors seem most consistent in differentiating those whose lives are judged to be successful from those whose lives are not: parental and family support for education; the presence of positive role models, particularly role models who demonstrate the value of schooling; a sense of responsibility that extends beyond oneself; and an active, goal-oriented approach to life. From the information in these eight cases, we can generate hypotheses about how the presence or absence of preschool influenced the subjects' early life experiences, their home and school environments, and their subsequent development into adulthood.

Basic family attitudes regarding **support for education** are probably already present when a child enters school, be it preschool or kindergarten. While preschool may not be able to change a negative family attitude, it does appear that it can reinforce or give concrete direction to a positive one. The Emersons, for example, clearly value education in general, and they credit the preschool experience in particular with giving Bonita the specific readiness skills she needed to do well in kindergarten. In another case, Jerry Andrews' mother valued the opportunity to be a preschool classroom aide. She downplayed her own contribution to Jerry's scholastic success, but Mrs. Andrews' involvement in the program may in fact have given her the very confidence and skills she needed to take an interest in and support her son's early learning. Gloria Henderson, a no-preschool child, was fortunate that her grandmother and mother encouraged certain skills—for example, playing word and number games—on their own. But in other cases, such as the Barnes family, exposure to preschool might have turned their vague ideas about the value of education as a means of economic advancement into more forceful and concrete support for Yvonne's actual schooling. Yvonne's parents might have encouraged her to do more than "hang out" in school if, by participating in preschool, they had been able to see how important specific activities, as well as attendance, were.

Role models are present or absent in the subjects' families regardless of preschool. However, in two cases, school staff (counselors and coaches) became specific role models for pursuing education and planning careers. The fact that nonfamily role models first appear most influential around

178

Table 33

SUMMARY OF CASE STUDY COMPARISONS

Success (+ or −)	Group (P or NP)	Name	Thumbnail Sketch	Parental Roles: Discipline	Parental Roles: Education	Attitudes Re Money: Degree of Importance	Attitudes Re Money: Why Unimportant	Role Models Presence: Who	Role Models: Type of Influence	Church & Religion: Family Activities	Church & Religion: Values	Sense of Responsibility: Self Only	Sense of Responsibility: Others: Who	Goal Orientation: Active	Goal Orientation: Passive
+	P	Jerry Andrews	Community college in engineering; mother involved in preschool program; teachers describe as highly motivated; uncles as role models; encouraged by high school counselor	Yes	Yes	High	Self-supporting	Yes; parents uncles counselor	Positive; education especially in engineering	No	Yes (has joined as an adult)	No	Yes; siblings, cousins, friends	Yes	No
+	P	Bonita Emerson	College graduate; wants to get master's degree in special education and open own school for black children; father (minister) and aunt (teacher) as role models; stresses importance of parent involvement in a child's education	Yes	Yes	Low	Only important as a barrier to achievement	Yes; father aunt	Positive; to teach and help others	Yes	Yes	No	Yes; black community and next generation	Yes	No
+	NP	Gerald Daniels	College graduate; athletic scholarship; self-admitted belated appreciation of education; majored in criminal justice; entering Army; plans to attend law school	Yes	Yes	Moderate	Symbol of achievement	Yes; mother coaches counselor	Positive; athletics & academics as an "out" from slums	No	No	No	Yes; siblings	Yes	No
+	NP	Gloria Henderson	College junior; plans to start own business in the black community; teenage parent; proud that she and her daughter are not on public assistance; mother an important role model	Yes	Yes	High	Get out of slums, raise own children "right"	Yes; mother grandmother	Positive; education, to make something of oneself	No	No	No	Yes; siblings, cousins, daughter, black community	Yes	No
−	P	Calvin Charles	High school dropout; serving prison term for breaking and entering; repeated arrests; disciplinary problems in school beginning in third grade; values money and material possessions	Mixed	No	High	Material goods, e.g., cars, clothes	Yes; Alexander Mundy (fictional)	Negative; (emulated as a thief)	No	No	Yes	No	Yes	No
−	P	Marlene Franklin	High school graduate; divorced with two children; receives AFDC and food stamps; former heavy marijuana user; older sisters with history of violence and drug abuse; hopes to find a "better" husband	Yes	No	High	Get off AFDC; material goods	Yes; sisters	Reverse; model of what to not be (drug addict, violent)	Yes	No	No	Yes; children	Mixed	Yes
−	NP	Dwight Gaines	High school graduate; four years in special education; raised mostly by extended family when young; unemployed; interested in auto mechanics; frequently skipped school to take odd jobs	Yes	No	High	Material goods, e.g., cars, entertainment	No	None	Yes	No	Yes	No	No	Yes
−	NP	Yvonne Barnes	High school graduate; poor academic and disciplinary records; time at school spent "hanging out"; lives at home with parents; unemployed; vague plans to "get a job" or "go to college" or "join the Army"	Mixed	No	Low	Father employed, material goods available	No	"No one influenced me!"	No	No	Yes	No	Mixed	Yes

junior high school suggests one way that preschool can indirectly affect life outcomes. To be exposed to these other role models, students must already be part of the school success flow. Gerald Daniels could be inspired by coaches and counselors because he was part of the school's athletic system. Yvonne Barnes could not; although athletic, disciplinary problems forced her to drop out of the flow. As data from the entire sample demonstrate, preschool significantly increases the odds of students remaining a part of that school success flow through the high school years. Having even slightly better grades, in some cases, may make the difference in being eligible to participate in athletics and other activities in which students have the chance to establish one-to-one relationships with potential role models on the school staff. Thus, success and role models appear to be associated with one another in both directions, that is, youngsters are successful because they have role models and they have role models because they are successful.

What effect can preschool have on one's **sense of responsibility** and **goal orientation**? The former seems so much a product of one's family values, while the latter appears to be a personality characteristic formed by a multitude of inner and outer forces. Yet preschool may again reinforce what the child already brings to the situation. Several parents spoke of their young child's initial adjustment to school in terms of separation from home. It may be that the preschool experience is an important early step on this road to independence. We see that successful young adults, along with having a sense of responsibility for others, believe they can take care of themselves and those for whom they feel responsible. In many small ways the preschool curriculum teaches children to be responsible for themselves and to look out for others in the classroom. Preschool can give youngsters a year or two to develop confidence in these social skills before facing the demands of attaining academic skills at public school entry.

Similarly, preschool may instill a certain confidence in a youngster that ultimately contributes to a more active goal orientation. All of the successful subjects we looked at viewed themselves, more or less, as self-made people. While acknowledging the importance of their families or other role models in their achievements, the young men and women always came back to their internal motivation. They believed in themselves, often more than others believed in them. Mrs. Andrews voiced surprise at Jerry's accomplishments, but *he* knew he could design a house. A counselor tried to discourage Bonita Emerson, but *she* knew she could graduate from a four-year college. Gerald Daniels talks about always having felt special and therefore knowing there was something better for him out there. Perhaps going to preschool can make other children feel special, giving them that extra confidence to reach for something more.

In short, it appears that preschool nurtures a child's potential, enabling him or her to acquire skills and confidence at an early age and ensure against their waste. Without preschool other nurturers may be found, but with preschool the odds of children realizing their potential are significantly increased. As the case studies and earlier chapters demonstrate, both individuals and society benefit when that potential is not wasted.-

Appendix
Supplementary Analyses

Alternative Analytic Approaches

Statistical analyses presented in the body of this monograph, with a few exceptions that are identified where they appear, are straightforward comparisons of values for the experimental and control groups; the analytic approaches used include both parametric techniques (F tests based on analysis of variance) and nonparametric ones (Mann-Whitney U test for ordinal variables, Fisher's exact test for nominal dichotomous variables, and the chi-squared test for nominal polychotomous variables). This approach to data analysis makes maximal use of the relatively strong experimental design of the study, offers a direct interpretation of results, and is consistent with the analytic approach taken in the study's earlier reports dealing with early adolescence (notably in Monograph No. 7, Schweinhart & Weikart, 1980).

The analyses presented thus far are in our judgment the most appropriate tests of our hypotheses regarding preschool education and the variables of interest. However, we recognize that statisticians and other users of statistics differ in their judgments of which statistical techniques are most appropriate to specific situations and variables. For example, regardless of the distribution of the dependent variable, some argue for the robustness of parametric techniques.

The question of which variables should have been used to frame the analysis could be debated endlessly. We strongly considered presenting all of our analyses for males and females separately, then decided that our sample should not be divided except into preschool and no-preschool groups, to emphasize the central purpose of the study. But given that decision, we could still have used gender as a covariate. By the same token, wave, IQ at project entry, socioeconomic status, and the important components of mothers' educational attainment and employment could also have served as important variables to divide the sample, for blocking variables in a factorial analysis of variance, or as covariates in a regression analysis. This appendix exists out of deference to the validity of these arguments.

In reporting prior to 1980, a number of other approaches to data analysis were taken, including three-way analysis of variance (with treatment group, wave, and gender as design classifications) and analysis of covariance (with variables representing child and family characteristics at program entry as covariates). In preparing the present monograph, we used a number of techniques to analyze the major study variables. Besides the results for one-way analysis of variance and for nonparametric tests, results for four additional parametric techniques are presented in tables in this appendix. In all of these, the principal hypothesis tested was that there is a statistically significant difference between outcomes for the preschool and no-preschool groups. The four additional parametric techniques are these:

Multinomial probit: a regression-like approach based on maximum likelihood statistics tests for effects of group, independent of wave and gender on dichotomous outcome variables.

Three-way analysis of variance: tests for main effects and interactions between treatment group, wave, and gender. Our use of this method is to ascertain whether there are effects of treatment group over and above all effects (main and interaction) of wave and gender.

One-way analysis of covariance: tests for effects of treatment after controlling for effects of gender and several variables at study entry—family socioeconomic status, mother's education, mother's employment, and child's Stanford-Binet IQ.

Three-way analysis of covariance: tests for main effects and interactions between treatment, wave, and gender after controlling for effects of child's IQ, family socioeconomic status, mother's education, and mother's employment at study entry.

All outcome variables already shown to have significant group differences (by using either nonparametric techniques or one-way analysis of variance) were also analyzed with the four techniques just described. The results are shown in Tables A-1 through A-3.

The general pattern of results from more complex analyses confirms the findings from simpler approaches presented in the body of the monograph: For 16 of the 27 variables, the p-values obtained from more complex analyses are statistically significant, being either the same or lower than those obtained in the simpler analyses. The most important of these 16 variables are proportion of years in special education, classification as mentally retarded, high school graduation, highest level of educational attainment, school costs, number of arrests and charges, self-support, and general welfare assistance. Other variables whose p-values maintain statistical significance are grade-point average, failing grades, absences, proportion of years in remedial education, months unemployed since leaving school and at age 19, savings, and persons with minor offenses. Group difference in self-reported involvement with police is statistically significant by all but one of the various analyses, and we are inclined to regard it as a robust finding across statistical techniques.

The fact that a group difference on a given variable is not found statistically significant by all of the techniques used does not necessarily cast doubt on the level of statistical significance reported earlier in this monograph, if the technique used earlier is indeed the most appropriate. For example, for dichotomous variables it may be argued that the multinomial probit technique is the correct multivariate procedure. So, for the dichotomous variables of age-19 employment and postsecondary education or vocational training, the statistical significance determined by the probit technique discounts the negative findings by the other multivariate techniques.

The design of the group by wave by gender analysis should be carefully considered in assessing the variables that did not maintain statistical significance in this analysis. With two groups, five waves, and two genders, this design has 20 cells and, with a sample size of 123, an average

Table A-1

P-VALUES[a] FOR DIFFERENCES BETWEEN PRESCHOOL AND NO-PRESCHOOL GROUPS:
EDUCATION AND RELATED OUTCOMES

Group Difference	Nonparametric Tests			Parametric Tests			
	Mann-Whitney U	Fisher's Exact Test	Multinomial Probit	One-Way Analysis of Variance	Three-Way Analysis of Variance	One-Way Analysis of Covariance	Three-Way Analysis of Covariance
Mean high school grade-point average	.0112	n/a	n/a	.0177	.0755	.0653	—
Mean number of failing grades (grade 7 on)	.0082	n/a	n/a	.0733	.0369	.0759	.0298
Mean days absent per year (grades K-6)	—	n/a	n/a	.0879	.0530	.0267	.0429
Proportion of years in special education	.0721	n/a	n/a	.0387	.0120	.0081	.0036
Classification as mentally retarded	.0168	.0138	<.05	.0161	.0167	.0071	.0093
Proportion of years in remedial education	.0240	n/a	n/a	.0252	.0421	.0713	.0741
Attitude toward high school	.0674	n/a	n/a	.0824	—	—	—
Graduation from high school	.0456	.0339	<.05	.0452	.0110	.0213	.0039
Post-secondary education or vocational training	.0368	.0288	<.05	.0363	—	.0686	—
Highest educational level attained	.0677	n/a	n/a	.0640	.0700	.0136	.0151
APL total score	.0134	n/a	n/a	.0249	—	.0590	—
Log of school cost per year attained (discounted at 3%)	.0500	n/a	n/a	.0378	.0120	.0081	.0036

[a] p-values are reported if less than .100, except in the case of the multinomial probit, for which p-values are reported as less than .05; italicized p-values are ones reported earlier in this monograph, unless otherwise explained; n/a means not applicable.

184

Table A-2

P-VALUES[a] FOR DIFFERENCES BETWEEN PRESCHOOL AND NO-PRESCHOOL GROUPS: ECONOMIC AND RELATED OUTCOMES

Group Difference	Nonparametric Tests		Multinomial Probit	Parametric Tests			
	Mann-Whitney U	Fisher's Exact Test		One-Way Analysis of Variance	Three-Way Analysis of Variance	One-Way Analysis of Covariance	Three-Way Analysis of Covariance
Working at time of interview	.0418	.0314	<.05	.0413	—	.0589	—
Months unemployed since leaving school	.0011	n/a	n/a	.0030	.0088	.0011	.0062
Months employed, age 19	.0295	n/a	n/a	.0147	.0134	.0090	.0143
Self-reported self-support	.0255	.0199	<.05	.0249	.0382	.0306	.0474
Self-reported use of government assistance	—	—	—	—	.0313[b]	—	—
Mean annualized assistance payment, 1981 dollars	—	n/a	n/a	—	.0240[b]	.0704	.0424
Use of general assistance: social services records	n/a	.0065	<.05	.0075	.0198	n/a	n/a
Saved some money	—	.0933	—	—	.0513	.0805	.0397
Level of satisfaction with work	.0740	.0552	<.05	.0739	—	—	—

[a] p-values are reported if less than .100, except in the case of the multinomial probit, for which p-values are reported as less than .05; italicized p-values are ones reported earlier in this monograph, unless otherwise explained; n/a means not applicable.

[b] The analysis reported in the body of the monograph is not duplicated in this table, but this (italicized) analysis is the one that resembles it most closely.

Table A-3

P-VALUES[a] FOR DIFFERENCES BETWEEN PRESCHOOL AND NO-PRESCHOOL GROUPS:
SOCIAL RESPONSIBILITY OUTCOMES

Group Difference	Nonparametric Tests		Multinomial Probit	Parametric Tests			
	Mann-Whitney U	Fisher's Exact Test		One-Way Analysis of Variance	Three-Way Analysis of Variance	One-Way Analysis of Covariance	Three-Way Analysis of Covariance
Ever arrested or charged	.0281	.0213	<.05	.0275	.0316	.0264	.0158
Ever arrested as adult	—	.0774	—	—	—	.0933	.0825
Ever arrested for property/violence offenses	.0998	.0730	<.05	.1000	—	—	.0811
Persons with minor offenses	.0071	.0063[b]	<.05	.0066	.0660	.0038	.0302
Persons ever fined	.0391	.0369	<.05	.0386	—	.0327	—
Self-reported involvement with police	.0340	.0260[b]	<.05	.0334	—	.0119	.0356

[a]p-values are reported if less than .100, except in the case of the multinomial probit, for which p-values are reported as less than .05; italicized p-values are ones reported earlier in this monograph, are otherwise explained.

[b]The analysis reported in the body of the monograph is not duplicated in this table, but this (italicized) analysis is the one that resembles it most closely.

cell size of 6. Thus there is the possibility of considerable variation from cell to cell that would not exist for a larger sample size.

Five variables that lost statistical significance in the complex analyses were based on low incidence counts: adult arrests, property/violence offenses, fines, use of government assistance, and amount of assistance payments. Three other variables that lost statistical significance were scale-score variables: high school attitude, satisfaction with work, and APL total score. If the relationship of any one of these variables to preschool had central theoretical significance, it would be important to conduct a longitudinal study with a larger sample size to increase our confidence that the effect found in this study can be generalized. However, the basic pattern of results is the same regardless of the disposition of these variables.

Analysis of Attrition

The two principal sources of data at age 19 were the subject interview and the school records. Of the 123 subjects in the study, 121 completed the interview—a 98 percent retrieval rate, with the missing 2 subjects both in the control group. Given the virtual absence of missing data on the interview, no analysis of the effect of missing data is necessary.

For school records, 112 of the 123 subjects had data, which means data were missing for 11 subjects. This constitutes a 91 percent retrieval rate. The analysis of attrition on school records is presented in Table A-4.

Table A-4

ANALYSIS OF DIFFERENTIAL ATTRITION
FOR SCHOOL RECORDS

Category	Records Present		Records Absent		p^a
	Preschool	No-Preschool	Preschool	No-Preschool	
Number in group[b]	54	58	4	7	—
% of group	93%	89%	7%	11%	—
% females	44%	38%	25%	57%	—
Initial IQ	79.4	78.4	82.3	79.7	—
Family socio-economic status	8.1	7.9	7.3	8.4	—
% single-parent families	46%	48%	25%	57%	—
Mother's schooling	9.4	9.4	9.8	9.6	—

[a]p-values are presented if less than .100.

[b]Numbers in groups were compared by chi-square analysis; other values for groups were compared by analysis of variance.

Table A-5

CORRELATION MATRIX FOR THE 12 VARIABLES IN THE CAUSAL MODEL

Variable	preschool	pretest IQ	family SES	gender	post IQ	mis- behavior	maturity	special ed	achieve- ment	attain- ment	arrests	mos worked
preschool	1.000											
pretest IQ	.075	1.000										
family SES	.079	.146	1.000									
gender	.066	.098	-.058	1.000								
post IQ	.424	.366	.218	-.001	1.000							
misbehavior	-.093	-.017	-.085	-.292	-.154	1.000						
maturity	.024	.184	.309	-.146	.336	-.218	1.000					
special ed	-.166	-.152	-.194	-.066	-.381	.157	-.465	1.000				
achievement	.178	.252	.435	.106	.481	-.269	.592	-.627	1.000			
attainment	.156	.133	.207	-.025	.350	-.208	.365	-.424	.489	1.000		
arrests	-.054	-.045	-.063	-.227	-.075	.410	.232	.237	-.240	-.438	1.000	
mos worked	.185	.169	.281	-.156	.144	.057	.216	-.176	.280	.371	-.199	1.000

Note. $n = 112$. See Chapter 5 and especially Figure 7 (p. 80) for a description of the variables and the causal model itself. A correlation coefficient is italicized if it is significantly different from 0. ($p < .05$).

The analysis of those with and without school records in either the experimental group or the control group revealed no statistically significant differences among the groups regarding group size or principal background characteristics. Inspection of group values for those having school records shows very little difference between experimental and control groups. For those not having school records, the experimental and control groups showed *percent* differences that appear large (for percent females and percent single-parent families) but the low *numbers* of subjects not having records (4 preschool and 7 no-preschool) negated the impact of these differences. We may conclude that differential attrition on school records had no discernible effect on the reported findings.

Correlation Matrix for the Causal Model

The causal model presented in Figure 7 (page 80) is based on the relationships among 12 variables, with assumptions made about the cause and effect relationships among these variables. Table A-5 presents the matrix of product-moment correlation coefficients for these 12 variables. This matrix presents the bivariate relationships between each pair of variables and makes no assumptions about cause and effect.

References

American College Testing Program. (1976). *User's guide: Adult APL Survey*. Iowa City, IA: Author.

Arthur, G. (1952). *The Arthur Adaptation of the Leiter International Performance Scale*. Beverly Hills, CA: Psychological Service Center Press.

Bachman, J. G., & Johnston, J. (1978). *The Monitoring the Future questionnaire*. Ann Arbor, MI: University of Michigan Institute for Social Research.

Barnett, W. S. (1984). *A benefit-cost analysis of the Perry Preschool program and its long-term effects*. Ypsilanti, MI: High/Scope Press.

Bissell, J. (1971). *Implementation of planned variation in Head Start*. Washington, DC: U.S. Office of Child Development, DHEW.

Blau, M., & Duncan, O. (1967). *The American occupational structure*. New York: John Wiley and Sons.

Bloom, B. S. (1964). *Stability and change in human characteristics*. New York: John Wiley & Sons.

Bronfenbrenner, U. (1974). *A report on longitudinal programs: (Vol.2). Is early intervention effective?* (DHEW Publication Number OHD 74 − 24). Washington, DC: U.S. Government Printing Office.

Chorvinsky, M. (1982). *Preprimary enrollment 1980*. Washington, DC: National Center for Education Statistics.

Consortium for Longitudinal Studies. (1978). *Lasting effects after preschool* (Final report, Grant No. 90C-1311, to the U.S. Administration for Children, Youth and Families, Office of Human Development Services, DHEW Publication No. OHDS 79-30178). Washington, DC: U.S. Government Printing Office.

Cronbach, L. J., Gleser, G. C., Nanda, H., & Rajaratnam, N. (1972). *The dependability of behavioral measurements: Theory of generalizability for scores and profiles*. New York: John Wiley & Sons.

Donaldson, M. C. (1978). *Children's minds*. New York: Norton.

Dropout rate falling here, statewide. (1982, July 18). *Ann Arbor News*, pp. A1, A3.

Dunn, L. M. (1965). *Peabody Picture Vocabulary Test manual*. Minneapolis, MN: American Guidance Service.

Elliott, D. S., Ageton, S. S., & Canter R. J. (1979). An integrated theoretical perspective on delinquent behavior. *Journal of Research in Crime and Delinquency, 16*(1), 3-27.

Espenshade, T. J. (1984). Investing in children: New estimates of parental expenditures. Baltimore, MD: Urban Institute Press.

Freeberg, N. E. (1974). *Development of assessment measure for use with youth-work training program enrollees, phase 2: Longitudinal validation* (Final Report, U.S. Department of Labor, Document No. ETS PR-74-1). Princeton, NJ: Educational Testing Service.

Freeberg, N. E. (1976). Criterion measures for youth-work training programs: The development of relevant performance dimensions. *Journal of Applied Psychology, 61*(5), 537-545.

Garber, H. L., & Heber, R. (1981). The efficacy of early intervention with family rehabilitation. In M. J. Begab, H. C. Haywood, & H. L. Garber (Eds.), *Psychosocial influences in retarded performance: Vol. II. Strategies for improving competence* (pp. 71-88). Baltimore, MD: University Park Press.

Gray, S. W., Ramsey, B. K., & Klaus, R. A. (1982). *From 3 to 20—The Early Training Project*. Baltimore, MD: University Park Press.

Haller, A. O., & Portes, A. (1973). Status attainment processes. *Sociology of Education, 46*(1), 51-91.

Hohmann, M., Banet, B., & Weikart, D. P. (1979). *Young children in action: A manual for preschool educators*. Ypsilanti, MI: High/Scope Press.

Howe, M. (1953). *The Negro in Ypsilanti*. Unpublished master's thesis, Eastern Michigan University, School of Education, Ypsilanti, MI.

190

Hubbell, R. (1983). *Head Start evaluation, synthesis, and utilization project* (DHHS Publication No. OHDS 83-31184). Washington, DC: U.S. Government Printing Office.

Hunt, J. McV. (1961). *Intelligence and experience.* New York: Ronald Press.

Irvine, D. J. (1982). *Evaluation of the New York State Experimental Prekindergarten Program.* Paper presented at the annual meeting of the American Educational Research Association, New York City.

Jencks, C. S., Bartlett, S., Corcoran, M., Crouse, J., Eaglesfield, D., Jackson, G., McClelland, K., Mueser, P., Olneck, M., Schwartz, J., Ward, S., & Williams, J. (1979). *Who gets ahead? The determinants of economic success in America.* New York: Basic Books.

Jencks, C. S., Smith, M., Acland, H., Bane, M. J., Cohen, D., Gintis, H., Heyns, B., & Michelson, S. (1972). *Inequality: A reassessment of the effect of family and schooling in America.* New York: Basic Books.

Kahn, G. (1982). *School enrollment of 3- and 4-year-olds by race/ethnic category.* Washington, DC: National Center for Education Statistics.

Karnes, M. B., Schwedel, A. M., & Williams, M. B. (1983). A comparison of five approaches for educating young children from low-income homes. In Consortium for Longitudinal Studies, *As the twig is bent...lasting effects of preschool programs* (pp. 133-170). Hillsdale, NJ: Lawrence Erlbaum Associates.

Klaus, R., & Gray, S. W. (1968). The early training project for disadvantaged children: A report after five years. *Monographs of the Society for Research in Child Development, 33*(4, Serial No. 120).

Kohen, A. I. (1973). *Determinants of labor market success among young men: Race, ability, quantity, and quality of schooling.* Columbus, OH: The State University Center for Human Resource Research.

Krech, D., Rosenzweig, M. R., & Bennett, E. L. (1960). Effects of environmental complexity and training on brain chemistry. *Journal of Comparative Physiological Psychology, 53,* 509-519.

Lazar, I., Darlington, R., Murray, H., Royce, J., & Snipper, A. (1982). Lasting effects of early education. *Monographs of the Society for Research in Child Development, 47*(1-2,Serial No. 194).

Levenstein, P., O'Hara, J., & Madden, J. (1983). The Mother-Child Home program of the verbal interaction project. In Consortium for Longitudinal Studies, *As the twig is bent...lasting effects of preschool programs* (pp. 237-264). Hillsdale, NJ: Lawrence Erlbaum Associates.

Levin, H. M. (1977). A decade of policy developments in improving education and training for low-income populations. In R. H. Haveman (Ed.), *A decade of federal antipoverty programs: Achievements, failures, and lessons* (pp. 521-570). New York: Academic Press.

Lindner, E. W., Mattis, M. C., & Rogers, J. R. (1983). *When churches mind the children.* Ypsilanti, MI: High/Scope Press.

Ludlow, J. R., & Allen, L. (1979). The effect of early intervention and preschool stimulus on the development of the Down's syndrome child. *Journal of Mental Deficiency Research, 23,* 29.

Maisto, A. A., & German, M. L. (1979). Variables related to progress in a parent-infant training program for high risk infants. *The Journal of Pediatric Psychology, 4,* 409-414.

Mallar, C., Kerachsky, S., Thornton, C., Long, D., Good, T., & Lapczynski, P. (1978). *Evaluation of the economic impact of the Job Corps Program* (First follow-up report 78-14). Princeton, NJ: Mathematica Policy Research, Inc.

McCarthy, J. J., & Kirk, S. A. (1961). *Examiner's manual: Illinois Test of Psycholinguistic Abilities, experimental version.* Urbana, IL: University of Illinois, Institute for Research on Exceptional Children.

Michael, R. T. (1975). Education and fertility. In F. T. Juster (Ed.), *Education, income, and human behavior.* New York: McGraw-Hill.

Miller, L. B., & Bizzell, R. P. (1983). The Louisville Experiment: A comparison of four programs. In Consortium for Longitudinal Studies, *As the twig is bent . . . lasting effects of preschool programs* (pp. 171-200). Hillsdale, NJ: Lawrence Erlbaum Associates.

Monroe, E., & McDonald, M. S. (1981). *Follow-up study of the 1966 Head Start program, Rome City Schools, Rome, Georgia.* Unpublished paper cited by Hubbell (1983).

Moore, M. G., Fredericks, H. D. B., & Baldwin, V. L. (1981). The long-range effects of early childhood education on a trainable mentally retarded population. *Journal of the Division for Early Childhood, 4,* 93-109.

Nam, C. B., LaRocque, J., Powers, M. G., & Holmberg, J. (1975). Occupational status scores: Stability and change. In *Proceedings of the American Statistical Association*, pp. 570-575.

National Association for the Education of Young Children. (1983). Progress report on the Center Accreditation Project. *Young Children, 39*(1), 35-46.

National Center for Education Statistics. (1980). *The condition of education—1980 edition.* Washington, DC: U.S. Government Printing Office.

National Center for Education Statistics. (1982). *The condition of education—1982 edition.* Washington, DC: U.S. Government Printing Office.

Nieman, R. H., & Gastright, J. F. (1981, November). The long-term effects of Title I preschool and all day kindergarten. *Phi Delta Kappan, 63*(3), 184- 185.

Palmer, F. H. (1983). The Harlem Study: Effects by type of training, age of training, and social class. In Consortium for Longitudinal Studies, *As the twig is bent...lasting effects of preschool programs* (pp. 201-236). Hillsdale, NJ: Lawrence Erlbaum Associates.

Phillips, L., & Votey, H. L. (1981). *The economics of crime control* (Sage Library of Social Research, 132). Beverly Hills, CA: Sage Publications.

Piaget, J., & Inhelder, B. (1969). *The psychology of the child.* New York: Basic Books.

Ramey, C. T., Bryant, D. M., & Suarez, T. M. (1984). Preschool compensatory education and the modifiability of intelligence: A critical review. In D. Detterman (Ed.), *Current topics in human intelligence.* Norwood, NJ: Ablex Publishing Company.

Ramey, C. T., & Haskins, R. (1981). The causes and treatment of school failure: Insights from the Carolina Abecedarian Project. In M. J. Begab, H. C. Haywood, & H. L. Garber (Eds.), *Psychosocial influences in retarded performance: Vol. II. Strategies for improving competence* (pp. 89-112). Baltimore, MD: University Park Press.

Rosenberg. M. (1965). *Society and the adolescent self-image.* Princeton, NJ: Princeton University Press.

Sameroff, A., & Chandler, M. (1975). Reproductive risk and the continuum of caretaking casualty. In F. Horowitz (Ed.), *Review of child development research* (Vol. 4). Chicago: University of Chicago Press.

Schweinhart, L. J. (1981). Comment on Intelligence Research and Social Policy. *Phi Delta Kappan, 63*(3), 187.

Schweinhart, L. J., & Weikart, D. P. (1980). *Young children grow up: The effects of the Perry Preschool program on youths through age 15* (Monographs of the High/Scope Educational Research Foundation, 7). Ypsilanti, MI: High/Scope Press.

Scott, J. P. (1962). Critical periods in behavorial development. *Science, 138*(3544), 949-957.

Sellin, T., & Wolfgang, M., E. (1964). *The measurement of delinquency.* New York: John Wiley and Sons.

Simeonsson, R. J., Cooper, D. H., & Scheiner, A. P. (1982). A review and analysis of the effectiveness of early intervention programs. *Pediatrics, 69*, 635-641.

Smith, M. S. (1973). *Some short-term effects of Project Head Start: A preliminary report on the second year of planned variation, 1970-71.* Cambridge, MA: Huron Institute.

Steiner, G. Y. (1976). *The children's cause.* Washington, DC: Brookings Institution.

Tobias, T. N., Baker, M. W., & Fairfield, B. A. (1973). *The History of Ypsilanti—150 years.* Ypsilanti, MI: Ypsilanti Sesquicentennial Committee.

U.S. Administration for Children, Youth and Families (1983). *Ninth annual report to Congress on Head Start services.* Washington, DC: Author.

U.S. Bureau of the Census. (1982a). *Money income and poverty status of families and persons in the United States: 1981* (Current Population Reports: Consumer Income, Series P-60, No. 134). Washington, DC: U.S. Government Printing Office.

U.S. Bureau of the Census. (1982b). *Trends in child care arrangements of working mothers* (Current Population Reports: Special Studies, Series P-23, No. 117). Washington, DC: U.S. Government Printing Office.

U.S. Bureau of Education for the Handicapped. (1976). *A summary of the Handicapped Children's Early Education Program.* Washington, DC: Author.

U.S. Department of Justice, Federal Bureau of Investigation. (1980). *Uniform Crime Reports.* Washington, DC: U.S. Government Printing Office.

U.S. Office of Special Education and Rehabilitative Services. (1983). *Fifth annual report to Congress on special education services.* Washington, DC: Author.

Weber, C. U., Foster, P. W., & Weikart, D. P. (1978). *An economic analysis of the Ypsilanti Perry Preschool Project* (Monographs of the High/Scope Educational Research Foundation, 5). Ypsilanti, MI: High/Scope Press.

Weikart, D. P. (Ed.). (1967). *Preschool intervention: Preliminary results of the Perry Preschool Project*. Ann Arbor, MI: Campus Publishers.

Weikart, D. P., Bond, J. T., & McNeil J. T. (1978). *The Ypsilanti Perry Preschool Project: Preschool years and longitudinal results through fourth grade* (Monographs of the High/Scope Educational Research Foundation, 3). Ypsilanti, MI: High/Scope Press.

Weikart, D. P., Deloria, D., Lawser, S., & Wiegerink, R. (1970). *Longitudinal results of the Ypsilanti Perry Preschool Project* (Monographs of the High/Scope Educational Research Foundation, 1). Ypsilanti, MI: High/Scope Press.

Weikart, D. P., Epstein A. S., Schweinhart, L. J., & Bond, J. T. (1978) *The Ypsilanti Preschool Curriculum Demonstration Project: Preschool years and longitudinal results* (Monographs of the High/Scope Educational Research Foundation, 4). Ypsilanti, MI: High/Scope Press.

Weikart, D. P., Rogers, L., Adcock, C., & McClelland, D. (1971). *The Cognitively Oriented Curriculum: A framework for preschool teachers*. Urbana, IL: University of Illinois.

Weisberg, H. I. (1974). *Short-term cognitive effects of Head Start programs: A report on the third year of planned variation—1971-72*. Cambridge, MA: Huron Institute.

Westinghouse Learning Corporation. (1969). *The impact of Head Start: An evaluation of the effects of Head Start on children's cognitive and affective development* (Vols. I-II). Athens, OH: Ohio University.

Wolfgang, M. E., Figlio, R. M., & Sellin, T. (1972). *Delinquency in a birth cohort*. Chicago: University of Chicago Press.

Wylie, R. (1974). *The self-concept: Volume 1. A review of methodological considerations and measuring instruments* (revised ed.). Lincoln, NB: University of Nebraska Press.

Commentary on *Changed Lives*

Marie Skodak Crissey*

I bin rich, an' I bin poor.
Rich is better. Much better.

attributed to Pearl Bailey

In the 1960s there developed a veritable explosion of studies, research activities, and experiments intended to test the theory that the cycle of poverty—from grandparent, to parent, to child—could be broken. Of particular interest here are the studies that examined the role of education in helping to break the poverty cycle. It is not known how many of these studies fell by the wayside. By the late 1970s, however, the Consortium for Longitudinal Studies was able to identify about a dozen studies that not only had endured but also had met the criteria for serious scientific research design, adequate data handling, and useful reports for dissemination. Among these was the Perry Preschool Project of Ypsilanti, Michigan. *Changed Lives* is the most recent in a series of monographs reporting on various stages and aspects of this study.

Briefly, the project is a study of 123 black youths, now over 19 years of age. They were selected at age 3 (age 4 for the initial group) from families of low socioeconomic status, over a span of four years (1962-1965). There were from 17 to 28 youngsters in each year's sample, all of whom had entry IQ's of 60-90. Each year's sample of children was equally divided into those who attended preschool and those who did not. The preschool and no-preschool groups were as closely matched as possible on such factors as sex distribution, parental education and employment, and residential status, and this comparability has continued for some 20 years.

The experimental group attended preschool from October to May, 2½ hours each day for the five-day week. In addition, a teacher visited each home for about 1½ hours each week throughout the year, including the summer months. The control group had no preschool program.

Both groups were given the same tests, same interviews and, after preschool, went on to attend public schools in the area. The preschool program varied somewhat from year to year and reflected the educational philosophies of the teachers and researchers. The objective at all times was the preparation of the children in those area considered to be significant for school success. Emphasis was on cognitive development, language, the broadening of information and experience, and the

---

*Dr. Crissey is one of the original "Iowa group" whose longitudinal and cross-sectional studies first highlighted the results of environmental deprivation and environmental enrichment on mental development. These studies challenged the prevailing "fixed intelligence" concepts of the early 1930s and have continued to contribute to the ongoing nature-nurture debate.

development of those social and behavioral skills associated with school adjustment. The program moved from a quite highly structured, cognitively oriented one, toward one with more child-initiated activities. The staff, teachers, researchers, and aides were not only highly competent, well trained, and well supervised but also exceptionally devoted to the project and to the children and families involved. There have been no losses of the participants and very few gaps in the test data, school records, interview summaries, or other information used in the various comparisons. This reflects not only the stability of the population but also the ingenuity of the research staff in locating the subjects and enlisting their continued participation over a score of years.

Evaluating the results of a study that extends over 20 years is uniquely complicated. Not only have the subjects passed from childhood through adolescence and into early adulthood with its special demands, but also the world around them has changed with a rapidity not predictable when the project began. Society has moved with lightening speed from a period when discrimination against blacks was common through the civil rights movements, integration, and the opening of employment opportunities; and all this darkened by periods of the severest economic crisis since the Depression of the 1930s. (Yet with all the changes, many things remained the same for the study sample. The community in which the subjects were born and raised remained basically black and economically depressed; its residents, largely unemployed; its crime rate, high.)

Along with the changes in the nation's social structure and climate came changes in basic ideas about the nature and objectives of intervention: Viewpoints evolved from hereditarian, to environmentalist, to interacting/transactional, to eclectic. Assessment devices and technology changed as these became age-inappropriate or as new ones became available. Not only the Perry Preschool Project, but all longitudinal studies suffer from these vicissitudes, which blur the clarity of conclusions and implications.

A good example of these changes is the evolution of the role of mental tests, that is, the convenient IQ. Originally devised as a screening technique for identifying Parisian children for special education classes, the Binet Intelligence Test was found to be useful in evaluating and classifying normal as well as mentally retarded children. In the course of standardization, it was found that the relative score (IQ) did not appreciably change on retesting. In the 1920s and 1930s the concept of the fixed IQ was compatible with the prevailing theory of inherited mental ability, more or less stratified by social class levels. In the 1930s and 1940s, however, evidence was found that significant changes occurred in mental ability when environmental conditions were markedly changed, particularly with regard to younger subjects. The criticisms regarding the results of mental (IQ) tests with culturally or racially different groups have, in the 1970s, challenged their use for various school-related purposes. Rather than measuring "innate intelligence," as believed for many years, an intelligence (IQ) test is a peculiarly sensitive achievement test, reflecting the individual's at-the-moment functioning level in reasoning, information, vocabulary, and so forth, as compared with the functioning of his or her age mates. It has a strong relationship (and is therefore of predictive value) to academic achievement as measured by school progress. It does not, however, measure a person's "street smarts," motivation, endurance under stress, or many other traits that affect life outcomes. Nevertheless, it is a convenient measuring technique—one of the few available in psychological and educational research. It is useful, but like any tool, it has its limitations.

The Perry Preschool Project, like all early intervention programs, used individual intelligence (IQ) tests both to identify and to describe the subjects. As in most studies of early intervention, marked improvement in IQ occurred among those attending preschool, bringing their mean score within the average range or approximately comparable to that found among mainstream school entrants. As with most studies comparing pre-entrance scores with kindergarten and first grade test scores, the initial increase in IQ was followed by a decline, and differences in IQ between experimental and control groups disappeared by about second grade.

In this report, no mental test scores are given for the 19-year-olds, the indirect evidence suggesting that both the control and experimental groups remained at approximately an 80-IQ level in spite of the differences in educational attainment. It would be of considerable interest to explore in more detail the careers of those who, as young adults, were in the 60-to-75-IQ range and those who were in the 90-IQ range and above. Since some members attended and/or completed college, it is unlikely that they did so with IQ's of less than 90—unlikely, but still possible, for example, with a special talent in athletics, or carefully selected courses, or a rank of 500 in a graduating class of 500. This is not to belittle such achievement but rather to point out that we do not really know what attributes a "survivor," or a "winner," may utilize to compensate for lack of intellectual qualities others may possess.

There appears to be no question that the preschool experience changed the participants. That this change was not necessarily reflected in IQ's of an elevated level should be neither surprising nor the basis for criticism. Nor should the change (as reflected by increase in IQ) observed during the preschool-stimulation period be expected to continue. Like the concentric ripples formed by a pebble thrown into a pond, the effects gradually fade away, and unless another pebble is thrown, eventually the pond becomes smooth again. It should be remembered that after the preschool experience, the experimental group joined the controls in a larger cohort of age-mates of similar cultural and economic status and received no more special attention in their daily lives. When the elementary school—and other environmental effects—are geared to the middle of the group, or to the lowest common denominator and the stimulation of preschool is not renewed at an appropriate level, it is inevitable that the brief exposure at ages 3 and 4 will fade.

In spite of the fact that experimentals and controls attended the same schools, had the same teachers, lived through the same street and neighborhood experiences, were exposed to the same TV shows—in spite of these commonalities—something of the preschool experience has remained with the experimental group and has influenced 15 years of their lives.

The monograph's interpretation of these effects as commitment to education, stemming from the child's early competence based on the cognitive development reflected by the rise in IQ, is logical. When a child knows and can use with confidence all (or nearly all) the skills and information a kindergarten or first grade teacher expects, the situation (and the consequent interaction between child and teacher) is quite different than it is when the child does not have these competencies. Not only will the child develop a different self-concept, and evoke a different attitude and treatment from adults, but also academic skills will be built on a firmer base than is the case when the child enters school with fewer preacademic and social skills. The pervasiveness of this commitment to education extends in various forms through the educational careers of the preschool group.

Thus, those who attended preschool, as compared with the control group, were found on the whole to have higher achievement test scores, higher grade-point averages, fewer failing grades, fewer absences, better attitudes and behavior, a higher rate of graduation from high school, more frequent enrollment in college or vocational training, and more satisfaction with their educational experience. Although more former preschoolers received remedial help in school subjects, fewer were retained in grade or identified as mentally retarded and placed in special education classes. There were economic advantages to taxpayers and society resulting particularly from fewer retentions and special education placements, as discussed in the Perry Preschool report. But apart from monetary considerations, there were effects for the preschool attendees that had both personal and general social values.

Interviews at age 19 included questions regarding employment, income, and future vocational plans. In spite of the high unemployment during the 1980-83 period, particularly acute for black young adults without training, or, in many cases, with a less than a high school education, it was found that 50 percent of preschool attendees were gainfully employed. Less than one third of the control group were then employed, and this group had, in addition, more than double the length of unemployment between jobs and earned less than half as much in terms of dollars. The aspiration level of both groups was low, primarily at the moderately skilled clerical or factory level. All things considered, these aspirations were probably realistic for most and did not apply to those who had college or special training or skills.

Not only were preschool attendees more likely to be employed (and pay taxes), they also utilized fewer public assistance resources, such as welfare, Medicaid, and food stamps. The economic implication of longer schooling and vocational preparation, better personal financial management, and less dependence on public support are discussed in the report. It should be noted that early establishment of a good employment record has cumulative favorable effects for the future. A 19-year-old who has a job in times of economic adversity and holds it for 2 to 4 years will have advantages in advancement and income gains that the 19-year-old who is unemployed for 2 to 4 years will be unable to match.

Two accompaniments of poverty, low socioeconomic status, and poor education are crime and illegitimacy (and/or larger family size). The subjects have now reached the age when the effects of early experience can be examined with regard to these areas of social responsibility. The assessment of criminal behavior is a peculiarly difficult one. The true extent and cost of crime is unknown (some crimes are undiscovered or unreported for a variety of reasons); crime is underreported (both by victims and in interviews with perpetrators); its seriousness is misclassified (by modifications of charges, plea bargaining, and so on); and evaluation of retribution is uncertain (judges vary in severity, for example). Even the careful scrutiny of records and sensitive interviewing of study subjects and of parents, friends, court workers, and police, would make this area a shadowy one. Furthermore, an experience in the preschool years, designed to enhance school-appropriate behavior and attitudes, does not necessarily emphasize the kind of internalized sensitivity to others that might be expected to influence law-abiding behavior in adolescence and adulthood. It has been generally accepted that criminal behavior is largely the result of family and peer group influences, with possible personality components. Some subjects in both the preschool and control groups engaged in illegal, antisocial, law-breaking behavior, but there is a persistent difference, not always statistically significant, but clearly consistent. Fewer experimental than control subjects were ever arrested; those who were had fewer offenses, were on probation for shorter periods, paid lower fines, had generally fewer involvements with the police, were involved in fights and violence less often. Relative success in school and commitment to the educational mores has served as an effective deterrent to delinquency. While the costs of involvement in the criminal system are discussed in the report, it is interesting to note that those who were free of such involvement were also spared the cost of lawyer fees, as well as the loss of pay during incarceration or trials, and had these resources available to spend in legitimate ways. Since the preschool group did include some individuals committing repeated serious offenses, this raises an interesting question regarding some obscure physiological components of antisocial behavior. Intensive study of markedly deviant individuals in both groups might be rewarding.

Large families, teenage pregnancies, and single-parent households characterize the poor and undereducated members of society. Among the preschool graduates this trend has been slowed, if not reversed, since the number of children is approximately half that of the controls. Since both groups were assessed between 19 and 24 years of age, this is only a preliminary indication of what may be a trend. It is well established that family size decreases with the improved educational and social levels of the parents.

In common with other longitudinal studies, comparisons of experimental and control groups with regard to more subtle aspects of civic behavior have been inconclusive. The small, usually statistically nonsignificant differences tend to be in favor of the experimental group. Such activities as church attendance, voting, membership in social or community groups, helpful behavior, and so on, are both difficult to measure and highly influenced by stresses not related to the original project objectives.

In addition to the report of the follow-up findings at age 19, the monograph has three significant chapters. In one (Chapter 6), the findings of seven studies of early intervention are compared and evaluated. It is concluded that in spite of differences in length of intervention, involvement of parents, and type of curriculum, "only early childhood programs of high quality produce long-term beneficial effects." In view of the apparent costliness of preschool programs, there is a temptation to cut corners. If one year produces the same results as two, if one teacher can influence 10 pupils as well as 5, if preschool alone does as well as preschool with added parent education—why not go with the less costly? As long ago as the 1930s the Davenport study[1] showed that 100 reasonably consecutive days of quality preschool experience were needed to produce changes in mental functioning, and that these changes would be fleeting unless continued for a substantially longer period.

Another chapter (Chapter 8) presents eight case studies of "successful" and "unsuccessful," men and women, preschoolers and controls. These were analyzed in an attempt to identify those life experiences that serve to offset subsequent success. The salient factors appeared to be as follows:

(1) Family support for education through encouragement, with emphasis on learning, not only on good behavior

(2) The presence of positive role models in the family, the school, or the community

(3) Active striving toward some goal, usually related to education

(4) A sense of responsibility beyond immediate personal needs

When these factors were absent, the chances for failure in education and continued economic dependency were increased.

A third chapter (Chapter 5) presents a major theoretical contribution explicating the way in which the preschool experience is eventually translated into the educational, economic, and social advantages seen at age 19. The interrelationships, utilizing the various statistical analyses that the data make possible, are presented in a causal model that accurately represents complex real-life events. It is a sophisticated example of how "one thing leads to another." It avoids the oversimplification that characterizes so many studies and illustrates the sensitivity of this group of researchers to the many real-world nuances for which research still does not have adequate assessment techniques.

In a flippant mood, it would be possible to summarize a study like this in three quotations: "I am a part of all I have met"—from the Aeneid; "As the twig is bent, so the tree is inclined"—an old English saying; and "The apple does not fall far from its tree"—an old German saying.

There is a more serious view, however, that this report richly deserves. Whether or not the project was originally intended to extend for the lifetime of its subjects, it now appears that the preschool experience has illuminated the lives of the participants even into adulthood. The preschool experience and the related teacher-parent contacts clearly resulted in skills and commitments that brought a measure of success in school and in society. The codes of behavior and life ideals that the schools exemplify have been incorporated into the lives and practices of the preschool participants. When the brevity of the preschool experience and its

---

[1]Skeels, H. M., Updegraff, R., Wellman, B. L., & Williams, H. M. (1938) *A study of environmental stimulation: An orphanage preschool project* (University of Iowa, Studies in Child Welfare, Vol. XV, No. 4).

minuscule part in the total life of the individuals is compared with their immersion in what can be seen as the negative influences of their life circumstances—of welfare dependency, unemployment, "street life"—it is indeed remarkable that any traces of the early influences can be found. No stronger testimonial to the efficacy of early intervention is needed.

Early intervention programs like the Perry Preschool program involve very little change in the social structure. They influence, but do not disrupt families. They nudge not only the immediate participant, but family members as well, toward middle-class, socially effective directions.

It is not difficult to show the cost-effectiveness of early intervention programs. The dollar values can be identified, even projected into the future. An even more significant return is to be found in the changed lives of people who are committed to education, to concern for a better future in their own and their children's lives, to living in a caring world with less crime and hostility. The results, over time, of studies like the Perry Preschool Project must have an impact on social policy.

Commentary on
Changed Lives

Edward M. Gramlich
Chairman, Department of Economics
The University of Michigan

Both as a program and as an evaluation, the Perry Preschool Project, reported on in *Changed Lives*, makes an important contribution. As a program, it provides a welcome counter to the prevailing pessimism that "nothing works." As an evaluation, the Perry Preschool study is very rich, with much data not usually available in programmatic evaluations.

The report itself admirably summarizes the project, the factual background, and the relevant theories of child development. It would be redundant for me to review the facts of the project and impossible for me, an economist, to analyze the theories of child development. Hence in my remarks I will focus on the Perry Preschool project as an evaluation. What does the evaluation say, how good is the evidence, and what should this project tell policymakers?

The evaluation of the Perry Preschool program, summarized in what is called the economic analysis in Chapter 5, uses a technique called benefit-cost analysis. Benefit-cost analysis is nothing more than its name suggests—an attempt to identify the project's benefits and costs, and then to compare them. In this, as in other evaluations, it is difficult to measure benefits, not quite as difficult to measure costs, but extremely difficult to compare the two. Comparison is difficult for any number of reasons— different people get the benefits and pay the costs, benefits and costs happen at different times, and benefits and costs come in different forms. Costs usually come in the form of dollars, benefits, in such forms as a better-educated population or a reduction in crime or teenage pregnancy. While the logic of benefit-cost analysis is straightforward, its implementation is anything but that.

Let me begin by describing for the uninitiated what happens when this technique of benefit-cost analysis is applied to the Perry Preschool program. I do this by reporting in the accompanying table the significant figures, taken from Tables 26 and 28 of Chapter 5. To simplify the table, all benefits and costs are per child, costs are labelled as negative benefits, all benefits and costs are given in dollars, and these dollar valuations are what is known as present values in 1981 dollars.

To go right to the bottom line, the numbers in the table's lower right hand corner indicate that the program is a winner. One year of the program yields net benefits of $28,933 per child; two years yield $23,769 per child. Either one or two years passes a gross benefit-cost test; presently I will explain how the results can be used to make precise policy statements.

We can go beyond this one-summary tally and look at the numbers in several ways. First, as to timing, most costs of the Perry Preschool Project were borne back in 1962-65, when the project started. Looking at the

NET PER-CHILD BENEFITS[a] OF THE PERRY PRESCHOOL PROGRAM

Benefits	To Participants		To Taxpayers and Potential Crime Victims		To Society	
	1-yr Preschool	2-yr Preschool	1-yr Preschool	2-yr Preschool	1-yr Preschool	2-yr Preschool
Measured (to age 19)	226	509	2,290	-2,389	2,515	-1,880
Preschool program	0	0	-4,818	-9,289	-4,818	-9,289
Child care	290	572	0	0	290	572
Educational cost saving	0	0	5,113	4,964	5,113	4,964
Earnings increase	482	467	161	156	642	623
Welfare reduction	-546	-530	601	583	55	53
Crime reduction	0	0	1,233	1,197	1,233	1,197
Predicted (age 19 +)	4,856	4,715	21,562	20,933	26,418	25,649
College costs	0	0	-704	-684	-704	-684
Earnings increase	19,233	18,674	4,580	4,446	23,813	23,121
Welfare reduction	-14,377	-13,959	15,815	15,355	1,438	1,396
Crime reduction	0	0	1,871	1,816	1,871	1,816
Total net benefits	5,082	5,224	23,852	18,544	28,933	23,769

[a]Present value discounted at 3%; 1981 dollars.

column labelled "To Society," we see that these costs would have amounted to $4,818 per child in 1981 for one year of the program, $9,289 per child for two years of the program. One of the benefits is immediate, the implicit value of the child care, amounting to $290 and $572 respectively in 1981 dollars. The rest of the benefits are only realized over time.

The first thing to consider about these subsequent benefits is that they are recurrent flows: a one-shot investment is made in 1962-65, and then crime rates are lowered, or earnings raised, in several subsequent years. Exactly how to measure these changes is a deep question in economics and econometrics, and the numbers should be viewed somewhat suspiciously. But whatever the gain, it should recur, and that is why the earnings increases loom so large in the totals.

The second consideration, partly offsetting the first, is that the recurrent increases appear later in time. A one-shot investment in physical capital would have also paid dividends over time, and this means that the recurrent gains must be discounted for the productivity of time between the date the human investment is made and the date the earnings increases begin to come on stream. Exactly what discount rate should be used in this calculation is another deep mystery about which hundreds of articles have been written by economists. In my view, the appropriate measure is close to the real marginal product of private capital, reasonably estimated at about 3 percent in the United States today. Fortunately, the Perry Preschool study, unlike many others, did discount benefits at this 3 percent rate.

The evaluation then breaks these present value increases into those that have been measured up until age 19 and those that are extrapolated into the participants' adult lives. Again examining the "To Society" column, we find that according to this breakdown, one year of the program, which would cost $4,818, has already paid for itself in the sense that the discounted sum of educational cost savings, earnings increases, and crime reductions exceeds the initial cost by $2,515. In business terms, the payback period for one year of the program is about ten years. But because the initial cost is much higher, two years of the program would not have paid for themselves by the time the subjects became 19—it would take another few years of earnings increases to bring them over the line. In my own view, this long payback period is not necessarily a drawback—an investment in preschool children is one of those programs that *will* have a long payback period—but critics with short time-horizons may use these data to raise questions.

The payback period analysis does bring up an interesting point about the Perry Preschool evaluation. It turns out that two years of the program cannot be shown to yield greater benefits than one year of the program. This suggests that the second year of the program is a clear waste—costs rise, while benefits stay the same. Net social benefits are 20 percent higher for the one year program ($28,933 vs. $23,769), and a strict reading of the evaluation would say that the second year of the program should be dropped. Putting it another way, instead of a second year being invested in the participants, the resources would better be devoted to putting a new round of children through one year.

Another interesting aspect of the benefit-cost analysis involves the identity of gainers and losers. I have until now focused on net social benefits, received by participants, taxpayers, and potential victims of crime, all added up. But that is a rather constricting way to give the numbers—politicians are also concerned about *who* gains and loses. The table gives the surprising information that participants themselves gain or lose relatively little from the program. It costs them nothing, they gain a bit from after-tax earnings increases up to age 19, but lose more than that in reductions in welfare payments. After age 19 the projected earnings increases are somewhat greater than the welfare reductions. If not for the margin provided by projected increases in adult earnings, participants in the Perry Preschool program should almost be indifferent between enrolling and not enrolling.

The greatest beneficiaries are others—largely taxpayers but also potential victims of crime. These groups did pay for the program, but they get much of that back fairly soon through savings in special education expenses within the schools. Then they gain from the welfare payment reductions and again from the taxes paid out of the earnings increases. By the end, nonparticipants gain almost six times their initial payment for the one-year program (23,852 + 4,818 divided by 4,818) and almost three times their initial payment for the two-year program.

This unexpected finding is exactly why one does a benefit-cost analysis—these analyses almost routinely turn up outcomes such as this one that could not have been anticipated. In my own view, I think the evaluators are right in saying that programs having as many net benefits as the Perry Preschool program appear to have substantial benefits for nonparticipants, whether they be taxpayers or people who would otherwise have been victimized by crime. In the particular details, my own guess is that the unexpectedly high returns to nonparticipants are at least partly due to implied reductions in welfare payments, which look implausibly high to me. But even if these implied reductions *are* high, this would affect only the distribution of benefits and not the overall summary tally, since a lack of welfare payments means only that a transfer from one group to another is not being paid.

A last matter involves the faith we should place in the numbers summarized in the table. My own guess is, not an inordinate amount. There are, after all, only 58 treatment students and 65 control students. Moreover, as we have seen, the big action in the benefit-cost analysis comes many years after the initial investment is made. Philosophically, this is disconcerting because one might expect these aging preschool graduates to have long-since forgotten however happy and enriched they were in their preschool years—this matter I leave to child learning specialists to sort out. Statistically, it is disconcerting because all estimates have large standard errors after so many years. But even though I would not place a high degree of faith in the particular numbers, the Perry Preschool study does provide very solid evidence in favor of preschool, particularly one-year programs. Though it can only be said with some uncertainty, it can be said that the program looks more like a winner than a failure.

Commentary on
Changed Lives

Julius B. Richmond and Milton Kotelchuck
Division of Health Policy Research and Education
Harvard University

Changed Lives: The Effects of the Perry Preschool Program on Youths Through Age 19 presents a very important demonstration that high quality preschool intervention can prevent developmental attrition and can make a positive impact on the future lives of its participants. This is definitely a story worth telling.

This book addresses one of the key social issues facing the American public today: that many children raised in impoverished environments show a decline in developmental functioning prior to entering school compared to more advantaged children. During birth and infancy, social class differences are not significant; yet by five years of age, the differences appear to be large and seemingly permanent. A culture of poverty has been initiated. An excellent description of the problem in nonquantitative terms was presented by Wortis and her associates:[1]

> Other elements than the child-rearing patterns in the environment were preparing the child to take over a lower-class role. The inadequate incomes, crowded homes, lack of consistent family ties, the mother's depression and helplessness in her own situation, were as important as her child-rearing practices in influencing the child's development and preparing him for an adult role. It was for us a sobering experience to watch a large group of newborn infants, plastic human beings of unknown potential, and observe over a five-year period their social preparation to enter the class of the least skilled, least educated, and most rejected in our society.

Many studies have documented this sad phenomenon—a phenomenon that we call "developmental attrition." Many problems cluster into this category: children suffering from learning disabilities, child abuse, lead paint poisoning, behavioral problems, and some categories of mental retardation. Individual therapeutic approaches based on individual diagnostic categories miss the commonalities of these children. These are poor children, programmed for failure. Developmental attrition simply refers to the fact that for a large number of these children their psychological and physical health does not develop to its potential.

The less than optimal developmental status is one of the more profound legacies of poverty—for it enriches neither the person nor our nation. Developmental attrition is not, however, a given. It can be and must be addressed. Our goal ought to be clear: to provide all of our nation's children who are at risk with an enriched environment to prevent devel-

---

[1]Wortis, H., Bardach, J. L., Cutler, R., Rue, R., & Freedman, A. (1963). Childrearing practices in a low socioeconomic group. *Pediatrics, 32*(2), 298-307.

opmental attrition and to maximize their intellectual and social potential. This is a goal that the Perry Preschool Project has attempted to achieve.

As a nation, we have developed intervention models and social strategies that can work. Starting in the late 1950s and early 1960s, several researchers and clinicians, such as Dr. Gray in Nashville, Dr. Caldwell and myself in Syracuse, Drs. Cynthia Deutsch and Martin Deutsch and Dr. Palmer in New York, and Dr. Weikart of the Perry Preschool Project in Ypsilanti, began small local intervention projects. Although each project was unique, certain common features predominated. Preschool children from impoverished backgrounds were exposed to an extensive preschool environmental enrichment program in a day care setting over a period of time, aided by parental support.

Whereas today we accept preschool intervention as the norm, in the early 1960s this was not the case. Many developmental psychologists then believed intellectual functioning was fixed and genetically endowed, and therefore such interventions were seen as useless. Moreover, many theorists assumed that maternal separation and maternal deprivation were intricately linked. Thus, they would argue that a preschool program would be harmful, since the child would be separated from mother and put into an "institutional" setting. By contrast, the early interventionists had a belief that intelligence was environmentally shaped and that one could halt the developmental attrition through a structured environmental enrichment. The initial results of the small intervention projects were promising; short-term cognitive benefits were seen without emotional trauma in children. By today's standards, these first research evaluations were modest, but they were also compelling. A new knowledge base was growing.

At that same historical moment, the War on Poverty had begun. The Johnson Administration was looking for a means of reducing the impact of poverty. The potential of this new research was understood and literally seized upon; the Head Start program had begun. Poverty would be fought, in part, by providing children from impoverished backgrounds with a "head start" to set them on a positive intellectual and physical path, so they would have an "equal opportunity" to benefit from subsequent public schooling, which in turn would ultimately lead to more equal economic opportunities when they reached adulthood. Poverty would be fought at its developmental base. The new national political will now supported the interventionist strategy, despite its limited research base. It was at this time that Julius Richmond was called to Washington by Sargent Shriver, the Director of the Office of Economic Opportunity, to help start a new national program incorporating the ideas that developmental interventionists had been demonstrating in their small projects. The national Head Start program commenced in the summer of 1965, five months after he was called to Washington in February 1965.

Thus, by the late 1960s we had a national goal to prevent developmental attrition, a social strategy for reaching that goal, the beginnings of a knowledge base, and strong national political support. Only today, 20 years later, can we begin to answer the question of whether preschool programs really achieved their goals of preventing developmental attrition and thereby positively impacting upon the economic and social realities of their participants when they reached adulthood.

Reports such as *Changed Lives* strongly suggest that we could and did achieve our aim of having an impact on these children's lives. While the Perry Preschool Project and others have previously documented positive impacts on scholastic, intellectual, and behavioral characteristics in adolescence, this new report begins to turn our attention to the impact in adulthood. *Changed Lives* demonstrates, possibly for the first time, the positive impacts of preschool intervention on the adult lives of participants—in terms of their early socioeconomic status, social responsibility, and intellectual abilities.

This monograph continues a tradition of reports on the long-term benefits associated with the Perry Preschool Project, focusing on its participant cohort, now at 19 years of age. The scientific strength of this study is enhanced by its being based on one of the strongest and most convincing of the preschool intervention studies. From the onset, it used a very strong random assignment study design, with excellent follow-up participation and methodology.

The benefits for young adults are striking. In particular, the improvements on the APL Survey suggest that the Perry Preschool participants, compared to their control group, have stronger adult daily living literacy skills. The participants' already improved socioeconomic situation is impressive, despite some postponement of earnings while furthering their education. It does not take an economist to be able to see that different economic paths are being taken by the two groups—and that this will strongly impact on their future earnings. The data on social responsibility are more modest, but still encouraging. Fewer teenage pregnancies and less involvement with the criminal justice system again suggest different paths in the lives of participants. Overall, a strong case is made by this study—that the young adult lives of preschool participants are changed and changed for the better.

The Perry Preschool study demonstrates that "prevention" works. It is a refutation of the charge that prevention is not possible. Nor is this study alone in its conclusion. The recent publication of the Consortium for Longitudinal Studies also shows a consistent pattern of long-term benefits—especially in better school placement, better scholastic achievement, and high rates of high school graduation. However, this publication is one of the first to consider the participants' post-graduation lives.

This study also makes the strong point that prevention is cost-effective and can pay for itself. While the economic facts do work in our favor in this case, a cost-benefit argument is not one I would generally make. I believe it is important to recognize that preschool enrichment programs may in fact *not* be cost-effective. Eradicating poverty's legacies may not be inexpensive. One should not defend humanitarian programs on the grounds of economic savings. Too often elaborate and complex cost-benefit analyses can draw us into tangential technical debates, while the real political question remains: As a society, are we or are we not going to devote sufficient resources to achieving our goal of preventing developmental attrition for our impoverished younger citizens?

This monograph begins to address the issue of how to influence public policy. The topic is not a simple one. I believe it is necessary for all of us in the child development professions to be more attentive to and analytic about this process. In several recent papers, I have suggested that three factors are necessary to influence public policy: the development of a knowledge base, the development of political will, and the development of social strategy (see accompanying figure). All three of these areas must come together before one can really talk about the development and implementation of public policy.

THREE-FACTOR APPROACH TO PUBLIC POLICY

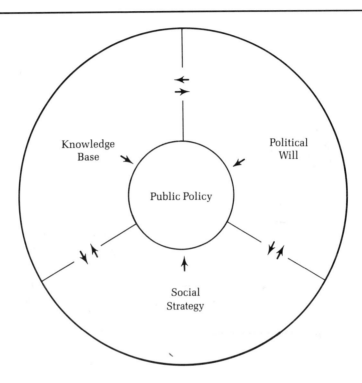

First, public policy depends on the existence of an appropriate **knowledge base**. A knowledge base provides the scientific and administrative data base upon which to make public health and education program decisions. It is fine to have as a long-term goal the prevention of developmental attrition, but without a firm knowledge base about the nature of intelligence, of intellectual growth, or of the epidemiologic effectiveness of different preventive strategies, we can only have a policy that proceeds incrementally in many directions. Many areas of developmental improvement must still await basic research. The knowledge base must be broad and multifaceted. Knowledge alone does not create public policy, but its absence will ultimately limit our capacity to make good public policy.

Second, public policy depends on **political will**. Political will is society's desire and commitment to support or modify old programs or to develop new programs. It may be viewed as the process of generating resources to carry out policies and programs. Often people in the child development professions know that there are better ways of dealing with a problem, but they may not succeed in bringing about change because they have not perceived the need to gain the political support for change. In order to effect improvements or changes, it is necessary to develop a constituency. The constituency for change may come from existing professional organizations or institutions that identify problems and help raise consciousness among decision-makers, or the constituency may come from the public that makes its aspirations and/or dissatisfactions heard through the legislative process.

Third, public policy depends critically on the existence of a **social strategy** or plan. Social strategy is a blueprint for how we are going to accomplish the worthwhile goals that we have established. It is the plan by which we apply our knowledge base and political will to improve programs; it is how we get from here to there. Just saying we want to cure learning disabilities or we want equity of access to employment does not mean we will accomplish it. A program must be developed that clearly outlines what our goals are and the means by which we are going to reach them.

In terms of this commentary, the Perry Preschool Project was the social strategy to prevent developmental attrition. The analysis presented in the book *Changed Lives* strengthens our knowledge base about the effectiveness of this preschool enrichment social strategy. The funding and other support for preschool intervention programs represent the political will that has sustained this project and that this project is attempting to enhance further. Let us go through each of these three topics, in more detail, in reference to *Changed Lives*.

Knowledge base: When the preschool enrichment social strategy was adopted as a national program by the Johnson Administration, there was very limited scientific evidence about its short- or long-term effectiveness or about the validity of the underlying theory that cognitive abilities were environmentally malleable. This monograph and the Perry Preschool Project are playing an important role in expanding our knowledge base. In particular, they suggest (1) that intervention can be effective, (2) that the impact can last for 15 years—through the period of schooling, into early adulthood, (3) that developmental attrition can be arrested, (4) that developmental level is not fixed but subject to the impact of intervention programs, and (5) that the impact affects many facets of a person's life—not just cognitive functioning. This monograph supports a growing list of studies that show the long-term benefits of preschool participation. And as noted before, it particularly provides information on young adult outcomes—a subject hypothesized to be a consequence of preschool participation, but heretofore unproven. This study, and others of a similar type, provide a resounding rebuttal to the simplistic and negative Westinghouse Report with its limited focus on IQ in early school years. This report will play a major role in providing the scientific support for future preschool enrichment programs.

Social strategy: At a generic level, this monograph shows that early preschool enrichment works as a social strategy to lessen developmental attrition and ultimately improve early adult life opportunities. However, there is much room for refinement in our social strategy. The evaluation of this project, although positive, shows we still have a long way to go until true social equality of opportunity exists in the U.S. For example, the APL scores of the Perry Preschool program participants, though much better than the scores of the controls, did not approach the national norms. Also, the high unemployment rate for the preschool subjects (the same as black youths nationally) is hardly indicative of equality of opportunity. And finally, the high rate of involvement with the police for all study subjects is quite dramatic and shows that a culture of poverty and racism is not easily transformed by one or two years of preschool enrichment.

The present preschool social strategy is positive, but not yet sufficient. Our interventions are not fixed in stone; we can adapt and improve upon them based on our long-term experiences of what strategies are most effective. We can take heart from the recent Head Start Synthesis Project, which appears to show that the cognitive benefits for the more recent ten years of the program (1975-1984) are stronger than for the earlier ten years (1965-1974). We are discovering what makes better programs and how to implement them. Head Start and related preschool programs are not dead, as some would assume, but in fact are getting stronger.

Many issues concerned with improving the preschool intervention social strategy can only be addressed by comparing this project to other similar projects. At what age should the intervention take place for maximal impact? For how long? Who should be included? If developmentally delayed children are included, what impact will it have on outcomes? What is the maximum student-teacher ratio? How can one measure the dynamic attributes of program quality? Should these programs be housed in the Departments of Education? What roles can pediatricians play? *Changed Lives* wisely touches on all of these issues of making the generic social strategy more beneficial. Though no single study can answer these questions alone (since by definition they only represent one unique set of experiences), each experience enriches our knowledge base. The Consortium of Longitudinal Studies and the Head Start Synthesis Project provide us with models of cross-study analyses that will allow us to improve on our preschool enrichment strategy.

Political will: Too often, we as developmental scientists overlook the importance of political will and assume that the mere presentation of scientific evidence will lead to change; this unfortunately is not true. Knowledge alone is not power. This monograph wisely suggests communication and outreach to the larger public as a form of political will. The authors recognize that we must actively make our knowledge base and social strategies known and that it is not improper academic professionalism to build political support for programs.

The Head Start program appears to have survived the recent period of federal human service cutbacks. President Reagan has argued that he supports the Head Start program because it is one of the federal programs that works. It is just as likely, however, that the Head Start program has remained intact because it has a powerful constituency in virtually every congressional district in the country. Parents and early educators are a powerful lobby fighting for a program they believe is important to the future of children and families (as this study demonstrates). This book provides a powerful tool for advocates in their efforts to maintain early intervention programs.

Unfortunately, developmental attrition still exists as a problem in the U.S. today. Developmental attrition is not solved through a one-time treatment. Rather, it is a struggle that must be fought for each child growing up in an impoverished environment. Recent statistics suggest that poverty, and especially the number of children growing up in poverty, is increasing. Indeed, without preschool programs such as Head Start or the Perry Preschool program, which can mitigate some of poverty's effects, many of the younger citizens of today would be facing an even bleaker future.

This book does show that "lives can be changed." We, as a nation, do have a strategy to ameliorate some of the developmental attrition associated with poverty. A knowledge base and social strategy exist. The question is, Do we have the political will? As professionals in child development we must struggle to influence public policy at all three policy levels. We must do more research to improve our knowledge base; we must develop our social strategies to produce more potent benefits, and as citizen-advocates, we must strengthen the political will to support preschool intervention programs. Publications like *Changed Lives* will make our tasks at all three policy levels much easier.